VULGARIANS
AT THE GATE

BOOKS BY STEVE ALLEN

Bop Fables (1955)

Fourteen for Tonight (1955)

The Funny Men (1956)

Wry on the Rocks (1956)

The Girls on the Tenth Floor (1958)

The Question Man (1959)

Mark It and Strike It (1960)

Not All of Your Laughter, Not All of Your Tears (1962)

Dialogues In Americanism (1964)

Letter to a Conservative (1965)

The Ground Is Our Table (1966)

Bigger than a Breadbox (1967)

A Flash of Swallows (1969)

The Wake (1972)

Princess Snip-Snip and the Puppykittens (1973)

Curses! (1973)

What to Say When It Rains (1974)

Schmock!-Schmock! (1975)

Meeting of Minds, Vol. I (1978)

Chopped-Up Chinese (1978)

Ripoff: The Corruption That Plagues America (1979)

Meeting of Minds, Vol. II (1979)

Explaining China (1980)

Funny People (1981)

The Talk Show Murders (1982)

Beloved Son: A Story of the Jesus Cults (1982)

More Funny People (1982)

How to Make a Speech (1986)

How to Be Funny (1987)

Murder on the Glitter Box (1989)

Passionate Nonsmokers' Bill of Rights (co-author, Bill Adler Jr.) (1989)

Dumbth: And 81 Ways to Make Americans Smarter (1989)

Meeting of Minds, Vol. III (1989)

Meeting of Minds, Vol. IV (1989)

The Public Hating: A Collection of Short Stories (1990)

Murder in Manhattan (1990)

Steve Allen on the Bible, Religion & Morality (1990)

Murder in Vegas (1991)

Hi-Ho, Steverino: My Adventures in the Wonderful Wacky World of TV (1992)

How to Be Funny (Re-Release) (1992)

The Murder Game (1993)

More Steve Allen on the Bible, Religion & Morality, Book Two (1993)

Make 'em Laugh (1993)

Reflections (1994)

Murder on the Atlantic (1995)

The Man Who Turned Back the Clock and Other Short Stories (1995)

Gullible's Travels (Audiotape, 1995)

The Bug and the Slug in the Rug (1995)

But Seriously . . . (1996)

Wake Up to Murder (1996)

Die Laughing (1997)

Dumbth: The Lost Art of Thinking (1998)

Murder in Hawaii (1999)

100 Song Lyrics by Steve Allen (1999)

Steve Allen's Private Joke File (2000)

VULGARIANS
AT THE GATE

Trash TV and Raunch Radio

Raising the Standards of Popular Culture

STEVE ALLEN

Prometheus Books

59 John Glenn Drive
Amherst, New York 14228-2197

Inquiries should be addressed to
Prometheus Books
59 John Glenn Drive
Amherst, New York 14228–2197
VOICE: 716–691–0133, ext. 207
FAX: 716–564–2711
WWW.PROMETHEUSBOOKS.COM

05 04 03 02 01   5 4 3 2 1

Library of Congress Cataloging-in-Publication Data

Allen, Steve, 1921–2000.
    Vulgarians at the gate : trash TV and raunch radio : raising standards of popular culture / Steve Allen.
        p. cm.
    Includes index.
    ISBN 1–57392–874–7 (alk. paper)
    1. Television broadcasting—Moral and ethical aspects—United States.
2. Radio broadcasting—Moral and religious aspects—United States. I. Title.

PN1992.6 .A38 2001
175—dc21   00-066471

Printed in the United States of America on acid-free paper

CONTENTS

Acknowledgments 9

Introduction 13

1. The Problem 17
   Do We Deserve Our Freedom? 32
   Starting Point 68
   Troubled Country 70
   The Role of Network Executives 73
   A Cause That Is Neither Conservative Nor Liberal 77
   Sumner Redstone 83
   An Ironic Twist 85
   Shasta McNasty 86
   Pushing the Envelope 88
   Shock-Jock Fired 89
   Late Night Raunch 90
   Pornography Available 91
   Just Shoot Me 93

VULGARIANS AT THE GATE

Awards Shows 94
The Tabloids 97
Peoria 101
Children 102
The Occasion of Sin 107
The Parents Television Council 110
Reaction to *Action* Should Be Revulsion 114
Self-Policing of Popular Entertainment 118
What Would You Think? 125
Weak Argument 127

2. The Denial of Responsibility 129
The Issue Is Misconstrued 130
The Fragility of Civilization 133
Judging 138
Influence of Media on Children 139
The Unabomber 142
Not Sex 144
Normal 146
Media Advisors 150
The Suburbanization of Television 151
Sexual Harassment 153
Advertisers Are Part of the Problem 154
Misplaced Industry Concern 159
Sen. Joe Lieberman 163

3. The Audience for Garbage 165
The Young 166
Children's Programming 171
Only Some Audiences Want Smut 173

4. The Offenders: A Closer Look
    at One Teen Idol   179
    Madonna   180
    Statement to Time-Warner   213

5. Shock Jocks and Confrontation TV:
    Howard Stern and Jerry Springer   219
    Howard Stern   220
    Jerry Springer   239

6. Popular Music and Recordings   243
    Music and Violence   268

7. Violence   277
    The Problem of Violence   278
    Statistics   288
    Evading Responsibility   289
    Stop Teaching Our Kids to Kill   292

8. Censorship   303
    Censorship/Humanism   317
    An Ancient Legal Principle   319

9. Conclusion   323
    The Print Media   329
    Pax Network   337
    The Function of a Parent   338
    Questioning versus Simply Rejecting Authority   340
    Bertrand Russell   342
    National Public Radio   345
    Restraints   346

Social Unrest and Delinquency	350
Dove Foundation Study	355
Better Alternative	358
Strengthening Moral Values	362
Humanitas Prize	365
The Power of a Letter	366
Picketing and Boycotts	368
The Religion Solution	369
Distribute Literature	370
Keep Files	370
Jack Valenti on Teaching Morality in Schools	371
Federal Trade Commission	372
More Good News	376
And Still More	378
The Power of a Star	379
Appendix A: Resource Organizations	**383**
Appendix B: Media Contacts	**399**
Recommended Reading	**407**
Index	**411**

ACKNOWLEDGMENTS

First and foremost, I wish to express my sincere gratitude to the thousands of people through the years, who have written to me, stopped me on the street, addressed me from my audiences or e-mailed me through my website to express their ever-growing frustration with the rising tide of violence and vulgarity in our popular culture. It is for them, and for all of our children and grandchildren, that I offer the thoughts in this book.

In preparing the manuscript, I am indebted to Janice Silver of my office staff for transcribing endless hours of dictated cassette tapes, since I do not use a typewriter, and for helping me verify so many of the facts and events referred to in the book. I am also grateful to my office managers, Gioia Heiser and Jim Walsh, for bringing order to my oftentimes chaotic professional life and for coordinating the dedicated members of my staff—Darryl Tanikawa, Susan Pasen, and Dayan Grubman—all of whom helped in either the gathering or organizing of the massive amount of research required to produce this volume.

I also wish to acknowledge the generous supply of data I have received from the staff of the Parents Television Council (including its chairman L. Brent Bozell, executive director Mark Honig, and their executive assistants Deborah Thomas and Tawnya Kemper. The Dove Foundation and its president Dick Rolfe have also kindly supplied me with valuable information through the years which has been helpful in preparing this text.

I would also like to take the opportunity to publicly thank the many reporters, columnists, and publications all of whom have graciously allowed me to include various portions of their thoughts and research on this troubling issue. The commitment of the more courageous among them to investigate and comment on the state of popular culture today, in the face of powerful media interests who cannot be pleased to receive such scrutiny, is encouraging.

As always, Steven L. Mitchell at Prometheus Books, has provided valuable editorial counsel throughout the process, and both Jonathan and Paul Kurtz are deeply appreciated for their willingness to publish my thoughts on this important subject.

ACKNOWLEDGMENTS

Finally, to my wife, Jayne Meadows, and our son, Bill Allen, who have provided me with both valuable insights on our entertainment industry and loving support as I have confronted many of its most powerful figures, I remain eternally grateful.

INTRODUCTION

Some social problems may be fairly well defined. For example, it was always in a sense outrageous that the hideous stench of tobacco smoke was permitted to befoul the air of eating establishments and airplanes, but in time, there was wide public attention paid to the problem and the matter was finally resolved.

The coarsening of our entire culture, however, is by no means so simple a matter. It is therefore more troublesome to oppose it. But oppose it we must, for the consequences of rearing millions of initially innocent children in a social atmosphere characterized by vulgarity, violence, brutish manners, the collapse of the family, and general disrespect for traditional codes of conduct is to chill the blood of even the most tolerant of observers. Nevertheless, the fact that working our way to a reasonable solution will be difficult should not delay us for a minute. All important projects involve great difficulty, and this one especially so, for we are not talking only about flagrant breaches of taste on the part of certain depraved individuals in the media. We are also wrestling with questions of law, freedom, democracy, social order, religion, morality, sex, philosophy, the free-enterprise system, and history. We are, in fact, talking about the ancient mysteries as to what it means to be human and what it means to be civilized.

Inevitably, in any such context, it will be necessary to hold up certain horrible examples. The few I've included have, in fact, already been subjected to public and professional critical scrutiny. My reference to them here, therefore, is by way of encouraging us to consider how some of the worst offenders rose to the position of prominence they now occupy. Perhaps dealing with such a question will tell us more about ourselves, and American society generally, than it reveals about the offenders. (It is ironic that, because of the necessity to quote concrete examples of the present period's cultural ugliness, in a work largely motivated out of concern for the tender sensibilities of children, I have produced a book that itself will not be suitable reading for children, although selected portions of it may properly be brought to their attention.)

INTRODUCTION

Anyone even casually familiar with history is already aware that the problem I address is not new. Thousands of years ago the scribes and philosophers of ancient civilizations were lamenting the disrespect for rules of the social game shown by the young people of their time. But I shall argue that there is a sense in which there is something new about today's offenses against law, morality, and even the generally more lenient standards of professional entertainment.

Ever since the arrival of the human species on our planet, there has been sexual misbehavior ranging from the moderate to the criminally outrageous. There has always, for example, been pornography, but it is only in the modern age that pornographic elements have been available in the mainstream media. Modern technology, in fact, makes possible—if not apparently inevitable—extrapolation of troublesome material, even if twenty-first–century humans are no more depraved than their distant ancestors.

The problem I shall address, namely, the dependence of popular entertainment on vulgarity and violence, is today so pervasive as to be almost inescapable. It is all too evident in video, for example, and it is now widespread on the Internet, frequently in the form of actual dictionary-definition pornography. It has become central to advertising, but I shall make only passing references to such media, having chosen instead to direct the reader's attention to the daily offenses in television, radio, motion pictures, and popular music.

Of the two visual media—films and TV—television is the more socially dangerous. This is not so because people who create television programs are personally more depraved than those who create films. Indeed, the degree of offensive material in motion pictures is often worse. But movies do not invade the home, at least initially, whereas television sets are almost permanently in the "on" position, in the same almost mindless way that electric lights, air-conditioners, and heaters are used. It is by no means an exaggeration to describe the present controversy as involving cultural warfare. That being so, we should not be surprised that large segments of the American population are angry to the point of demanding action. Increasingly, their refrain is that of Peter Finch's TV anchorman from the brilliant film, *Network*: "I'm mad as hell, and I'm not going to take it anymore!"

1
THE PROBLEM

Like a child acting outrageously naughty to see how far he can push his parents, mainstream television this season is flaunting the most vulgar and explicit sex, language, and behavior that it has ever sent into American homes.
> —New York Times, April 1998

Can you find more than an hour-and-a-half of TV that you'd want your kids [to watch]?
> —Susan Sarandon

On Wednesday, July 21, 1999, an important blow was struck for responsibility and decency when the following appeal was publicly announced by a group of respected leaders at a media conference in our nation's capital:

VULGARIANS AT THE GATE

American parents today are deeply worried about their children's exposure to an increasingly toxic popular culture. The events in Littleton, Colorado, are only the most recent reminder that something is deeply amiss in our media age. Violence and explicit sexual content in television, films, music, and video games have escalated sharply in recent years. Children of all ages now are being exposed to a barrage of images and words that threaten not only to rob them of normal childhood innocence but also to distort their view of reality and even undermine their character growth.

These concerns know no political or partisan boundaries. According to a recent CNN-USA Today-Gallup poll, 76 percent of adults agree that TV, movies, and popular music are negative influences on children, and 75 percent report that they make efforts to protect children from such harmful influences. Nearly the same number say shielding children from the negative influences of today's media culture is "nearly impossible."

Moreover, there is a growing public appreciation of the link between our excessively violent and degrading entertainment and the horrifying new crimes we see emerging among our young: schoolchildren gunning down teachers and fellow students en masse, killing sprees inspired by violent films, and teenagers murdering their babies only to return to dance at the prom.

Clearly, many factors are contributing to the crisis—family disintegration, ineffective schools, negligent parenting, and the ready availability of firearms. But, among researchers, the proposition that entertainment violence adversely influences attitudes and behavior is no longer controversial; there is overwhelming evidence of its harmful effects. Numerous studies show that degrading images of violence and sex have a desensitizing effect. Nowhere is the threat greater than to our at-risk youth— youngsters whose disadvantaged environments make them susceptible to acting upon impulses shaped by violent and dehumanizing media imagery.

In the past, the entertainment industry was more conscious of its unique responsibility for the health of our culture. For thirty years, television lived by the National Association of Broadcasters [NAB] Television Code, which detailed responsibilities to the community, children, and society and pre-scribed specific programming standards. For many years, this voluntary code set bound-aries that enabled television to thrive as a creative medium without causing undue damage to the bedrock values of our society.

In recent years, several top entertain-ment executives have spoken out on the need for minimum standards and, more recently, on the desirability of more family-friendly programming. But to affect real change, these individual expressions must transform into a new, collective affirmation of social responsibility on the part of the media industry as a whole.

We, the undersigned, call on executives of the media industry—as well as CEOs of companies that advertise in the electronic media—to join with us and with America's parents in a new social compact aimed at renewing our culture and making our media environment more healthy for our society and safer for our children. We call on industry leaders in all media—televi-sion, film, video, and electronic games—to band together to develop a new voluntary code of conduct, broadly modeled on the NAB code.

The code we envision would affirm in clear terms the industry's vital responsibilities for the health of our culture; establish certain minimum standards for violent, sexual, and degrading material for each medium, below which producers can be expected not to go; commit the industry to an overall reduction in the level of entertainment violence; ban the practice of targeting of adult-oriented entertainment to youth markets; provide for more accurate information to parents on media content; commit to the creation of "windows" or "safe havens" for family programming, including a revival of TV's "family hour"; and, finally, pledge significantly greater creative efforts to develop family-oriented entertainment.

We strongly urge parents to express their support for this voluntary code of conduct directly to media executives and advertisers with telephone calls, letters, faxes, or e-mails and to join us at www.media-appeal.org. And we call on all parents to fulfill their part of the compact by responsibly supervising their children's media exposure.

We are not advocating censorship or wholesale strictures on artistic creativity. We are not demanding that all entertainment be geared to young children. Finally, we are not asking government to police the media.

Rather, we are urging the entertainment industry to assume a decent minimum of responsibility for its own actions and take modest steps of self-restraint. And we are asking parents to help in this task by taking responsibility for shielding their own children and also by making their concerns known to media executives and advertisers.

Hollywood has an enormous influence on America, particularly the young. By making a concerted effort to turn its energies to promoting decent, shared values and strengthening American families, the entertainment industry has it within its power to help make an America worthy of the third millennium. We, as leaders from government, the religious community, the nonprofit world, and the private sector, along with members of the entertainment community, challenge the entertainment industry to this great task. We appeal to those who are reaping great profits to give something back. We believe that by choosing to do good, the entertainment industry can also make good, and both the industry and our society will be richer and better as a result.

STEVE ALLEN, author, entertainer

WILLIAM J. BENNETT, co-director, Empower America

DAVID BLANKENHORN, president, Institute for American Values

SISSELA BOK, distinguished fellow, Harvard Center for Population and Development Studies

FREDERICK BORSCH, bishop, Episcopal Diocese of Los Angeles

BILL BRIGHT, founder and president, Campus Crusade for Christ

L. BRENT BOZELL III, chairman, Parents Television Council

THE REV. DR. JOAN BROWN CAMPBELL, general secretary, National Council of Churches

SEN. SAM BROWNBACK (R-Kan.)

JIMMY CARTER, former U.S. President

LYNNE V. CHENEY, senior fellow, American Enterprise Institute

STEPHEN R. COVEY, co-founder and vice chairman, Franklin Covey Co.

MARIO CUOMO, former governor of New York

VULGARIANS AT THE GATE

JOHN J. DiJULIO JR., professor of politics, University of Pennsylvania

PAMELA EAKES, founder and president, Mothers Against Violence in America

DON EBERLY, director, the Civil Society Project

AMITAI ETZIONI, professor, George Washington University

VIC FARACI, senior vice president, Warner Brothers Records

GERALD R. FORD, former U.S. President

WILLIAM GALSTON, professor and director, Institute for Philosophy and Public Policy, School of Public Affairs, University of Maryland

ELIZABETH FOX-GENOVESE, professor of humanities, Emory University

MANDELL I. GANCHROW, M.D., president, Union of Orthodox Jewish Congregations

NORTON GARFINKLE, chairman, Oxford Management Corp.

ROBERT P. GEORGE, professor of jurisprudence, Princeton University

GEORGE GERBNER, telecommunications professor, Temple University, dean emeritus, Annenberg School for Communications, University of Pennsylvania

PATRICK GLYNN, director, Media Social Responsibility Project, George Washington University

OS GUINNESS, senior fellow, Trinity Forum

ROBERT HANLEY, actor, writer, director; founder and president Entertainment Fellowship

STEPHEN A. HAYNER, president, InterVarsity Christian Fellowship

ANDY HILL, president of programming, Channel One Network

GERTRUDE HIMMELFARB, professor emeritus of history, City University of New York

MARK HONIG, executive director, Parents Television Council

JAMES DAVISON HUNTER, professor of sociology and religious studies, University of Virginia

KATHLEEN HALL-JAMIESON, dean and communications professor, Annenberg School for Communications, University of Pennsylvania

SEN. KAY BAILEY HUTCHINSON (R-Tex.)

REP. HENRY HYDE (R-Ill.)

NAOMI JUDD, entertainer

JACK KEMP, co-director Empower America

SEN. JON KYL (R-Ariz.)

VULGARIANS AT THE GATE

RABBI DANIEL LAPIN, president, Toward
Tradition

CAROL LAWRENCE, actress, singer

SEN. JOE LIEBERMAN (D-Conn.)

SEN. JOHN McCAIN (R-Ariz.)

E. MICHAEL McCANN, district attorney,
Milwaukee County, Wisc.

MICHAEL MEDVED, film critic, radio host

THOMAS MONAGHAN, chair, Ave Maria
Foundation

RICHARD JOHN NEUHAUS, president, Institute on Religion and Public Life

ARMAND M. NICHOLI JR., M.D., associate
clinical professor of psychiatry, Harvard
Medical School

SAM NUNN, former U.S. senator from
Georgia

NEIL POSTMAN, professor, New York University

ALVIN POUSSAINT, M.D., director, Judge
Baker Children's Center, Boston

GEN. COLIN L. POWELL (ret.)

GEN. NORMAN SCHWARZKOPF (ret.)

GLENN TINDER, professor emeritus of political science, University of Massachusetts

C. DELORES TUCKER, chair, the National
Political Congress of Black Women

JOAN VAN ARK, actress, producer, director

JIM WALLIS, editor, *Sojourners* magazine;
    leader, Call to Renewal Program
DAVID WALSH, president, National Institute
    on Media and the Family
JERRY M. WIENER, professor emeritus of psy-
    chiatry and pediatrics, George Washington
    University
ELIE WIESEL, professor of humanities, Boston
    University
JAMES Q. WILSON, professor emeritus, UCLA
ALAN WOLFE, professor, Boston University
DANIEL YANKELOVICH, president, the Public
    Agenda

Although networks and production studios deny responsibility, their reasoning is no more complex than that which made the executives of America's tobacco companies lie through their teeth for decades when they were privately perfectly aware that their product was addictive and injurious to health as well. Even after it had been clearly established that well over 400,000 Americans were dying every year from the effects of tobacco smoke—with uncounted millions throughout the rest of the planet—the lying continued. Do not be confused, therefore, by the evasive denials now emanating from those who create and market our various forms of public entertainment.

VULGARIANS AT THE GATE

Parents and other concerned adults are under a moral obligation to provide themselves with basic relevant information. For example, according to the A. C. Nielsen Company the average child (age 2 through 11) watches nearly *four hours* of television per day. In August 1999 the American Academy of Pediatrics recommended that children under the age of two not be permitted to watch television at all, on the grounds that doing so deprives them of social interaction which is critical for early brain development. The same physicians' organization recommended that older children sleep in media-free bedrooms to reduce their exposure to questionable references. And yet more than half of all children in America have a television set in their bedrooms. A 1994 study by the Center for Media and Popular Culture reports an average of fifteen violent acts being televised per channel per hour between 6 A.M. and midnight, an increase of 41 percent in only four years. In his 1999 national address on media violence after the student massacre at Columbine High School in Littleton, Colorado, President Clinton reported that "by the time the typical American child reaches the age of eighteen, he or she has seen 200,000 dramatized acts of violence and 40,000 dramatized murders." And there are scores of reliable studies suggesting that television violence may contribute to aggressive behavior.

My purpose in writing this book, therefore, is to provide responsible adults with the ammunition they need to wage a successful cultural war for the attentive consciousness of America's children.

• • •

The reality of what is actually out there for the public to view and hear in the media seems rarely to be addressed publicly and in a coherent and substantive way. The majority of Americans agree, albeit with varying degrees of emphasis, that something must be done about the vulgarity and violence in our media. But this great and understandably acrimonious debate involves, among other things, a challenge to capitalism, to our free-enterprise system.

I support this point by starting with what is obvious, that the primary reason for the existence of the moral garbage presently being marketed to children and adults alike is that there is profit in it. There is indeed, for the professional offenders have discovered not only that there is a clear though relatively small market for explicit material, but that even among the majority of Americans who are not themselves morally hopeless there are classic human weaknesses to which media marketers can appeal and exploit.

That the nature of free enterprise allows for very low incidence of restriction and is harmonious with freedoms generally is obvious enough, but surely there is no defender of capitalism naïve enough to believe that a free market is literally perfect. We must now concentrate on the relevant imperfections. One of them is that the lust for profit is now the primary energizer of the debasement of our entire society and culture. The most shockingly vulgar recordings reap multimillions in profit, and the same is true of sleazy radio, television, and films. To read some of the social commentary of, say, a quarter or half-century ago an impartial observer might be forgiven for assuming that all we had to do was to defeat Communism and a good many if not all of our troubles would be behind us. Well, Communism, at least in the strength it boasted before the collapse of the Soviet Union, no longer much troubles us. While we may no longer have those half-comic, half-tragic nightmares about Communists under the bed, the ironic thing is that there are indeed monsters in our midst, and they are us. And a shocking reality whose gears are meshed with this first understanding is that it is America's major corporations that are funding a large part of the social damage we are suffering.

This is a point with which, at least to my knowledge, even the conservative community of well-organized think tanks has not adequately dealt. But I see hope in this very fact, for if we assume that our industrialists have an invisible protective shield that blinds them to criticism coming from liberals, surely the same cannot be said if similar criticisms come from the industrial world's chief philosophical defenders.

So far I have spoken only of the responsibility of those who create and produce violent entertainment. I'm certainly not alone in this; the majority of the American people are demanding that the marketers of mass-entertainment carefully consider the negative effects of their product. But that leaves unanswered an awkward question: What about the public demand for aggressive, violent material? It is perfectly fair to point this question directly at the reader, the film-goer, and the TV watcher. If we even go so far as to impress upon our children that we have personally recognized the harmful nature of such unhealthy modern entertainment, we will have made some progress. But still, the primary offenders, those who create the objectionable material in the first place, must stop blaming the audience, as if they themselves are somehow morally opposed to what they are forced to market. On this complex and troubling question there is more than enough guilt to go around.

DO WE DESERVE OUR FREEDOM?

Historically there has long been a certain tension between the arts and social policy. Humankind has always been practiced at breaking the moral law, but poets, novelists, philosophers, dramatists, and journalists have at least attempted to transmit positive messages, often by specifically criticizing what is vile and criminal in society. What we are witnessing today, by way of contrast, is the apparently willing cooperation—sometimes even the enthusiastic leadership—of the practitioners of popular culture to degrade an already deeply disturbed society. It is unclear why we had to wait until the 1990s for this to be generally perceived as a vital concern, but it is at least a hopeful sign that the degree of cultural depravity is now becoming widely recognized.

There has always been a market for vulgarity and licentiousness; but at present it is undeniable that motion pictures, theater, television, radio, the recording industry, and to a lesser degree, journalism are enthusiastic participants in the general collapse of standards and behavior. Some people may find it hard to believe that television, to refer to only one venue, was a morally admirable medium as recently as the 1950s. With a few exceptions it was largely administered by gentlemen and ladies, and although it was, from the first, apparent that inferior cultural merchandise was likely to become quite popular, given the notorious imperfections of human nature itself, television programming in general at least consisted of fare that could be watched by the entire family. Whether one approves or disapproves of the wholesome nature of early television, it is clear that the medium has changed. A surprising amount of programming, in both daytime and evening hours, is now sadly unfit for children, by any societal standard of the last millennium. Individuals might behave abominably, but societies once did sincerely attempt to maintain general standards, if only on the quite sensible grounds that the alternative invariably leads to social anarchy and chaos in which the civilized conduct of human affairs becomes an essentially losing proposition for literally all participants.

Among those who once formally guarded the moral and ethical ramparts were the corporations, consisting chiefly of men who had been reasonably well educated and were by-and-large responsible citizens—the conservative country-club set, in other words—but their role as moral guardians now appears to have been almost totally abandoned. Corporate America, granting exceptions, has not only largely given up its former admirable participation in the maintenance of society's general sanity but has joined those who would undermine it and is, in fact, funding them in large measure.

This is nowhere more clear than in the context of TV and radio. The owners of television and radio stations, and the networks by which they are strung together, are apparently so concentrated on the bottom line—to use the tiresome phrase—that they simply turn a blind eye to what is nothing less than the partial collapse of their own society. As a result not only is television awash in foul language and repulsiveness, but the owners—those holding the most power—are not just permitting but encouraging their creative representatives to further extremes of muck and mire. Once it became clear that there is a definite cause-and-effect relationship between the schlockiest forms of sexual display and achieving higher ratings, the battle was over.

I await the cries of anguish from my fellow philosophical defenders of the free market, but I do not intend to hold my breath until I hear them.

If ours were a more rational society it might be thought that the current wave of countercriticism would at least have led the chief offenders, corporate or private, to slightly pull in their horns. But precisely the opposite has taken place. Television, which has now been roundly criticized for its increasing vulgarity during the decade just past, continues to be more deliberately shocking than ever. When it was first introduced, the witless spectacle known as *Married . . . with Children*—a deliberately vulgar situation comedy aired on the Fox network—was considered a daring exception. Instead, it turns out to have been the forerunner of an actual cultural movement.

In 1990 an editor for the *Los Angeles Times*, having learned of my criticisms of the wave of vulgarity that had become so dominant in American entertainment, asked me to write a brief commentary for the paper. I quote it here from its September 17, 1990, publication because it enables me to make a rather happy point.

> The producers of a new sitcom, incapable of creating actual wit of the sort weekly provided by *Cheers* or the *Cosby* show, decide to go with the current flow, despite the fact

that that flow is carrying us all along right into the sewer. They make an innocent five-year old say, "It sucks." The very sort of language parents forbid their children to use is now being encouraged not only by anything-goes cable entrepreneurs but the once high-minded networks. We may therefore paraphrase the ancient moral admonition about money to read: Love of Ratings Is the Root of All Evil.

We're not just talking about television here. Much of modern entertainment already involves vulgarians addressing barbarians. But the underlying questions are vastly more important. Why are ratings important? Because they translate into dollars. The bankers, corporate executives, and country-clubbers who own network stock, plus advertisers, far from resisting the present aesthetic and ethical collapse as their class would have in times past, are actually abetting the ugliness.

Marketplace factors are already largely responsible for having thoroughly debased popular music, a billion-dollar industry, since the tastes of poorly educated teenagers with discretionary income dominate the field. Most of today's punk and heavy-metal lovers have yet even to hear such names as George Gershwin, Cole Porter, and Richard Rodgers. Forget Ludwig von Beethoven.

The best humor, when it is not simply purely playful, says something witty and wise about the issues it confronts. Among the horrifying problems of American civilization at present is the collapse of the American family, which has assumed such proportions that many now react to the word *family* as if it were just another noun like *roller skates* or *television*. Humans can do without roller skates or TV but they literally cannot long survive, as a rational, emotionally healthy species, without a secure family structure.

The reason, to belabor the obvious, is that the family is the soil in which each year's new crop of humans grow. It is mostly the failed family, therefore, which has produced our present millions of prison inmates, rapists, drug addicts, burglars, muggers, sexual psychopaths, nonprofessional whores of both sexes, and general goofolas.

Very well—agreed; that is the problem. The solution of today's comedy specialists, with few exceptions, is to make vulgar light

VULGARIANS AT THE GATE

of what is, in reality, tragically heavy. As for those trying to treat as deep a wound as our society has ever suffered, far from encouraging them, today's comics deride them. That even those who acknowledge the right rules of conduct will often fail to live up to their own honestly professed codes is sadly clear.

But what the dominant voices of our culture—with their access to popular music, radio, TV, and the comedy concert circuit—are now saying is "F--- virtue."

If you think our society is sick now—stand by.

This relates, of course, to the debate about censorship and the question as to whether the large segment of American society that perceives the moral dangers in totally unrestricted artistic expression has any say at all concerning the use of public funds by the National Endowment for the Arts. The question is a perfectly fair one: Though artists have the creative right to produce work that may even express racial, sexual, or religious hatred, does the state have the correlative obligation to endorse such expression with already inadequate taxpayers' money?

The matter is by no means justly resolved by reflexive condemnations of censorship, which in any event already exists in law, or are slander and libel perfectly acceptable?

Even the maligned networks do censor their programs. When the prince of filth of a few years ago, Andrew Dice Clay, appeared on that bastion of free speech, *Saturday Night Live*, several of his more revolting remarks were, quite properly, censored. High time.

When I entertain, I almost invariably spend the first twenty minutes or so responding to questions submitted by members of the audience. At a recent awards luncheon sponsored by a Toastmasters group three different participants brought up the same subject matter. A woman asked, "What's your opinion of current-day comedians who mostly shout and insult the audience and have no intellectual or entertaining ideas?" A gentleman from Thousand Oaks, California, asked, "Has humor gone too far?" And a man from Torrance, California, wrote, "You've spoken of certain infamous public personalities who 'scrawl graffiti on the national dialogue.' How do we let these participants know how far off-base they are? How do we get them to cease and desist?"

VULGARIANS AT THE GATE

In the process of telling these folks a story about a guest on my television show in the 1950s who accidentally used a vulgar term, I said "Perhaps I should explain to younger people here today that while television now permits almost any sort of vulgarity, especially on its talk or comedy shows, for much of TV's history nothing of the sort was permitted. We just laughed at Sid Caesar, Jackie Gleason, Red Skelton, and those other wonderful comedians because they were funny." And then I added, quite casually, "It might be interesting sometime, just as an experiment, to go back to that system." To my surprise, the result was thunderous applause.

Perhaps the time has come to determine, by standard polling methods, what percentage of the American audience actually relishes the incredible daily barrage of vile language that has come to be so characteristic of modern comedy. Note that I am not referring here to the sort of innocent and cutely naughty humor that was common in old burlesque, although never in vaudeville, where it simply was not permitted because theater owners catered to a family audience.

It has been possible for modern American viewers to see instances of this sort of humor, almost always involving baggy-pants comedians working with pretty young women, because of the availability on our tele-

vision sets a few years ago of that delightful production, the *Benny Hill Show*. Mr. Hill was in the grand tradition of the English music hall, in which there has
always been a great deal of comic leering at attractive
showgirls, almost invariably by comedians with naturally funny faces, but our burlesque entertainers never
stooped to the ugly vulgarity that one hears now even
on daytime television where children can and do see it.

It is certainly relevant to consider that those still
regarded as the great comic entertainers of the century did not resort to the gutter-language heard today
in every comedy club in the land. We simply laughed
at Charlie Chaplin, Stan Laurel and Oliver Hardy,
Buster Keaton, Bob Hope, Fred Allen, Victor Borge,
Milton Berle, Phil Silvers, W. C. Fields, and the others.
Even the most depraved viewers never appealed to
our great comedians to deal in obscenity and language that would shame a drunken sailor.

Show business is, of course, a business in some
respects like any other, and if American popular taste
generally has fallen to such a low estate that millions
of dollars can be made by catering to it, then it would
be difficult to address the broad issues constructively
or to hope for much improvement. But the will of the
majority is also an important factor in our political
and social system. Let us assume that polls and sur-

veys would reveal that most Americans are disgusted by the degree of ugliness in modern comedy; wouldn't it be reasonable to expect that that fact—if it were so—would be reflected in the marketplace?

For that minority who apparently cannot get enough vile concepts and terms in their popular entertainment, perhaps a sub-market could be established for their convenience, something like my proposal for comedy clubs: Filth Night Monday, Wednesday, and Friday could be advertised, and Clean Nights be made available on Tuesday, Thursday, and Saturday. The various content-rating systems for television, movies, and music lyrics, of course, are an attempt—though weak—to do something about the otherwise constantly descending level of ugliness to which we are presently subjected.

I wish I could report that the simple publication of my original complaint in the *Los Angeles Times* led to a moderately detectable movement for reform. Nothing of the sort happened, but I did learn that I had a good many supporters *within the entertainment community*. The morning the article appeared, a call came in from the witty and original comedian Mort Sahl. He not only expressed a number of compliments but did so heatedly and implored me to keep repeating the same message, explaining that he was personally disgusted by the drift of modern comedy away from meaningful social commentary and toward empty schlock, rudeness, and sleaze.

A few minutes after Mort called, another comedian, Gary Morton, was on the phone. In his later years Morton was better known as the husband of the late Lucille Ball but in his younger days he had been a stand-up comic, and a funny one. He, too, resoundingly seconded my motion. "It's about time," he said, "that somebody inside the business said what you did this morning. It's driven me nuts for years, and Lucy used to get so angry that she switched off the TV. She couldn't stand all the garbage she was seeing." (It should be noted that Lucy's hilarious and completely clean *I Love Lucy* series is still enjoyed by millions each day throughout the world.)

I quickly realized that these calls and others I received that day were more important, in terms of their source, than if I had received congratulatory messages from Billy Graham or the late Mother Teresa who, of course, would have deplored the present degree of vulgarity in entertainment. The fact that so many of my friends—all of whom, like myself, are just regular guys on the morality scale—voiced the same concerns was even more significant.

VULGARIANS AT THE GATE

An early and courageous critic of the "anything goes" school of comedy was the late Henny Youngman who, writing in the *New York Times* of July 31, 1990, said, "A guy I'd thought was my friend played me a tape of Andrew Dice Clay, this hot-shot kid comic from Brooklyn with the filthy mouth. After listening to a few gags I realized Clay needs no introduction. What he needs is an act." Youngman even denied that some of Clay's laugh-lines were jokes at all. They're not, he said, "they're ugliness."

Another relevant incident occurred in 1998 when I attended a lunch meeting in Beverly Hills' Spago Restaurant with a dozen or so of my fellow members of the Friars Club. Comedians have always been considered the glamour-members of the fraternal organization, which is famous for its "roasts" of various celebrities.

Over the course of several decades such professional funnymen as Milton Berle, Georgie Jessel, Jack Carter, Sid Caesar, Dean Martin, Norm Crosby, Buddy Hackett, Johnny Carson, Red Buttons, Jan Murray, and Henny Youngman—to name only a few—have staged all-star comedy fests in which, at least on many occasions, true heights of hilarity were reached. It is important to note here that not all of the jokes that emerged in such settings could be described as suitable family entertainment. Indeed, for many years the Friars did not even permit women to attend those of its productions called "stag" shows. This was not done out of any male chauvinist bias but rather out of respect for the more presumably tender sensitivities of women. I stress this point because it relates importantly to what I am about to say.

At the Spago lunch Jack Carter, an unfailingly amusing gentleman, happened casually to mention that he had just seen a new TV situation comedy that he described as "so dirty you wouldn't believe it." He quoted a few sample lines, which were indeed even more vulgar than much of what one sees on evening television. Finding it hard to believe that even the now shameless networks could have authorized the telecasting of such lines, I said "Which network?"

"Oh, it was on HBO," Jack said.

Sid Caesar, who was sitting to my left, agreed with Carter's assessment of the show, which is called *Sex and the City*. So here again, we have an example of long-time progressive practitioners of the comedy trade, by no means altar boys or candidates for the rabbinate themselves, expressing revulsion by what now is considered, at least by some broadcasters, acceptable entertainment.

It turns out that Jack Carter described the program

accurately. On an early episode of the series a married man "flashes" (exposes himself to) a young woman. It is noteworthy that Darren Star, who created not only this particular series but also *Beverly Hills 90210* and *Melrose Place*, said at a public press conference of the HBO cable service, "I can't think of another place that would give us the freedom to produce this candid and comical take on contemporary sex and relationships."

Incidentally, a critic named Stacey D'Rasmo, writing in *US* magazine, made an important observation in saying, "the reason for the popularity of this show *Sex and the City* on HBO is not raw sex—you can see more humping on the average soap opera—but the raw analysis of male-female relations, a courtesan perspective." Another noteworthy comment was made to the *New York Times* by Sarah Jessica Parker, the attractive and talented star of the series. "Oh God, the scripts are salty and ribald! This is something I've never done before. Since the pilot the writers have accommodated my more prudish side."

"For one thing," says *New York Times* reviewer Gini Sikes, "they've all but eliminated Miss Parker's use of a particular four-letter word that she says is not part of her vocabulary." Let us be grateful for even small favors. The most intriguing parts of Ms. Sikes's April 1998 review/commentary are as follows:

Seeking freedom from the restraints of network censors and advertisers . . . [Wait a
minute; *what* restraints?] Mr. Star first tried
to sell *Sex and the City* as a comedy series
pilot to HBO last year. . . . "The network
brought me in to attract younger demographics, then changed its mind, making
me re-tool the show." Star says, "That experience taught me a great lesson. I'd rather
not work for ten years than write to serve
network dictates."

Given the recent increase in the number of Americans outraged about the vulgarity level to which the
three once-respected major networks (ABC, NBC,
CBS) have descended, it would appear that the
undoubtedly talented Mr. Star, and the many other
writer/producers who think like he does, are now
properly the subject of considered critical analysis.
Consider for example, his comment that "In terms of
creative freedom, HBO is the best place to work right
now in TV. You're allowed to write the way people
speak in the real world, which you can't on the networks because *they're run on fear*" (italics added).

Apparently Mr. Star considers the emotion of fear
itself, though it is the product of millions of years of
physical evolution, a somehow shameful human

attribute that ought to be stamped out, along with such excess baggage as respect for morality itself. I will pay at least a few network executives the compliment of assuming that they hold the uglier four-letter words to a minimum in their telecasts simply because even some quite depraved people find such language unpleasant and degrading, especially when it is employed in a casual way. The point is that in a legitimate drama such as HBO's brilliant series, *The Sopranos* or ABC's equally outstanding *NYPD Blue* there may be a literary justification for the inclusion of the kind of language characteristic of prison, ghetto, military, or Mafia life. But it is far more characteristic of modern comedy entertainment that the standard verbal rough stuff is inserted into situation comedies partly because writers just want to see how much they can "get away with." Perhaps in a utopian society, Mr. Star might be sentenced to write a five thousand-word essay on the meaning of the term *creative freedom*.

One begins to wonder, given the adulation and publicity with which *Sex and the City* was greeted by the print media, why there are so few journalists willing to deal, in specific terms, with the rawness of the program's story-lines? It's important to note that, although adjectives such as *steamy*, *spicy*, *ribald*, and *bawdy* are used, there is rarely even the faintest suggestion that the critics take a dim view of the extremes to which the program resorts. A modified exception came in the August 2, 1999, issue of *Newsweek* which used the words "obscene," "raunchy," and "shockingly explicit" in describing the conversations between the lead characters. According to the *Philadelphia Enquirer*, episodes of *Sex and the City* have included uninhibited discussions about "penis size, oral and anal sex, and how a sudden onset of flatulence can destroy a romantic interlude."

Ms. Parker herself comes across in print as the likable and bright person she is in reality. Her observations in response to reporters' questions have a general reasonableness about them. But occasionally, like the rest of us, she is simply out-and-out wrong, as when she says of the program, "I don't think it's vulgar." Ms. Parker, it's *supposed* to be vulgar.

This may not come as disturbing news to Star, who, I have little doubt, knows exactly what he's doing. Vulgarity is in, folks. It's quite another question, of course, as to whether this is marvelous social news or suggests something rather ominous about America's future.

Producer Darren Star was quoted in the same August 1999 *Newsweek* story as saying something that is refreshingly candid, but morally horrendous. In explaining why he decided to bring *Sex and the City* to HBO he said, *"I wanted to do an R-rated show about adult sexual relationships that had no kind of censorship, moralizing, or judgment"* (italics added). There was more to his explanation, but to include it here would be perhaps to dilute the reader's concentration on something that one hopes will serve to bring us to a clearer understanding of precisely what this book is about, and what has so many millions of Americans up in arms. On the assumption that Mr. Star is not a one-of-a-kind phenomenon, it follows that there are some television producers who actually *want* to create and transmit R-rated material into our homes.

Second, Mr. Star has now clearly established the existence of a school of thought that simply does not want to be encumbered with moral considerations. His forthright assertion therefore has brought us to a point of decision. If any appreciable number of television program-creators agree with Mr. Star on the point he has raised, are the American people prepared to let the no-morals-or-censorship-gang get away with it?

The real harm this program will do is that its four glamorous principals will no doubt be adopted as role-models by some impressionable teenage girls. And I'm sure that's all we need now, yet another powerful influence for our teenagers to sleep with almost anybody, smoke heavily, drink too much, and talk like hookers.

In one scene alone the word *shitty* was used about a dozen times. A significant thing about the use of such terms is that they are rarely employed in a traditional context, which is usually to express such strong emotions as anger, contempt, or pent-up frustration. They are now used in the same quite casual way that not very many years ago would have involved such words as *damn* or *hell*.

Considered in the context of the broader nighttime schedule of HBO programming which includes the pornographic documentary series *Real Sex*; the voyeuristic backstage look at strippers, *G-String Divas*; and the utterly tasteless comedy *Arliss, Sex and the City* may be considered relatively mainstream by some. But it is again its potential to influence teen behavior which leads me to devote these pages to it.

• • •

For the past several years I have continued to speak my mind on the issue of vulgarity in television, comedy, and music, and have, again and again, been gratified to see how much cheering comes from within an industry that some critics may perceive as almost completely uninterested in morals and manners. There is surely no shortage of offenders but if they constitute a majority at all I believe it is a slim one. In early 1999 I was part of a panel of entertainers interviewed by talk show host Larry King on his popular CNN program. My three companions were Milton Berle, Sid Caesar, and Art Linkletter. At one point it emerged that all four of us agreed in deploring the wave of ugliness that has come to characterize so much of American comedy. Add to the list of those comic entertainers who also have voiced dismay at the emphasis on vulgarity the names of Danny Thomas, Jackie Gleason, Andy Griffith, Bob Newhart, Bill Cosby, and Bob Hope. Some of these gentlemen in their personal appearances—in other words *not* on radio, television, or films—have occasionally indulged in off-color material, but the distinction they made is of enormous importance. They simply have had the good sense to know that the great American audience—which includes millions of children—is not suitably entertained by the schlock-shock fare now so common.

What these and thousands of others within show-business are trying to bring about is certainly not the outlawing of that ancient staple of human discourse, the "dirty joke," and they are not demanding anything so absurd and irrelevant as that all practitioners of the comic arts live personally spotless lives. If American comedy had never until now been exhibited in clean and inoffensive forms, and if, let us say, it had always been as degrading as much of it is at present, then at least a certain level of abstract debate might be conducted (Resolved: There should be less vulgarity in entertainment). But that is not the situation we face. From the beginning of this century, throughout the days of minstrel shows, vaudeville, motion pictures, radio, television, and even, for the most part, in the rougher night clubs, the glorious creativity of Will Rogers, black comedian Bert Williams, W. C. Fields, Joe E. Brown, Charlie Chaplin, Laurel and Hardy, Harold Lloyd, Buster Keaton, Fibber McGee and Molly, Amos and Andy, Smith and Dale, Ed Wynn, Bert Lahr, Danny Thomas, Sid Caesar, and other popular comedians never depended on cheap shock to get laughs. So that should settle part of the debate once and for all. Clean comedy can be successfully marketed simply because it has been, and for a very long time.

In 1951, after I had arrived in New York to do television work for CBS, I happened to be walking down Broadway one afternoon in the company of a young woman and suddenly realized we were passing Charlie's Bar, an old-fashioned saloon famous among jazz musicians as a quiet, relaxed hangout and meeting place. "Hey," I said, "I've been hearing about this place for years. Let's go in for a few minutes, okay?"

The time was about one in the afternoon and the place was empty except for one lone customer at the far end of the bar. My friend and I seated ourselves near the entrance, ordered soft drinks, and continued our casual conversation. Somehow it was exciting, as I looked about the room, to realize that hundreds of the world's greatest jazz stars and big band musicians had occupied that same space over a long span of years. There was nothing particularly impressive about the room itself, nothing of the modern Planet Hollywood tourist-trap ambiance. All-in-all the experience was casually pleasurable, right up until the point when the lone alcoholic at the other end of the bar began to talk—to no one in particular—but loudly enough to intrude on our consciousness. Life almost daily presents worse problems, but the fellow was using ugly language. I would have paid no particular attention had I been alone, but in that pre-*Sex and the City* day it was not considered acceptable to use such language in the presence of women. Even this was not a matter of major concern since my companion and I had planned to remain on the premises for only a few minutes. Unfortunately the loudmouth, wrapped in his own loneliness and negativity, began to increase his volume. At this the bartender, without saying a word, approached the man. Suddenly curious as to what he might say to the offender I followed him with my eyes as he walked to the far end of the bar. Speaking softly, he leaned in very close to the drunk and said, "Hey, man—modulate."

My friend and I laughed heartily, I left the bartender a good tip, and we returned to the street.

Is there no one in radio or television to so address today's vendors of vulgarity? Evidently not. Consider that in 1998 Howard Stern was hired by the once proud CBS to bring his daily festival of radio filth to late night TV.

Bear in mind that the decision to accord even more riches and "honor" to Stern is not at all the result of an idea by some tasteless lieutenant who risks reprimand from his superiors for having added new and particularly objectionable sleaze to the network's schedule. It is now the superiors themselves—the owners—and the leading stock holders who make or enthusiastically support such decisions. The

VULGARIANS AT THE GATE

Time-Warner company has taken a great deal of public criticism for its willingness to ignore moral and ethical considerations in turning a profit. Within the context of television, the Fox network would appear to hold the same distinction.

This is interesting on its face but even more so upon analysis. Ordinarily when either an individual or an institution is criticized it responds by slightly pulling in its horns and trying to put some sort of acceptable face on what has been widely recognized as offensive or harmful. Fox TV, by way of contrast, appeared determined to become even more offensive.

In the short-lived 1995 series about four men having relationship problems, *Misery Loves Company*, not only was there a scene where a tall, attractive-looking blonde woman walks into a public men's room and stands, visibly using a urinal, but this was the specific clip Fox used as the "coming attractions" example, implying that such moments were not only typical of the program but revealed it at its best.

Multiply this by—oh, fifty—and you need no additional evidence to dismiss the suggestion that networks can police themselves.

It would be an interesting experiment—don't you think?—to approach these leaders in their capacities as associates of one philosophical tradition or another. Some of them, after all, are Catholics, Protestants, Jews, Conservatives, Democrats, or Liberals. This question should be put to them: "As one affiliated with a social bloc that boasts a long and honorable ethical tradition, do you personally approve of the vileness of a program you have recently added to your schedule?"

I sent a letter of precisely this sort not long ago to media mogul Rupert Murdoch, owner of the Fox network and one of the most powerful and socially influential men on earth, after learning, from a magazine article about him, that he was not only very proud of his position as a political conservative but also a sincere Christian.

Dear Mr. Murdoch,

In connection with an article I am preparing for publication I would like to put to you what I perceive as an extremely simple question.

I pose it against the background of a wave of public sentiment in the United States that is becoming almost violent in its proportions and energy—and expresses the true sense of outrage felt by the majority of Americans, though not all, at the degree to which popular culture in our country has become cheapened.

VULGARIANS AT THE GATE

Although the Christian Right—with which I understand you are in substantial philosophical agreement—is perhaps the loudest of the critics of the present sordid state of affairs, they are by no means alone in expressing their displeasure at the current daily barrage of vulgarity, obscenity, blasphemy, and general sleaze.

As a Christian yourself, I assume you take a dim view of the general ugliness and immorality of much of popular culture.

So far, in this letter, I am sharing information rather than presenting a question. But now I'll get to that. The fly in the ointment is that Fox television is widely viewed as not only a participant in the general marketing of sleaze but—in fact—one of the worst offenders. [What I had chiefly in mind was Fox's high-rated program *Married . . . with Children*, a sitcom about an atypical American family celebrating vulgarity.]

I enclose, in this specific connection, a copy of a letter I sent some months ago to a man named John Matoian. As you will see, I expressed hope at, and hearty approval of, the hiring of Mr. Matoian since the fact that he had joined your corporation suggested that someone in a position of authority had become so concerned about the marketing of truly vile material, that they had brought the honorable gentleman into the picture as a way of doing something productive about the problem.

But the fact is—as I assume you are aware—Mr. Matoian was quietly dismissed not long after he had been hired.

Since no reason was given for his firing, it is reasonable to at least suppose that it might have been because he did, in fact, try to strike a few blows for decency and social responsibility but was—for that very reason—perceived to be a threat to those who had taken your telecasting empire into the lamentable direction that has given it its present reputation.

It now occurs to me that I'm really presenting two separate, though related, questions to you. Are you, or is any member of your team, prepared to explain why Mr. Matoian was hired and fired so quickly? And second, do you perceive what to casual observers seems glaringly evident—that there is a flat contradiction between your avowedly Christian, conservative principles on the one hand and [on the other] the sort of merchandise that has become so closely associated with the name Murdoch, at least in the United States?

You are perfectly within your rights to leave me with nothing, in response, except being able to say "Mr. Murdoch declined to comment," but since I will pay you the compliment of assuming that you take your journalistic and other responsibilities seriously—and are not so morally monstrous a creature as to be interested in nothing but profit—I am naturally hoping—as my readers will eventually—for a more detailed and rational response.

Cordially,
Steve Allen
Enc: Matoian letter

2 October 1995

Dear Mr. Matoian,

As a person busy enough myself to work seven days a week, I always wince a bit when I receive a letter running more than two pages. With your own workload you probably have the same reaction. I wish I could spare you the attendant discomfort, but the message I have to communicate is of such importance that I believe spending the extra few minutes in reading it will be worth your while.

Well, not so much your own while—or mine, for that matter—but that of the nation. The preceding sentence was not a deliberate exaggeration made for dramatic effect. I refer to something the importance of which has, at distressingly long last, come to be generally perceived.

For whatever the point is worth, you are the first television network executive I have ever presumed to offer personal and professional advice. When I was much younger, I profited in a number of instances when older and wiser gentlemen extended to me the same favor. They thought I was in a position, because of my employment in television, to achieve more than the usual rewards that result from success in the entertainment field. Norman Cousins and Robert Hutchins were such personal mentors; they both became good friends as a result.

I am not seeking to intrude on either your personal or professional time—we're both too busy for that—but I am moved to communicate with you after reading the "School Spirit" article by Jennifer Pendleton in the September/October 1995 issue of *Emmy* magazine. At last, I thought, a television programmer who realizes there is more at stake than achieving impressive ratings and profits. To save a bit of time here I will [include] an article I wrote a few years ago at the request of the *Los Angeles Times*, ["TV Humor: Barbarians Are Storming the Gates . . . ," included in this volume on pages 35–39] since it will show you "where I'm coming from."

In writing the piece, I was just getting a strongly felt emotion off my chest, but I was surprised and gratified by the reaction. The very day the article appeared I began to get phone calls and letters from people, mostly within the industry—seconding my motion. During the next few years, although I discovered I was one of a large army making the same public complaints, the background situation nevertheless continued to worsen.

Both the radical right and the more responsible intellectual wing of the conservative movement expressed themselves repeatedly and in no uncertain terms. So did liberal and centrist spokespeople. And in time, as you know, the attention of Congress was drawn to the issue.

I was approached by an admirable pro-family media organization called the Dove Foundation, and have been helping them in various ways in recent years. A couple of weeks ago I received a mailing, enlisting my support, from William Bennett's group.

I enclose at this point a second op-ed piece for the *Los Angeles Times* ["It's Time for Comedians to Clean up Their Act"], again written at that newspaper's request. . . .

The fact that you, a professional educator and responsible citizen, have been placed as boss of Fox TV is as if a priest has been put in charge of a whorehouse. In that case I suppose the gentlemen would try to close up the operation, so the analogy is imperfect. But you are certainly in a position to reform Fox.

No doubt it has already occurred to you that Fox stands very much in need of reforming. Its production of *Married . . . with Children* alone requires such a judgment. That series is truly lousy as entertainment—compared to the great examples such as *Cheers*, *All in the Family*, and others —but what is also vile is the deliberate sniggering emphasis on sexual references. If some people want or need actual pornography, it is their right to have access to it. At least they're honest in their demands. But programs like *Married . . . with Children* cannot even claim that modest defense.

You personally are in no way responsible for many of the serious offenses that Fox has already committed but, to return to my thesis, I'm pleased that you have been placed in a position to do something about the problem.

I can think of no way in which I can be personally helpful to you in your reform campaign, but if you think of one, feel free to let me know.

I am aware that, even assuming you have such an intention yourself, the task will not be easy. There is a depressing correlation at present between schlockiness and sleaze on the one hand and high ratings on the other. Even the most superior examples of the sit-com form such as *Seinfeld*, *Mad about You*, *Frasier*, and others have a degree of sex-emphasis that would have been unthinkable only a few years ago.

Someone in an audience asked me recently if I didn't think there was too much double-entendre in television comedy. I responded that I wish there was more double-entendre; what offends me is the now common *single*-entendre, in which the vulgarity is blatant and deliberate.

Ms. Pendleton referred to the "old-fashioned values that guide" you. Good for you. (On a relevant point, I'm enclosing a copy of my latest book [*The Man Who Turned Back the Clock*], a collection of short stories. You need not bother to read all of them but I have marked with a paperclip one in particular entitled, "One Reason Television Is So Terrible." The story happens to be true.)

I've been addressing the general theme of social collapse in my writing since the 1950s. Having been involved with comedy, in either the sketch or talk-show form, I was happy to cooperate with another early mentor, Pat Weaver, NBC's programming chief in the early 1950s, who encouraged all of us providing programs for that network in his day to feel free to sprinkle at least a bit of enlightenment and education into our entertainment fare.

Congratulations on both your new assignment and your expressed ideals.

Cordially,
Steve Allen

VULGARIANS AT THE GATE

Since Mr. Murdoch's letter of response, though cordial and even complimentary, was marked "Not for publication" I will not reproduce it here, but there is no harm in referring to a few of its points. Mr. Murdoch expressed some agreement with my concerns regarding popular culture in general, and, in his own defense, he pointed out that certain of his top shows, such as *New York Undercover*, a crime drama; *The X-Files*, a sci-fi favorite; and *America's Most Wanted*, a reality series, are not part of the vulgarity problem and have in fact been much praised. Mr. Murdoch also denied that Mr. Matoian had been dismissed. He reported that Mr. Matoian chose to leave to pursue other interests.

• • •

It might be instructive if we briefly shift our attention away from the close-up view of the vulgarity issue and enlarge our vision to include society itself, in the general sense. Can there be any informed adult at present who is not aware that our social predicament may accurately be described as dangerous? Despite enormous sums of money spent on such campaigns as the "Just Say No" antidrug effort, the fact is that many in the under–forty-five generation do not perceive narcotics addiction as a problem! In 1970 there were over 300,000 drug arrests in our country according to the Federal Bureau of Investigation. As of 1999 the number was over 1.5 million! And, of course, such incidents do not exist in isolation but are related to street-crime generally, the decay of our cities, and the growing numbers of the homeless.

As for irresponsible sexual behavior, granting that it has always been a human problem, it has now assumed massive proportions. According to the National Center for Health Statistics, in 1940, the proportion of births to teenagers ages 15 to 19 that occurred out of wedlock was 13.5 percent. By 1984 it had risen to 75.9 percent! Divorce is now as common as marriage, and in every case in which children are involved the consequences are tragic.

There is also the problem of what has been called the dumbing down of America, which I dealt with, at considerable length, in my recent book *Dumbth: The Lost Art of Thinking (and 101 Ways to Reason Better and Improve Your Mind)* which documents the fact that the American people are getting dumber.

Our prison population continues to grow alarmingly, the number of those living in abject poverty is enormous—but is it really necessary to recite more details of the sort that assail us every day through the news media? And is there anyone so blind as not to see a connection between the social chaos now characteristic of American society and the junkyard aspect of much of American entertainment?

STARTING POINT

When I began my personal and admittedly unscientific study of modern television programming, of which this book is one result, I assumed that what was chiefly at issue was the willingness of some in the entertainment field to sacrifice principle for expediency, to abandon long-accepted industry norms for the sake of a few additional ratings points that might be earned by resorting to vulgarity, violence, or other forms of cheap sensationalism. That initial perception, it turns out, was perfectly sound. But I did not initially perceive its anything-for-a-buck shallowness. That is indeed involved but there is a great deal more at issue, for behind the obvious outrages and disgusting breaches of taste there is something deeper and far more ominous. The more dangerous offenders, I have only gradually perceived, are not simply well-intentioned country-clubbers willing to get away with what they themselves realize are breaches of taste on a narrow, what-the-hell basis. More serious is the fact that some of the offenders are quite prepared to advance a philosophical rationale for the evil they do. This is, to start with, unprecedented in my personal experience, and I have been involved with controversy about important social and critical issues for over half a century. I have engaged in debates with Communists and Nazis. I have even publicly opposed powerful organized crime leaders. I mention this not in any boastful sense, but simply to demonstrate that I have never shrunk from either opposition or criticism. But I have never before encountered the outspoken ugliness, the bared-fangs rhetoric, or the shameless defenses of the indefensible that are now coming to the surface.

Since the beginning of history and, it is reasonable to assume, even before that impossible-to-define point, wherever there was an attempt at organized, rational thinking, and the development of a method of writing to retain it, there was always a sense of codes of behavior, all based on the general perception of a natural moral law, which starts with the simple awareness that some behaviors are right and others are wrong. There has always been the general assumption that something identifiable as righteousness or virtue was, at the very least, preferable to evil.

VULGARIANS AT THE GATE

There is nothing the least bit primitive and therefore inferior about such philosophical perceptions. They are still alive; the various forms that the struggle for social justice takes bear witness to that simple fact. Indeed the pure ideal of justice itself can exist only in such moral contexts. But in recent decades such once-common perceptions have not only begun to erode, they have come under conscious attack.

TROUBLED COUNTRY

Although Americans like to quote a statement attributed to Jesus, "Ye shall know the truth and the truth shall make you free," when actually confronted with new truths a good many of us tend not only to run away from them but to pause just long enough in our intellectual flight to give the truth-teller a good sound pummeling. Although we think of our mighty nation as the leader of the civilized world, not many of us are aware that the United States leads the world in the percentage of children born outside of marriage. Because the news and educational media for most of our history tended to ignore the violence and lawlessness which has been part of our history from Colonial days, the assassinations of Pres. John F. Kennedy, Martin

Luther King Jr., Sen. Robert Kennedy, and Malcolm X, followed by the attempted killing of presidents Gerald Ford and Ronald Reagan finally did force upon us an awareness that we are the only nation on earth that has a gun-violence problem the dimensions of which are now brought to our attention almost daily.

There is no longer any serious debate about the tragically destructive effects upon children resulting from their parents' divorce. Once again, we lead the world in the number of broken homes that occur within our borders. Consequently, nearly two-fifths of our children no longer live with their fathers. Moreover that disturbing statistic has doubled over the last quarter-century. As Sylvia Ann Hewlett and Cornel West report in their book *The War against Parents,*

> Of the 15 million children without fathers, almost ten million are the products of marital separation and divorce, and the remainder are the products of out-of-wedlock births, still primarily concentrated in the poor black population. Divorce, on the other hand, crosses class lines with impunity and now wreaks havoc throughout society. In 1950, one out of every six marriages ended in divorce; by 1995, the figure had risen to one in two marriages. Divorced

fathers often lose all contact with their children, as the data show. Two sociologists at the University of Pennsylvania, Frank Furstenberg and Kathleen Mullan Harris, for example, followed a representational national sample of 1,000 children from divorced families between 1976 and 1987 and found that 42 percent had not seen their fathers at all during the previous year.

I strongly recommend that anyone interested even casually in the general welfare of our society read Ms. Hewlett's and Mr. West's sobering report. My purpose in introducing the subject-matter here is simply to remind the reader of what by now should be obvious enough, that there is *a direct connection between such depressing realities on one hand and the constant exposure to television on the other*. As mentioned earlier, literally no other institution in our society—not the church, not our schools, not government, not books and newspapers, not even parents exercise such influence on American children as does television.

For decades America's tobacco growers and manufacturers brazenly lied to the public about the harmful effects of their product. Television was helpful in finally exposing such a deceptive industrial campaign. It is sadly ironic now that our vast entertainment industry is guilty of precisely the same sort of denial of responsibility it earlier criticized.

There are those, and their number is growing, who see the present outrages as a deliberate, conscious intent to plunge our culture—and therefore, inevitably our society—into a state of depravity of the ugliest sort. But I feel that, while the ultimate results may be the same, what has really been taking place in recent years is a moral numbing, a growing, blind, and even stupid insensitivity in which many have lost their awareness of evil to such an extent that we no longer give much of a damn about questions of right and wrong.

Naturally I do not suggest that this process has been fully accomplished; we do retain the capacity to be disturbed by terrorist bombings and gun rampages in schools, but as regards less atrocious offenses we appear to have reached a state of dulled tolerance.

THE ROLE OF NETWORK EXECUTIVES

That there has always been a great deal of evil in the world is clear enough, but our response to this disturbing generality and to the specific offenses that dramatize it is often to relieve ourselves of responsibility by blaming others.

We must face all facts, however depressing they may be. There are others who deserve blame but we make a serious mistake if such finger-pointing serves to absolve us of our own participation in what we deplore. If we are personally so virtuous that we are not perpetrating a specific evil we may still contribute to it simply by standing back, doing little or nothing in the way of opposition. Concerning the blatant breaches of taste and judgment on the part of the executives of radio and television networks, they certainly deserve criticism, but most of us do not appreciate the precariousness of their position. They rarely receive credit for the excellence of some programs they choose and, even when they do, such honors have no relevance to whether they are continued in their assignments or relieved of their duties. The only factor that determines their professional fate is that of the ratings and the revenues of the programs they authorize.

While free competition is an integral part of the economic system of most nations, and properly so, its effects on many individuals are catastrophic. We read a great many stories of those who are successful in the marketplace but little attention is paid to those who, often through no fault of their own, are ground up and spit out by the massive engine of our economy. One thinks in this connection of the great comedian Fred Allen's description of television as a "tread-✓ mill to oblivion," although he was referring only to the fate of performers.

I have known scores of radio and television executives and I have found many of them to be law-abiding and admirable ladies and gentlemen, but because they labor under the disadvantage of being members of the human race they do at times make mistakes. For example, while no network executive would ever publicly admit anything of the sort, with few exceptions they hold unflattering opinions of the viewing public, which is to say, the American people. Consequently it sometimes happens that they will proudly boast of and vigorously promote programs that they originally rejected with unmasked contempt.

Readers interested in supportive details should consult Les Brown's classic *Television: The Business behind the Box*. In complimenting an advertising executive named John Allen, Brown observes that he had been instrumental in breaking down CBS's resistance to two groups of programs, the now-famous and much loved Charlie Brown animated specials and *National Geographic* magazine's superb nonfiction anthologies, "both of which had become proud offerings of the network, playing four times a year with unfailing ratings potency. The Charlie Browns (based on the *Peanuts* cartoon strip of Charles Schultz) had become perennials, minor family classics with the unusual history of attracting larger audiences for the repeat shows than for the originals. *A Charlie Brown Christmas*, in its fifth annual showing, pulled a phenomenal 53 percent share of audience in December 1969. As for the *National Geographic* programs, they were a revelation in an industry which had long held to the principle that nonfiction did not appeal to a mass audience. The success of these specials and of the occasional Walt Disney nature shows on Sunday opened the way to wildlife, travel, and anthropology documentaries, both on the networks and in syndication. Since both series were novel ideas when they were proposed to CBS by Allen—Charlie Brown for his client Coca-Cola, the *National Geographic* shows for another client, Encyclopedia Britannica—they were stubbornly resisted by network executives. The verdict from the CBS program department when the first Charlie Brown cartoon was screened was negative: too thin a story, the animation too slight, better left as a comic strip. The exact opinion expressed by one of top programmer Mike Dann's lieutenants had a familiar ring: " 'Piece of s--t.' "

What this disturbing little drama clearly establishes, sad to say, is that the American television audience was vastly more wise, in this context, than the so-called experts at the networks. And bear in mind that when the two program ideas were presented for their consideration both came complete with sponsors, a rare phenomenon when producers are seeking network approval for a new program.

A CAUSE THAT IS NEITHER CONSERVATIVE NOR LIBERAL

Those who, to their credit, happen to take an interest in one social problem or another often start out thinking that they are dealing with one isolated issue, but they should quickly begin to suspect that there are no isolated issues. Every individual social difficulty is part of a large and disorderly collection of interrelated problems. Depending on our own social biases we sometimes assume that the present debate about the ugliness and vapidity of many aspects of our culture boils down to a liberal-versus-conservative issue. Life, unfortunately, is too complex to conform to so limited a view. The debate on our cultural collapse is a matter of troubling complexity that often transforms opposing views into strange bedfellows. I suggest that where unity of effort is possible, among otherwise contending philosophical camps, it ought to be encouraged.

A gifted scholar named Jean Hardisty, a founder and president of an independent, not-for-profit research center, Political Research Associates, wrote an important book published in September 1999 titled *Mobilizing Resentment*. She responded to my letter about it with an insightful comment. "You mentioned that in the matter of the degradation of modern culture you agree somewhat with the 'social conservatives.' I concur, to a large extent. What we now see and hear in the commercial media world is not progressive, though it does inflame the Right's leaders. I often say that, during the last twenty years, *both* sides have lost the culture war, and the real winners are commercial media interests."

There is a famous story which I have encountered in various mutually exclusive contexts, that I assume has continued to be told because it makes an important comment on human nature. A number of gentlemen of note, gathered at a social function at a royal palace, were engaged in a debate about morality. "Gentlemen," said one member of the company, "we could argue the point endlessly, but perhaps we can settle it quickly by putting some questions to Madame de La Salle," whereupon they approached that grand lady of the court.

"Madame," one of them said, "we were just debating a question you can perhaps resolve for us. If you will forgive an indelicate question, would you sleep with His Majesty for 100,000 livres?"

"Well," said the woman, "doing so would certainly be against my principles but, in all fairness, when I stop to think of the great social power such an amount of money would confer, I confess that perhaps I would."

"Thank you, Madame," the gentleman said "but now a further question. Would you be willing to sleep with His Majesty for only ten livres?"

The woman drew herself up haughtily and said, "Sir, what do you think I am?"

"We have already established that," the gentleman said. " Now we're just trying to determine the price."

I introduce this tale because it relates to a question about corporate virtue. When I started analyzing vulgarity, sleaze, sex, and violence in the media, a process which at that early stage was quite casual and certainly not seriously analytical, I assumed that the chief perpetrators of the present wave of vulgarity were particular members of the media's creative community. There has been, of course, no reason whatever to alter that perception, given that there could be nothing like the present wave of sleaze and ugliness unless it had been created by various writers, directors, producers, and sanctioned by studio executives. But what I failed to recognize at the outset was that the corporate community is equally guilty. Although the reader may think less of my intelligence when I confess that such awareness did not come immediately to mind, the fact is that it did not. I very naively assumed that what I call the country-club class stood in some sort of loose philosophical opposition to "Hollywood" and could therefore be expected to call the worst miscreants to account.

What a dunce I was to harbor any such prejudices.

We shall perhaps never know whether, in the early phases of this particular drama, when what is now a cultural deluge was at first only an occasional trickle, the studio, network, and advertising bosses (those who held the ultimate authority simply because theirs was the money) might have had some personal misgivings about the wisdom of assaulting the national consciousness with the present mixture of pornography, vulgarity, and violence. In any event, it quickly turned out that they were perfectly willing to sleep with His Majesty when the price was right.

It is fortunate that the present phase of the dialogue did not take place a quarter of a century ago when there was still a semblance of serious debate about the relative strengths and weaknesses of capitalism on the one hand and doctrinaire socialism on the other. The corporate community, after all, already had a thoroughly besmirched reputation because of its frequent disregard for our planet's water, air, and soil. The Marxists had already picked up the weapon provided two thousand years ago in the observation of the Apostle Paul that love of money was the root of all evil. (Parenthetically, the famous attribution must have been in part a misquotation or translation error since it is obvious that, while a lust for money is the root of a great deal of evil, there are other forms of evil with which it has no connection.) But there had been actual offenses, outrageous crimes committed as part of the imperialist, colonial expansion—several centuries of slavery being only one of them—and formidable philosophical defenders of free enterprise had to be rallied around to respond seriously to such charges.

We are fortunate that Communism eventually collapsed of its own weight, if not yet in every part of the world, so that we can at least contain the debate within the philosophical domain. But, that the critical process itself absolutely must continue—unless we are prepared to totally discard moral considerations—there can be no doubt. Just as in the one case we finally were forced to admit that, yes, specific corporations and industries were guilty of the most gross and selfish pollution of natural resources, we now have come to the equally sobering realization that *it is again large corporations—today vastly more powerful than ever before—that are in part responsible for the present plague of cultural pollution.*

Formerly the heroic critics of the desecration of natural resources were all left-of-center, whereas today the chief and perhaps most effective critics of the creation of a cultural wasteland are right-of-center. But I hope that we will not be so blinded by team-loyalties that we will now make ourselves deliberately oblivious to principles. As regards this particular issue, it happens that the conservatives are right, and it would be a mistake to oppose them simply because one may also differ with them as regards gun control, women's reproductive rights, affirmative action, or the minimum wage. I'm constantly running into nonconservatives who are just as revolted by today's ugly vulgarity as is any Southern Baptist.

Because conservative speakers, writers, and publishers have long been, to their credit, outspoken critics of the high percentage of tasteless fare in popular culture, some observers have erroneously assumed that only conservatives are troubled by today's popular culture. Since this is not the case, it ought not to be believed. As long ago as 1988 the Planned Parenthood organization, working with the Louis Harris polling company, released a stinging criticism of American television. Said Planned Parenthood's president, Fay Wattleton, "TV leaves teenagers with the very dangerous impression that sex is something that people are swept away by. . . . We cannot help but assume this has a tremendous impact on young people's beliefs and habits."

SUMNER REDSTONE

It occurred to me several years ago that there are a few executives in the entertainment industry who, because they control such vast media empires, have the power, if they chose to act in concert, to resolve the vulgarity-and-violence problem, literally over one weekend. Unfortunately any such virtuous act will almost certainly never happen for the simple reason that the gentlemen in question—whose reputations depend on their ability to master the current market-place—would apparently not dream of risking a diminishment of their own profits.

According to Don Kaplan, critic for the *New York Post*, media mogul Sumner Redstone, chairman of CBS Viacom (which also owns the MTV and Show-time cable networks), speaking on TV vulgarity, said in 1999 "I don't consider that gross. Violence is bad, sex is good." Is Mr. Redstone being deliberately devious here? Of course sex is good, but I doubt that when Mr. Redstone engages in it he invites children into his bedroom to witness the event. In case the essential point here hasn't quite gotten through to today's defenders of cultural garbage, sex is not only good, it's wonderful. But what we are talking about in this context is not sexuality's essence, which is obviously necessary even for the continued existence of our species. The point is that not all forms and aspects of sex can be described as good. Everything depends on the surrounding circumstances.

I know so little of Mr. Redstone that I have no idea if he is married. If he is, what would he think if someone proposed to report to his home at some convenient time and physically, sexually assault his wife? I assume that he would heatedly object to such a scenario. His objection would of course be based *on moral grounds*, on the simple recognition that some things are right and other things are wrong. Teenage pregnancy is wrong. Rape is wrong. Incest is wrong. Adultery is wrong.

No doubt Mr. Redstone would claim that we should not depict rape, incest, or adultery as good. I quite agree. Unfortunately the ugly fact remains that when many television programs deal with the subject of sex, particularly in a dramatic context, they depict certain sexual offenses and crimes in such a way as to titillate viewers, particularly the young among them. A recent *USA Today* study of scenes depicting sex on the four major broadcast networks (ABC, CBS, NBC, and Fox) found that only 9 percent were between married people. The other 91 percent of the sex scenes featured adulterous, teen, homosexual, or otherwise nonmarital sex. With the average American now said to view approximately 14,000 TV references to sex each year, this should be a cause for true concern.

AN IRONIC TWIST

Perhaps nothing so clearly reveals the cynicism of television's networks and production studios as the fact that even though they are prepared to bring back such morally neutral programs as *The Brady Bunch* they are deliberately restructuring them with full components of sleaze.

It would be a mistake to assume that this and similar offenses are happening because the television production industry has largely fallen into the hands of personally immoral individuals. Although the entertainment industry may have a higher percentage of such creatures than the rest of the population averaged-out, the explanation for the continuing outrages is not quite so dramatic. What is involved is nothing more than the anything-for-a-buck mindset that even Adam Smith, who was, after all, a moral philosopher, recognized as the central problem of free-enterprise capitalism. Its ability to produce profits and a high standard of living has never been in doubt; the question is, can it do so without corrupting its practitioners and the societies in which they function?

SHASTA McNASTY

In early October 1999, the UPN television network added to its all-too-common offenses by introducing *Shasta McNasty*, an alleged teenage comedy about a hip-hop band. *Daily Variety* critic Ray Richmond quite correctly called this garbage by its right name in saying

> If *Shasta McNasty* doesn't hammer the final nail into the family-hour coffin, then probably nothing can. A parrot scream[s] "jack off" and chomp[s] somebody's crotch before getting pummeled to pieces. . . . *Shasta McNasty*'s message to adolescent guys is that if they don't want to be branded as losers, they should seek out chicks to ogle and make certain to avoid even the thinnest attempt at pro-social behavior. The show probably won't live long, facing as it does, slot competish . . . *but the damage it can do to good taste will be incalculable.* (Italics added.)

TV Guide's 1999 fall preview issue was equally condemning, describing the show as a "raunchy romp" and "the season's lowbrow watershed." Executive producer Neal Moritz was quoted as saying "I'm sure some people will be offended but I think the main audience is young men and women under 22." Regardless of for whom Mr. Moritz thought he was providing the series, *Shasta McNasty* was rejected by the television viewing audience and ultimately cancelled by UPN.

VULGARIANS AT THE GATE

PUSHING THE ENVELOPE

Our modern society is the most cliché-ridden in history. The problem with clichés is not that they so quickly become tiresome but they eventually become used as substitutes for thought. A good example of recent vintage is "pushing the envelope." In the context of the present problem the most unfortunate thing about the phrase is that it seems invariably to apply to going beyond the boundaries imposed by simple common sense and even tolerant good taste. The harm is compounded by the fact that in the language of social critics and others who comment upon the culture of the moment, pushing the envelope seems never to involve a clear reference to reprehensible and sometimes truly revolting conduct or language. The total absence of ethical or moral comment represents an instance of dumbth of its own.

On April 7, 1999, Fox aired a program called *Banned in America: The World's Sexiest Commercials.* The word *sexiest,* of course, was employed as a commercial come-on. What it really meant was the world's most *vulgar* commercials. *TV Guide* described the show in its guidelines section simply as "a saucy collection of foreign ads that *push the envelope"* (italics added). It quoted the show's producer in the same issue as saying "It's very twisted." An apt description, the program was precisely the sort of fare that is making increasing numbers of television viewers give up watching altogether, on the assumption that the present offenders who are profiting from the avalanche of sleaze are beyond hope of reform.

SHOCK-JOCK FIRED

The obvious central danger of conducting the affairs of a society on an anything-goes basis, which at least theoretically might make sense if most of us were ladies and gentlemen, is that since far too many of us now are not, the new class of talentless sensation-mongers seem to have literally no internal moral monitors at all. In the earlier radio and television days, had such people emerged, they would have been immediately fired. Now such discipline is rarely imposed. But it did happen in February 1999 when Doug "Greaseman" Tracht of Bethesda, Maryland, rock station WARW played part of a recording by Lauryn Hill, a Grammy Award–winning black recording artist, then commented, "No wonder people drag them behind trucks."

The reference of course was to the brutal torture

and death of African American James Byrd Jr., who was decapitated while being dragged behind a pick-up truck driven by white supremacist John William King of Jasper, Texas.

Reportedly Tracht was initially only suspended by his station management but, after a chorus of protests from listeners and black leaders, he was fired the very next day. Mr. Tracht subsequently issued a formal public apology for his comments.

LATE NIGHT RAUNCH

By 1998 the wave of criticism about television's sleaze was already so evident that it might have been assumed that the networks, if only out of self-interest, would pass the word along to the producers of their programs that they might profitably consider at least diminishing somewhat the amount of vulgarity for which they have now become notorious. On the contrary, the targets of national ire have seemed to become even more defiant.

Regarding late-night entertainment, the argument can at least be made that few children are watching at such hours, but on one of the popular shows in early December the host appeared in a comedy costume in the imaginary role of a popular Christmas toy. Playing straight for him were two adorable children who appeared to be about six or seven years old, a boy and a girl. As accustomed as I am to television vulgarity, I was shocked when the subject matter of one of the jokes—again, with children in the sketch—was based on the fact that their mother might prefer to use the toy's batteries for her own vibrator.

PORNOGRAPHY AVAILABLE

In some cities that have public-access TV channels it is now possible to watch actual pornography. I do not refer to programs that concentrate on sex to such an extent that critics carelessly use the word "pornography" to describe their content. Rather I refer to actual pornography of the most explicit sort. For the last few decades there has been a general understanding that for those who are either addicted to or merely pruriently curious about pornography a market exists to satisfy such demand. What is new about the situation is that such material is now available on television. And what is socially dangerous about the new permissiveness is that children are being exposed to it.

VULGARIANS AT THE GATE

Time-Warner's cable system in the San Fernando Valley suburbs of Los Angeles, for example, has carried a program hosted by a lingerie-clad Dr. Susan Block, who appears in bed offering sex advice to phone-in callers on a wide variety of sex acts and fetishes. "I know some people think this is awful, this is pornography, we should be prosecuted," concedes Block's producer, Max Lobkowicz, who is also her husband, and a *veteran of some thirty years in the pornography industry*, according to *Los Angeles Times* columnist Sandy Banks, who has written of her deep shock at coming across Block's program by chance while channel surfing. The most alarming part of Banks's report in the January 12, 1999, *Times* is the revelation that among the program's viewers children are included.

"We hear from kids all the time," Lobkowicz says. "They flick through the remote until they find us." Much modern journalism simply reports such things and seems to consider it unprofessional to evaluate them morally. To Ms. Banks's credit, she concludes by saying "I cringe at the thought of my thirteen-year-old stumbling upon Block's show. . . . It's hard enough to tune out all the talk about sex that dominates our days. Do we really need to see it on display?"

JUST SHOOT ME

In the case of the prime-time comedy series *Just Shoot Me* on NBC (whose original premise I believe ironically dealt with a journalism graduate taking a job with her father's fashion magazine hoping to raise its standards but being met by continual opposition) what is being criticized is not its comedy credentials. I have admired David Spade's work since I first saw him on *Saturday Night Live,* and his present producers have assembled a thoroughly professional comedy writing staff; but the degree of the program's funniness has no relevance to the point of the criticism that has quite rightly been directed at it. What is at issue here is that the deliberate and explicit vulgarity goes far beyond the boundaries of even the overly permissive standards that have prevailed in recent years.

In one particular episode, Spade's character, Dennis, returning from a Jamaican vacation he took with a new girlfriend, hints to his co-workers that things got steamy ("The tide wasn't the only thing going in and out") but soon admits she snubbed him. "It's not like I didn't see her naked," Dennis adds. "I was just pretending to be asleep while she was getting it on with the tennis pro." Later in this same episode, co-worker Elliott tells Dennis that he's "going to do to her what she did to you," to which Dennis replies, "Give her a painful, seventy-two-hour erection?" But instead, Elliott has sex with the same woman, who gives him "the hottest, wildest, oiliest night of crazy, freaky, monkey sex this side of Bangkok." In explaining the sexual particulars, Elliott says, "She's amazing. I felt like I was with three women—and I've *been* with three women."

Who sponsored this particular episode of *Just Shoot Me* (the material of which is, by the way, indicative of much of the series)? Companies perceived to be family-friendly, such as Milton Bradley, Target, and Toys Я Us were among the list of advertisers making this episode possible. When company dollars send this kind of depravity into the home at the early hour of 9 P.M., something is dreadfully wrong with the equation.

AWARDS SHOWS

Certain means of measurement may be more instructive than others for purposes of demonstrating how far television entertainment has fallen. A particularly disturbing instance is that of the prestigious awards shows such as the Oscars (for motion pictures), the

Emmys (for television), and the Tonys (for theater). In addition to the inevitable glamour and celebrity-power of such telecasts the one quality that was most typical of them, during the earlier period, was that indicated by the simple word *class*. The hosts were generally chosen for their air of authority and dignity and encouraged to officiate the proceedings with an appropriate degree of decorum.

A new low was reached on the 1998 Tony Awards show when many found fault with the work of the mistress of ceremonies, otherwise gifted comedy actress Rosie O'Donnell. As one friend of mine, a radio veteran experienced at comedy, put it, "She emceed the whole show as if she were introducing acts at a schlocky comedy club." The other objection-able area concerned her indulgence in the grossest sort of vulgarity (for example: A tasteless joke about feminine napkins and the brilliant musical *Ragtime*) that made one long for the days when Angela Lansbury hosted such ceremonies.

I emphasize that this is by no means only my own opinion, but represented the consensus among show-business veterans at the time. Veteran Broadway producer Alexander Cohen, who had served as the producer of the program from 1967 to 1986, was quoted by *Daily Variety* as complaining, "They have robbed the Broadway theater of its heritage and sense of occasion, and substituted it with a crude vulgarity which demeans, embarrasses, and infuriates those professionals who really care."

The 71st Annual Academy Awards in early 1999 were also roundly criticized, in this case for the shameless behavior of host Whoopi Goldberg. While I was one of Ms. Goldberg's first fans in Hollywood, even I was shocked that she would use the occasion of the Oscar ceremony to make crude jokes about female genitalia and masturbation. An executive of the ABC network, which broadcast the ceremony, was quoted as saying "Ms. Goldberg was a complete disaster and she should not be the host of the program ever again. . . . She was way out of line."

As of September 1999, not only was the tidal wave of schlock assuming ever-larger proportions, there literally seemed to be no getting away from it. On the Emmy awards program an animated character from a Fox TV series actually said, while introducing a cartoon clip reel, "It's tribute time, or as we call it in my house, time to go take a poop." The fact that the words seemed to come from a cartoon character would have made them of even more interest to children, millions of whom must have been watching the program, but of course the line was written by a human being and apparently was considered within the bounds of conventional taste by the program's producers and the executives of the network that carried it.

At a time when we are trying to show the world and our kids the very best that film, television, and the theater have to offer, the presentation ceremonies are tainted by sexual innuendo and vulgarity. What image does *that* send to the world?

THE TABLOIDS

Among the worst offenders of good taste are the early-evening programs which, oddly enough, do not originate or create the vulgar material they exhibit on our television screens but nevertheless they do bring it to our attention. I refer to programs such as *Extra!* and *Access Hollywood*, which are usually described by the adjective "tabloid." Here most of what is aired is offered during the hours when children are watching, by the way.

They not only report news, they also occasionally express an editorial opinion. But when the subject matter is sex—in practically any and all of its manifestations—that editorial opinion seems literally never to be critical. What is usually involved is a woman announcer—often quite a pretty one—

smiling suggestively herself and using such terms as "steamy," "hot," "spicy," or "sexy." The actual meaning of such references, if you break them down analytically, is "We don't want you to *miss* something that is definitely vulgar and erotic."

The verbal references are of course accompanied by objectionable visual components, given the family dinner hour airtime of most of these programs. But it is not only the early-evening tabloid shows that distort the ethical perceptions of our children. Local news shows, too, if you can believe it, are now part of the problem.

I quote here part of a letter I was moved to send in 1997 to the management of a Los Angeles television station—one affiliated with the ABC television network.

> On Thursday of this week in San Diego I was the keynote speaker at the first Character Education Project convention to take place outside of Washington, D.C.
>
> I'm assuming, in this connection, that you noticed that the President referred to character education in his State of the Union Address.
>
> In all such contexts I am constantly hearing the most scathing and sad-to-say well-deserved criticism of television, which

is unremittingly teaching lessons, concerning morals and ethics, precisely the opposite of what our culture has for centuries tried to inculcate, and clearly the opposite of what concerned scholars—including both religious believers and atheists—recommend now.

In this connection has it by any chance even remotely entered the mind of any of you at Channel 7 that it is pretty stupid to treat the visit of Howard Stern to Los Angeles as a legitimate news item concerning which, in fact, you wasted valuable air time with a "special report"?

Not only did you carry this segment—which was, as expected, utterly inane and unfunny—but your station wasted additional valuable air time, incredibly enough, with four separate "stay tuned" promos about it.

It is obvious that even someone like Mr. Stern could be a legitimate object of news interest. So—what was the rationale here? Out-and-out free promotion for Stern's movie, with a typically Howard Stern title, *Private Parts*.

Sir, is what I'm saying here a total surprise to you? Do you think I'm some far right-wing religious nut who's pestering you when you are minding your own business and telecasting nothing but perfectly legitimate fare?

If so, you really had better wake up and smell the coffee. I think you ought to appoint some consumer affairs specialist to attend a few parent-teacher conventions.

It is now generally agreed—on the political right and left—that our whole culture and society is sliding, at an increasing rate of speed, down into a moral sewer.

It is also a matter of very common agreement that television is among the causative factors.

When I perform my comedy concerts—which I'm constantly doing around the country—I get my chief laughs by answering actual questions from my audience, and one of the subjects that comes up literally every time now is the role television and films play in contributing to this big problem that I can assure you concerns every intelligent parent in the country.

So—in connection with something I'm preparing for publication on this issue—what's your story?

I received no answer.

PEORIA

I've been recommending to associates in the entertainment industry for about fifteen years that they actually take a trip into the Midwest or to any of America's thousands of rural communities to find out what the preponderance of Americans think about the present state of affairs.

They certainly found out a few years ago when a combination of television executives and public officials from Washington asked Midwestern parents what they thought of the new content-rating system (V for violence, S for sexual situations, L for coarse language, and D for suggestive dialogue).

It should perhaps be explained that the ever-increasing complaints about television's objectionable content had created a demand for something like the film-ratings procedure to be instituted for television programs. Unfortunately, even with such a system the harmfully bad programs would not be one bit improved, but at least potential customers would be warned about excessive violence or vulgarity and therefore have only themselves to blame if they watched the labeled shows.

The meeting was deliberately scheduled for Peoria, Illinois, long assumed to be a typical American community. As the *Hollywood Reporter* said, the parents involved didn't devote much time to commenting on the rating system; "Instead they gave the TV and political people an earful about the content itself." One woman said, "You can't even watch cartoons anymore. What are you going to do? Why have you let TV go this far?"

Republican Representative Billy Tauzin, from Louisiana, brought his telecommunications subcommittee to town, where he heard one young woman, a mother, say "I was horrified by some of the things I saw on TV, and the ratings they were given."

To that remark the entire hall erupted in loud applause.

CHILDREN

There's one aspect of this large debate that does not appear to have been adequately dealt with by the networks or the studios. I refer to a quite specific element, namely, the involvement of children in the viewing audience. The moral weaknesses of adults, who interact with other adults, are, insofar as they don't affect me personally, none of my business. I have enough trouble with my own shortcomings. But societies in all parts of the world have rules that at least attempt to guide adult conduct. This is not a situation in which all virtue is on one side of a sharply defined line and all evil on the other. There are complicating factors. For example, even if we all could agree—concerning our private behavior—on what is virtuous conduct of a sexual nature, for example, very few of us want the government—either local, state, or federal—to be involved in policing us. But of course *that is exactly what happens whenever any law is enacted.* Again, it is some form of government that is making an attempt—a legitimate one if the law is properly enacted—to control our conduct. The philosophical rationale for it is often that the attempt does conform to the will of the people—either the majority or at least the better, wiser elements of the people. It can never conform to the total popular will because the narcotics sellers want to be permitted to continue to sell their deadly product, bank robbers take a dim view of infringements on their freedom to steal other people's money, rapists think the police have a lot of nerve to try to interrupt their form of pleasure, and so on.

But there is one particular area where there is a remarkable unanimity of opinion and that concerns crimes or offenses of various sorts of which children are the victims. Even in the degraded context of prisons the most hardened criminals have a particularly low opinion of those among their number who have murdered, beaten, or raped children. Even behind bars those who abuse children are considered the scum of the earth.

So to return to our basic subject, the influencing of children is the crux of the difficult problem with which television, Congress, and the nation are presently wrestling.

Please understand, we are dealing here not only with my own opinion. Poll after poll has shown that it is the opinion of the majority of the American people that show business and television have gotten too dirty. You could argue that the majority of Americans are wrong. You might say that you personally can't get enough dirty jokes or innuendo, and happily for you there are places you can go to get more of it. I don't question your right to have actual pornography made available to you. I don't care if it's video tapes, magazines, photographs, whatever you want. I may think less of you for wanting it, but it's none of my business if you do. But we're talking here about specialized markets in connection with which it is considered by everyone to be important to keep such materials away from children. There's virtually no debate about this. But in the case of TV the tricky factor is that it's not specialized, except in the obvious sense that there are different channels. When a show is on the air it's being projected with the intent of the network to be seen in as many homes as possible.

What angers many parents or other concerned adult Americans is that not only do they personally find a lot of the jokes and other elements of modern entertainment highly offensive, they are made additionally uncomfortable by the fact that many of us do still sit down and watch these programs with children.

So the ball is really in the networks' court. I say networks rather than the studios because the studios will market anything as long as they think they can sell it. But there's no law that says the networks have to accept whatever the studios put in front of them. And of course in many instances the networks are creating their own programming.

Consider now what has been the networks' reaction to being so widely criticized, especially the last few years, for the vulgarity of some of their programs. Has any programming executive exhibited the slightest tendency toward contrition? Has anybody said, "Well, maybe there is a point here. Maybe on some of our shows we've gone a little too far"?

On July 16, 1997, there was a front-page story in

VULGARIANS AT THE GATE

Variety quoting programming chief Leslie Moonves of CBS—a talented and likeable fellow—giving his frank comments on the issue. He made it clear that he didn't like the criticism and apparently felt it was simply not deserved. As he put it, quite specifically, the new television content code adopted a week or so earlier "will not influence our programming one iota."

Was this perhaps a momentary exaggeration that Mr. Moonves might have subsequently regretted? We've all had experiences of that sort: We overstate our case and are later a bit embarrassed at having done so.

No, apparently not at all. To make his point even clearer, Moonves said, "The ratings will not affect anything we do, for one second. We think it will have zero effect. The whole point is to inform parents about what's on our schedule, not to edit what we're putting on the air." If we assume that Mr. Moonves's comments represent the views of his associates at the networks, then the chief result of his thinking is going to be to amplify the roar of criticism, which I've been warning my associates in the industry about for more than a decade.

THE OCCASION OF SIN

More and more in recent years I find myself thinking of an ancient theological concept, the occasion for sin, referring to social contexts from which individuals attempting to reform themselves would be well advised to stay away. Examples: A recovering alcoholic ought not to spend time in saloons. Someone trying to kick the curse of drug-addiction ought not go to parties where pot and cocaine are freely passed around. A man wrestling with a sexual compulsion shouldn't go to houses of prostitution or singles bars.

In today's culture it sometimes seems that our entire society has become one massive occasion for sin. Such a thing was never technically possible in former times, but now, when we live in an environment bombarded morning, noon, and night with messages from films, television, radio, recordings, and other means of mass communication, it is almost impossible to escape encouragement to act in ways that have traditionally been the province of the libertine, the thuggish, and the depraved.

The result? We now have twelve-year-old schoolchildren walking down the street blithely singing lyrics that advocate the rape and violent abuse of women, the killing of police officers, and other forms of social madness, while at home they watch teen drama *Dawson's Creek* and the animated comedy *South Park*, to name but two of the productions now featuring moral disorder and tastelessness. Meanwhile, the latest R-rated movie opens with a splash at the cinema down the street, only to turn up on HBO or at the neighborhood video store a few months later. MTV pours out its slick, seductive images and the radio blasts its shock-jock crudities and soul-destroying music.

Some modern folk are made uncomfortable by such terms as "sin." Personally I don't care if we refer to such morally heedless, destructive cultural productions as simply "bad stuff," but we had better agree on some set of terms to discuss the profoundly disturbing realities of our present social predicament. As I've indicated, there was a time when we might have been able to ignore the worst of all this since it was once at the margins. But it is now in the mainstream, and the evidence is everywhere, certainly on the Internet but especially on TV, the most pervasive medium in the history.

Although such humorists as Mark Twain, Will Rogers, Robert Benchley, S. J. Perleman, and the theatrical team of George S. Kaufman and Moss Hart made us laugh hysterically without sexual references, there's hardly a sitcom on TV today in prime time that doesn't depend on them, crudely and explicitly. As Mary Tyler Moore has said, "In today's television, on all the sit-coms, if the A story is not about sex, the B story is." And there is apparently no longer a debate about the sleaziness of soap operas. As for cable TV, many of its shows should be rated double-V for violence and vulgarity. Some are plain pornography.

Luckily, increasing numbers of people are disturbed by this collapse of standards and values in the popular arts. Civilization has faced such decadence before, of course. It is said, for example, that during the reign of the Byzantine emperor Justinian in the seventh century the arts became so depraved that the church often refused religious burial to anyone connected with them. Today's clergy are more compassionate, but they are nevertheless gravely concerned.

And they are not alone. All across the political spectrum thoughtful observers are appalled by what passes for entertainment these days. No one can claim that the warning cries are simply the exaggerations of conservative spoil-sports or fundamentalist preachers. Even people who fall far short of a state of personal sanctity—myself included—are revolted.

What are we to do? An old rural joke from the turn of the century concerns a farmer who had a particularly obstinate mule. A stranger came along one day and said "I can work on that mule for you." The farmer told him to go right ahead, at which point the fellow picked up a club and gave the animal an unmerciful blow to the head.

"Why did you do that?" the farmer said.

"Well," said the man, "first you've got to get their attention."

THE PARENTS
TELEVISION COUNCIL

For more than a dozen years I've been trying to get the industry's attention by quietly communicating with friends and associates in the entertainment business, warning them about the mounting chorus of complaints and the various forms of censorship to which continued excesses could lead. Friendly persuasion hasn't worked, so in recent years I've served as a spokesperson for the Parents Television Council, which has long stood for family-friendly programming. The PTC has placed a series of full-page ads in newspapers across the country appealing to the television executives who are personally responsible, along with sponsors and others, for the present coarsening of American culture. The ads frankly declare that "TV is leading children down a moral sewer," call on the sponsors of degrading shows to withdraw their support, and invite readers to back the PTC's efforts with a contribution with which more ad space is purchased. To judge both by letters from several corporate sponsors and by what I interpret as embarrassed silence from the studios and networks, we've gotten their attention.

The Parents Television Council membership has rapidly passed the 600,000 mark and continues to grow daily, adding to the millions of Americans telling us they want sponsors to stop bankrolling television filth. With the help of these people our national full-page advertisement has appeared in over 500 papers across the nation. And though still in its infancy—as of October 2000—the PTC has expanded its project of public awareness from a $100,000 campaign to one of more than $3.8 million.

In May 1993, Ken Auletta wrote an insightful feature in the *New Yorker* reporting the answers of the film industry's top executives to the simple question of whether they would want their own children to see some of their productions. Many of the executives dodged and weaved—and implicitly answered no. Since then the problem of cultural coarsening has only gotten worse. Mr. Auletta's question must continue to be asked.

Our radio and TV stations and networks, after all, are not owned by pornographers like Larry Flynt or Al Goldstein—the former being the publisher of *Hustler* while the latter published *Screw*—who at least do not disguise what they are doing. The offenders often turn out to be the country-club elite, many of whom are Republican, and some of whom are proudly conservative and church-going.

Let us, by all means, direct the beam of our ethical concern on this until now dark corner. Let us see who scurries away, or—if we are lucky—who vows to mend their ways. This will happen, though, only if the finger of public disapproval is pointed at specific individuals and entities. The PTC is doing its part, but surely there are other organizations that might join in. The occasion for sin, it turns out, is also the occasion for doing the right thing.

The networks and studios cannot claim they were surprised by the 1999 wave of criticism that reached a short-lived crescendo. On September 17, 1995, the *Omaha World-Herald* published an important editorial titled "How a Nation Teaches Its Young: TV Drowns Other Voices." Clearly the editors had

decided that the time had come to tell it like it is. "Once-taboo words, expressions, and subjects have flooded the family-viewing hours—not only on movie channels and the Fox network but also on the big three networks. . . . References [are made] to "screwing" and barnyard terms for urination and the anal orifice. [Included are] graphic discussions of the character's sexual urges. Nudity. Breast jokes. Penis jokes. Characters that once won fans with witty, humorous roles now talk about jumping into bed with each other. . . . Virtues such as modesty and politeness have been replaced with dirty-dancing and gutter-level quips."

REACTION TO *ACTION* SHOULD BE REVULSION

In the Summer of 1999, Parents Television Council Chairman L. Brent Bozell III warned readers of his weekly syndicated column about an upcoming Fox series whose content was shockingly vulgar even by that network's standards. What is most disturbing about his account is how the early reaction to the program from media insiders was so positive, and how conscious was Fox's attempt to further lower the standards of American television. Here is an excerpt from Bozell's cautionary column.

> Almost every year, television's fall schedule boasts at least one program that generates a great deal of talk—"buzz," as they say in Hollywood—before it premieres. Usually, shows attain buzz status by featuring some sort of envelope-pushing material.
>
> The current buzz series is Fox's *Action*, and apparently justifiably so. Press reports have indicated that this sitcom, set in the movie industry, features all manner of objectionable content, including a protagonist who "utters bleeped-out profanities at will," a call girl as a major character, and a homosexual studio executive who "surrounds himself with gay studs." As is to be expected, the ultrahip showbiz set is eating this up. "I loved [*Action*], but some advertisers are going to have a problem with it," prominent media buyer Paul Schulman told *TV Guide*.
>
> *TV Guide* states that Fox entertainment boss Doug Herzog, who, while at Comedy Central, brought the obnoxious *South Park* to that cable network, "was looking to push the content envelope" when he joined Fox a

few months ago. So he green-lighted *Action*. Some Fox executives, fearing controversy, didn't want the series on the fall schedule, but Herzog prevailed: "I said, 'Guys, this is why we're in the business. If this works, we've moved the ball forward.' "

Herzog's football metaphor sums up the modern prime time mentality: increased raunch equals progress . . . this is how most of Hollywood thinks. A recent *Entertainment Weekly* article said that after *There's Something About Mary* struck box-office gold, "it was like a permission slip for moviemakers everywhere to share their sickest, smelliest, suckiest toilet humor with the rest of the class." To illustrate that point, the author cites *Austin Powers: The Spy Who Shagged Me*, wherein the title character "sips a diarrhea daiquiri" and has "gerbils appear to pop out of his butt."

Fortunately, there's no guarantee that "shock television" has any staying power. After its relentlessly hyped first year, ratings for *South Park* have dropped by almost two-thirds. Howard Stern has lost 67 percent of the audience for his syndicated TV show since it began last August. According to the *New York Post*, back then 79 stations carried

Stern's show; now only 55 do. Indeed, sex-crazed prime time has been in an ever-worsening ratings slump for several years.

What *Action*—and Fox—deserve is public humiliation. More to the point: the show's sponsors, whose funding makes this garbage possible, should be held accountable. Let's see who sponsors *Action* and we'll know who is responsible, directly responsible, for the sewage being thrust on America's families.

As its premiere approached in September 1999 *TV Guide* designated *Action* a "Fall Preview Favorite," saying, "The season's most talked-about comedy doesn't just push envelopes [can we get a new cliché here?], it scorches them." *TV Guide* predicted that *Action* "could be huge," but also acknowledged that viewers could be "turned off by its relentless viciousness and self-absorption." I suspect viewers were turned off by more than that. *Action* failed to attract a sufficient audience and was cancelled quickly.

VULGARIANS AT THE GATE

SELF-POLICING OF POPULAR ENTERTAINMENT

The history of self-policing in the entertainment industry shows that the trend has been away from the industry's limiting what can and can't be included in its product and toward simply labeling the product to warn consumers when it contains material they may find objectionable.

As for television, the networks have long had standards-and-practices departments—censors—to determine what is and isn't suitable for airing, but in the 1990s these departments have become toothless or closed up. For example, the NBC program standards in effect in the early 1990s stated that "coarse or vulgar language should be avoided." Anyone who watches much of NBC's prime-time fare these days knows that this guideline is no longer followed.

In 1975, the networks, though only as a result of prodding from Congress and the Federal Communication Commission, agreed to set aside the first hour of prime time for all-ages programming. Who could complain? Well, the Writers Guild of America, of which I am a member. They and other groups went to court and successfully challenged this restriction on First Amendment grounds. In January 1997, the industry, again spurred by the possibility of federal intervention, implemented age-based parental-guidance ratings (TV-G, TV-PG, TV-14, and TV-MA) for much of its programming. These ratings were supplemented in October 1997 by content ratings. These ratings added more information about the content of a rated program in an attempt to clarify why it was rated as appropriate viewing by a certain age group. (More than one study has demonstrated that in practice, both types of ratings have done a poor job of informing parents about which shows are and aren't appropriate for all-ages viewing. In fact, according to the Annenberg Public Policy Center, nine out of ten parents they surveyed didn't even know the age ratings for programs that their children watch.)

Popular music has fared no better. In 1985, in response to public pressure from such citizens groups as the Parents Music Resource Center, the Recording Industry Association of America (RIAA) began its voluntary program under which companies were urged to label releases (tapes and CDs) containing "strong language or expressions of violence, sex, or substance abuse." The RIAA introduced the uniform "Parental Advisory: Explicit Content" sticker in 1990.

But recordings have since become even more offensive. Some artists and music executives have suggested that the existence of a ratings system actually allows them to provide even more outrageous material under the theory that the presence of warning labels provides parents and other consumers with the only "protection" needed.

The debate about the practice of warning potential customers—children or adults—about certain merchandise that is vulgar, violent, obscene, or otherwise degrading, is trickier than it at first appears. Consider the analogy of cigarettes. It took a great deal of congressional pushing and shoving, not to mention the deaths of millions of Americans from smoking, to finally force tobacco manufacturers to quote on the labels of their product a warning, from the Surgeon General's office, that cigarette *smoking is dangerous to health.* Now consider the same kind of warning but this time on a videocassette or a musical recording.

An ideal response to the Surgeon General's warning on packs of cigarettes—a clearly rational result— would have been that tens of millions of Americans who were *already* smokers would have *stopped* the next morning. Of course nothing of the sort ever happened. In fact there are those who feel that it was in the tobacco companies' interest to include the Surgeon General's warning because, in the event of a future lawsuit by a smoker who because of the manufacturer's product had become seriously ill, the tobacco merchants could at least say, "We're not to blame for your own stupidity. Every pack of cigarettes now carries a clear-cut warning about possible dangers to health. So if you started smoking *after* the date of that first imprint then you have only yourself to blame."

It is sadly obvious that not all American parents are responsible and loving enough, indeed even intelligent enough to take serious steps to protect their children against negative influences from the popular arts. And even when children are lucky enough to have concerned parents, such admirable individuals cannot possibly personally supervise every minute of their children's watching or listening to audio or video material.

And what of the millions of American children who spend long afternoons or weekends at the homes of friends and sometimes make overnight visits? Too often parents know little or nothing about what is considered appropriate material for viewing or listening in the homes of their children's friends.

• • •

An earlier example of content codes was the Hays Office Code for motion pictures. It was born in the

1930s when Will Hays was the president and chief executive officer of the Motion Picture Association of America. He installed a man named Joe Breen as the head of the censorship department.

A catalog of "do's and don't's" was sent to all film-makers and studios. It was a stern document literally outlining what was not permissible on the screen, such as open-mouth kissing. Any couple in bed, even if they were married, had to have one foot on the floor before any kind of affection could be shown; all films had to show that crime does not pay. In order for a picture to pass muster it had to get a seal of approval from Mr. Breen and his associates.

Because the major studios, members of the MPAA, owned all of the first-run theaters in America, without a seal no filmmaker could get a play date. As a result, Mr. Hays and Mr. Breen had supreme authority over what could and could not be displayed in films.

In 1949 a number of independent theaters went to the U.S. Justice Department to protest the monopoly of first-run theaters. The Justice Department filed an antitrust suit against the studios/theater owners. In 1950 the U.S. Supreme Court decided in favor of the Justice Department and the major studios were forced to sell their theaters to independent businesspeople.

This seminal event broke the back of the Hays Code. Though it stayed in effect for another fifteen years, in reality the screen was not as rigidly policed as it had been because now independent filmmakers could get their pictures shown without the seal of approval.

By the late 1960s, filmmakers were straining at the leash to open up the screen and many major studios were creating new distribution company logos to distribute films that did not have a seal of approval. In 1968, the third head of the MPAA, Jack Valenti, abolished the Hays Code and in its place inserted the Voluntary Movie Rating System. But, in its day, the Hays Production Code was a remarkably effective example of the entertainment industry's ability to police itself.

In addition to the thou shalts and thou shalt nots I have already mentioned, some of the other elements on the Hays list of eleven "don't's" and twenty-five "be careful's" included taboos against "licentious nudity," trafficking in illegal drugs, and ridiculing the clergy. Producers were warned to be careful about depictions of bloodiness; "lustful kissing"; "the deliberate seduction of girls"; and extremely violent destruction of buildings, vehicles, and the like.

One thing that seems never to have been controversial was the insistence that films make it clear that crime does not pay—which meant that all evildoers must be punished in one way or another. That is by no means the case today.

I have little sympathy when today's producers whine that the strict old rules would inhibit good art. Some of the greatest pictures ever made were created under that original production code. *Casablanca*, for example, and *Citizen Kane*, *The Maltese Falcon*, *Mutiny on the Bounty*, and many others. In fact, on June 18, 1995, *Washington Post* entertainment critic Rita Kempley argued that while the old Hays Code may now sound "quaint," it "just might have been the midwife of Hollywood's Golden Age." That's because the constraints "forced writers, directors, and performers to tax their skills and to use their imaginations. Filmmakers evoked everything from sheer terror to sexual longing—in some cases unforgettably—without resorting to excesses of profanity, flesh, blood, or grandiose effects."

Today's unbridled freedom of expression has "only limited the moviemakers' vocabulary," argues Kempley. "The more they show, the less they create." Sex and violence are resorted to heavy-handedly as a "simplistic way to manipulate audiences."

Kempley notes that the architects of the Hays Production Code expressed concern over "the effect a too-detailed description of these may have upon the moron." Today, she warns, the morons are at the gates.

But it's not too late. With a little common sense, decency, and forbearance, America's entertainment producers could develop a voluntary code of conduct that would largely eliminate the antisocial elements of today's programming without cramping their art.

WHAT WOULD YOU THINK?

What would you think if you were in some public place, perhaps a busy airport, in the company of your young children or grandchildren, and a perfect stranger came up to you and began to express himself in incredibly vulgar terms, employing the traditional four-letter words, and as if that were not objectionable enough, the stranger's female companion began to expose portions of her anatomy and do a deliberately erotic dance? Obviously anyone, even if he were personally depraved, would strenuously object to such a situation.

But now let us further assume that when you protested such shocking behavior, in the presence—I repeat—of children in your family, the offenders asserted that they had a perfect right to their behavior on the grounds that the United States Constitution guaranteed them such freedom of speech. Your objections, it is clear, would not have been without reason. There are, after all, simple principles that would make your protests not only justified but inevitable.

Now will somebody please explain to me, why, when exactly the same offenses and those that, as we all know, are often far worse occur not in a public place, open to all, but in the privacy of our own homes, and when the offenders transmit their ugly messages through our television sets, we are suddenly supposed to be helpless to defend ourselves against such onslaughts.

The defensive argument that "If we are offended by something on television all we have to do is turn the set off" is so ineffectual that it must be advanced simply as a delaying tactic. It is clear enough that turning off one's own TV set only puts an end to such provocations in that one location, and only for the time being. But it certainly cannot be argued that the background problem is thereby solved. Similarly offensive material will likely still be present when you eventually turn the set back on, and in the meantime the very material you found atrociously offensive will still be sent into millions of other homes in God-knows-what surrounding circumstances—children watching without any parental or adult supervision, or visiting children already contaminated by early exposure to such material.

WEAK ARGUMENT

One of the weakest arguments advanced by those who, in effect, say "I can do anything I want on television or other media, no matter how disgusting, because of the First Amendment" involves pointing out that the great majority of those exposed to morally corrosive vulgarity and violence never actually proceed to commit rape, murder, or any other serious crime.

So what? A majority of those who have smoked cigarettes nevertheless do not eventually die of lung-cancer or heart disease either. But it is still a fact that the small percentage of Americans who *do* die from the poisonous effects of tobacco-smoke number well over 400,000 per year!

It is instructive to note that once our society began to fully grasp such tragic facts, two things happened: (a) laws and other restrictions on smoking were enacted, and (b) the people who made a living by selling tobacco products simply went on lying on a daily basis in defense of a business they were perfectly aware often had lethal effects.

VULGARIANS AT THE GATE

As regards vulgarity and violence in entertainment, thousands of responsible studies have shown what was apparent enough all along. And yet this same pattern of denial is precisely what we have seen in recent decades from the entertainment industry. As far back as 1972, U.S. Surgeon General Jesse Steinfeld issued a report and testified before Congress that television violence "does have an adverse effect on certain members of our society" and yet the Hollywood corporate and creative community have consistently denied any responsibility whatsoever for the past thirty years.

2
DENIAL OF RESPONSIBILITY

Hollywood and popular culture must be fought. The movies, the media, and the popular-music industry offer their own heroes—most of whom are disdainful of normal life, hard work, and fidelity. Instead, they glorify violence, excitement, and aberration. The cumulative effect of such indoctrination is incalculable, but frightening.
> —Peter Gibbon, headmaster,
> Hackley School, Tarrytown, N.Y.

The day after a teenager guns down the sons and daughters of studio executives in Bel-Aire or Westwood, Disney and Time-Warner will stop glamorizing murder.
> —Greg Easterbrook,
> *The New Republic,* May 1999

VULGARIANS AT THE GATE

THE ISSUE IS MISCONSTRUED

Because almost all of us are guilty, and on a daily basis, of instances of irrational thinking, it should come as no surprise that we so often think hazily as we engage in the present debate over standards for television, radio, movies, and other types of entertainment. The purveyors of vulgarity sometimes respond to even the most justified criticisms by acting as if those who take issue with them wish to affect their personal conduct. This is an astonishing misperception. The individual behavior of those members of the creative community who are doing the most shameful work may be admirable, par-for-the-course, or shockingly depraved. For those who might have a special interest in the third category, it has been well-documented not, as the impartial observer might expect, in conservative journals, but in such liberal publications as *Spy* and *Buzz*, two ultra-hip and free-swinging general-audience publications.

But there are sinners, if one may use so out-of-fashion a word, in the conservative camp, too. Not because they are conservative, but because they are human. Even in the professions that specialize in the subject of morality—those of priests, ministers, and rabbis, for example—we hear endless tragic stories of clergy who have succumbed to the very weaknesses and/or appetites against which they warn the rest of us.

But all of that, as I say, has no direct relevance to the issue at hand. The offenders may live as they wish, in private. Indeed they may even so live in public in our tolerant times without being denied invitations to very many dinner parties. What the American majority—itself particularly moral or not—is trying to get them to stop doing is heedlessly promoting their own low standards to America's youth through television, radio, films, and theatrical arts generally.

I know, I know; the theater is separate from television and radio. The latter two invade our homes. In fact, all too often they dominate our homes. It is by now, I assume, common knowledge that our children spend much more time attending to television than they do communicating with their parents. Indeed many of them develop an ability to tune out the voices of their parents even while in their physical presence. There is no evidence that they turn so deaf an ear to television, radio, and popular recordings.

The counterargument is sometimes proposed that no one is forcing American viewers or listeners to consume any particular programming. That is so obviously true that an entirely appropriate response to it is this: So what? No one forces anyone to become addicted to heroin or to rot one's brain and other internal organs by repeated excessive use of alcohol either. Should we therefore abandon all public criticism of narcotics and alcohol addiction? What we need is not less but a far more formidable combination of parental and general adult responsibility, private personal and corporate responsibility, and—if necessary—yes, more laws to safeguard the hearts and minds of our children. This will require, needless to say, the cooperation of many professional disciplines. America's magazines—especially those sold from grocery store racks, should be forced to admit that they are part of the national problem. Ever since Helen Gurley Brown took over the popular American institution called *Cosmopolitan* magazine— for which, come to think of it, I wrote a regular column back in the mid-1950s—and turned that once family-oriented periodical into a deliberately salacious magazine by concentrating on sex, it's become difficult if not impossible for editors of rival publications to publish anything whatever of a moral nature, however mild. It has apparently come to be considered "hip" to snigger and joke about every sort of home-wrecking behavior that has troubled humankind for thousands of years.

DENIAL OF RESPONSIBILITY

Fortunately some individual journalists have gotten the message and, particularly in the last few years, there have been admirable instances of writers for major and minor newspapers calling things by their right name, but at the same time the notorious cancer that always gnawed at the heart of the free-enterprise economy, the anything-for-a-buck problem, makes it ever more difficult to stop promoting evil and crime so long as they are perceived as merchandisable commodities which can be—and are—turned into massive profit.

THE FRAGILITY OF CIVILIZATION

There is a strong tendency on the part of those who live in technologically advanced cultures to assume, probably because of the high visibility of the accouterments of civilization, that it is securely fixed in place. Civilization, in fact, is pathetically fragile. Forms of technology are likely to persist, or return if destroyed, but the sense of even minimally shared values that is the essence of civilization is quite capable of being blown away in a short period of mindless passion.

If we arbitrarily assume that the only human history worth the name covers a roughly three-thousand-year period, it is immediately apparent that the sort of policies generally described by the adjectives *progressive, liberal,* or *reformist,* have held stage for a very small percentage of the total time. It by no means follows that living conditions for the masses in earlier ages were generally so pleasant or just as to preclude revolutionary sentiment. Quite the reverse was the case. Conditions were so deplorable that neither the majorities nor their presumptive spokespersons saw any hope at all of ameliorating their circumstances by political means other than violent rebellion. But when in more recent centuries it finally became possible to at first dream of change and then attempt to peaceably bring it about, a pattern emerged that persists to the present day and presumably will far into the future. Starting from the background of disgracefully unjust circumstances, social philosophers initiate change by laying a rationale for it, after which champions of justice—many of whom pay dearly for their efforts—set about the long, slow process of protest, debate, and legislation in an effort to gain fairer treatment for the suffering majority. Far from being welcomed and thanked for their efforts, however, the pioneers of progress are invariably firmly opposed. Nevertheless, glacial status quos do finally begin to crack, melt, and crumble; changes, both major and minor, do take place, in the context of a contest of wills between opposing powers. But the factor of moral persuasion, weak as it sometimes seems when pitted against guns and tanks, and armies quite prepared to employ them, often does have an affect on the conscience of those guilty of sustaining the old, oppressive regimes. This is not, alas, always the case. Moral arguments, even in their sweetest forms, had not even the possibility of any helpful effect when they were preached to Nazis, Stalinists, and Fascists.

It has been recognized that India's revered Mahatma Gandhi succeeded in his incredible accomplishment of bringing a degree of freedom to India and releasing it from the British yoke. His efforts were possible only because, as a moral spokesperson, he was able to appeal to the conscience of the English who, despite what was often their personal selfishness and rigidity, at least were Christians of one sort or another, and who were aware of the necessity of preserving their own good names, something they could hardly do if they simply said, in effect, to hell with the poor, whether in the British homeland or the colonies they controlled. But when we speak of appealing to the conscience of those in positions of power, we are talking about a process with two separate factors: (a) the simple, direct reference to commonly accepted moral standards and (b) stimulation of acute personal guilt on the part of those largely responsible for having so long maintained the cruelties of the established order.

The old saying "The pen is mightier than the sword" refers to the same process. An assassin's dagger or the bullets of a firing squad can quite easily exterminate a given philosopher or activist who calls for social justice, but such weapons can have no effect on the thinker's ideas.

The same general dynamics were, of course, at work regarding the long battle, within the United States of the nineteenth century, to do away with the monstrosity of slavery. The only proslavery argument that retained any "sense" at all was the economic one since it is obviously to the benefit of an employer if he can, by whatever means, simply avoid paying his workers. But all the moral strength was on one side of the argument, and those loyal sons of the South to whom fell the job of defending the indefensible had the thankless task of opposing the ultimately invincible. It is important to review such factors now, as we enter the twenty-first century, because while it is obvious that slavery has been legally abolished, it by no means has followed that its ugly residue has been completely swept away. There are still dark corners, and in far too many hearts, where the contempt that made it possible to treat other human beings as if they were mute beasts of burden in the first place still lingers, if only hazily articulated. This is quite clear from the truly sickening literature of the far-right racist wing whose members by no means try to disguise their anti-Semitic and anti-black sentiments but, such is the horror, proudly flaunt them. They can do this and still sleep peacefully at night only by dehumanizing those they hate simply because if the objects of their scorn were perceived as humans, with the same rights as themselves, the haters would be consumed with paroxysms of guilt.

Unfortunately for the fate of the nation, some of the haters on the right are as impervious to the normal human emotion of guilt as are the Islamic terrorists who hold the tragic belief that they not only perform virtuously but literally assure themselves a place in heaven by their bloody slaughters of innocent victims in the many bombings they have perpetrated around the world in recent years.

VULGARIANS AT THE GATE

JUDGING

We judge the human race by the actions of both its best and worst representatives. The evaluation is made more difficult, alas, by the fact that the actions of the worst tend to be much more dramatic than those of the best. If there is only one murderer in a village of one hundred people and you have the misfortune to become the object of his interest you are still dead, even though the other ninety-nine bore you no ill will whatever.

Motion picture lobbyist Jack Valenti, among others, has argued, in effect, that most television producers and executives are good old boys and that the admitted excesses are committed by a minority of offenders. This variation of the "few-bad-apples" argument is worth only passing attention. Those producing the foulest entertainment may indeed constitute a minority in the statistical sense. The uncomfortable fact is, however, that for quite a few years now they have not only been permitted to function in the marketplace, they have come to dominate that marketplace. Moreover, they are the ones who are giving the rest of the industry a bad name. I personally will have more sympathy with the rest of the industry when I hear them beginning to criticize the offenders in the same spirit in which millions of Americans are now doing.

INFLUENCE OF MEDIA ON CHILDREN

Important matters, even those that deal with narrowly specific matters, are essentially philosophical. One such question with which everyone in our society should be profoundly concerned is this: Do the entertainment and communications media—radio, television, newspapers, magazines and books, motion pictures, and recordings—have any influence at all on the popular consciousness?

When the question is stated in such simple terms the answer is so self-evident that it seems a waste of time to have brought up the matter. At this basic starting-point there is literally unanimous agreement that, yes, we bother to write, to speak publicly, to communicate in various technological ways not only in the remote hope that we will be able to influence the perceptions and thinking of others but with confidence that we will do so.

As regards television and radio specifically there has never been the slightest doubt that they are effective and powerful means of communication. Otherwise they would not be the mega-dollar industries they are. There is a relevant clue in the fact that we use such terms as the *movie business*, the *television business*, or the *radio business* in referring to such fields. In a business there is always a product or service made available in the marketplace. Those who need that service, or perceive some way in which it can be put to use for their personal advantage, buy its wares in the same simple way in which a homemaker buys a loaf of bread or a pound of tomatoes. Since all of this is so obvious there is a particular fascination in the twist that dialogue on the matter takes when the evidence we are considering is not sales figures on the number of automobiles, pain remedies, or athletic shoes sold but rather the *effects on the popular consciousness of the unremitting exposure, through the media, to material that obviously transgresses common moral assumptions*. The motion picture industry, at least in the early days of its development, without any imposition of outside censorship, without the necessity of advice from organized religion, simply recognized the social wisdom of making clear, in its films, that illegal, immoral, or otherwise destructive conduct had to be called to account. The at least semiheroic on-screen protagonists had to be rewarded and the evil-doers punished. Obviously powerful moral lessons were inculcated in that simple way.

In the context of war there was never any question about the remarkable power of films, radio, and eventually television to unify the common will for the end of defeating the enemy, invariably shown as a dangerous and despicable creature who deserved to be vanquished.

It is unnecessary to cite additional examples. But against this almost monolithic perception certain subsidiary questions began to be raised of a *more complex nature*. These dealt with sex and violence.

No one has ever argued that we are totally immune to the appeal of pornography. Indeed a vast and profitable industry has been erected on the fact that in our capacity as animals literally programmed to propagate our species, we are easily aroused by exposure to stimuli of a sexual nature. And of course it is not only professional pornographers who take commercial advantage of this fact. The advertising industry knowingly employs sexual material, not so much with the conscious intention of weakening the moral fiber of a nation but merely to sell merchandise. I doubt that anyone has ever seriously argued that the purpose of *Sports Illustrated* magazine's "annual swimsuit issue" is to enlighten the public about the benefits of swimming or the latest developments in beach couture.

All of this is clear enough, so clear, in fact, that one marvels at the blank-faced "who-me?" denials now commonly advanced by networks, production studios, the corporate giants that own them, and product sponsors when they are criticized for the daily barrage of blatant images to which they are subjecting America's children.

THE UNABOMBER

One background factor that greatly worsens our present predicament is the recent quite mysterious difficulty in making moral judgments, even when considering moral outrages. One particularly annoying factor of the social problem we are considering is the seeming inability of a great many of Hollywood's executive and creative community to criticize even the most revolting examples of offensive material. Their predicament is, to a degree, understandable. They may often meet the offenders socially at the same dinner parties or public functions. They may even work side-by-side at the same studios or networks. As we used to say in the Army, "I feel for ya but

I can't quite reach ya." The longer people who are well-qualified to speak out refuse to do so because of a sort of social cowardice, the longer millions of Americans will tar them with the same brush as the worst miscreants.

Additionally disturbing is the fact that the same unwillingness to criticize evil is now detectible in many areas of society. Social critic Terry Teachout, in reviewing David Gelernter's 1997 book, *Drawing Life*, makes an important and certainly relevant point. Gelernter was one of the victims of the Unabomber, Theodore Kaczinski. "Mr. Gelernter is not interested in understanding the beast who nearly killed him. His interest, rather, is in how America responds to the works of such creatures and their lesser brethren. He believes that by elevating tolerance to the status of a cardinal virtue, our intellectual elite has created an environment in which ordinary men are deprived of the ability to recognize evil when they see it—or do it." It is inevitable, he argues, that vile crime should flourish when a "squalid cutthroat coward" such as the Unabomber is automatically assumed to be mad rather than evil, and the making of moral judgments is viewed not as a responsibility but as a sin. "A society too squeamish to call evil by its right name," he writes, "has destroyed its first, best defense against cutthroats. Our best line of defense against crime is to hate it. . . . No free society can defeat crime by force. If we fight it (as we are doing) with force alone, it overwhelms us." My own view is that Kaczinski is both mad and evil, but Gelernter's point deserves our careful consideration.

Make no mistake, what the champions of cheapness and sleaze are doing is not simply a matter for judgment according to taste. While their offenses are not in a sense as dramatic as the sickening crimes of the Unabomber and other violent terrorists, they are nevertheless evil and therefore should be opposed as such.

NOT SEX

Those who have commented defensively, over the ages, on controversies over sex, violence, and vulgarity, often imagine that what critics are saying is, essentially, that sex itself is evil and that, therefore, almost all manifestations of it should be vigilantly discouraged. The misperception is understandable, given the all-too-frequent historical instances of religious fulminations against the dangers that sexual behavior presents. Indeed the writings on the subject of some of the early church fathers sound pretty peculiar to us today, and to many religious believers as well. It is not necessary here to review the relevant classic works but we can see traces of them in the fact that Christianity, one of the world's most significant religions, still argues that total chastity and virginity are not only ideals but among the highest to which humans can aspire. In the Catholic Church, for example, priests and nuns are literally forbidden to indulge in any form of sexual activity and therefore encouraged to feel the deepest sort of guilt when they do.

The Bible is unfortunately unclear on a long list of moral and social questions and sex is one of them. On the one hand, there are expressions of admiration for the reportedly virgin mother of Jesus, but other portions of scripture speak quite accommodatingly of polygamy. To the present day a not insignificant percentage of believers in the Mormon religion see nothing wrong in taking multiple female marriage mates. This tolerant view of polygamy, of course, is generally limited to men of the Mormon faith, all of whom would be presumably horrified if any of their women decided to co-habit with several husbands.

VULGARIANS AT THE GATE

NORMAL

A number of social critics in recent years have commented on the question as to what is or is not "politically incorrect." The adjective *political* does not always properly apply but I take it that we know what we're talking about here. While the perception has been widely criticized in recent years—particularly by conservatives—it is essentially virtuous in its social intentions. It was the concept of political incorrectness, after all, that finally discouraged the once-too-common indulgence in Polish and "little moron" jokes, which leads to consideration of the once-uncontroversial word *normal*. It is not encountered nearly as often in recent years as it once was, originally out of sympathetic concern for the sensibilities of those who, in fact, are not normal. The question, then, boils down to what may or may not be properly described as "normal." Surely no informed person could argue that we should give up the perception of normality totally in discussions of human behavior, if only because certain extreme forms of behavior— e.g., serial killing, bulimia, necrophilia, the sexual abuse of children, etc.—could not possibly be described as normal.

To say that something is normal does not, by any

means, convey that it is necessarily either socially acceptable or admirable. When human beings are driven to extreme anger, let us even assume anger that is justified by surrounding circumstances, a large percentage of them will eventually respond by striking out physically, perhaps in self-defense at one extreme and in sadistic abuse of their tormentors at the opposite pole. Such behavior may, sad to say, be normal enough, but it is certainly wrong and/or illegal.

Our present predicament, however, tends to err as regards a reluctance to apply the words *normal* or *abnormal* to certain forms of deviant behavior. Indeed the word *deviant* itself has become part of the larger debate. But we must never be so foolish as to permit our charitable concern with the sensitivities of others to rob us of legitimate elements of judgmental language.

Generalities are often abstractly acceptable but suddenly become problematic when they are applied to individuals. We should walk carefully through this particular philosophical minefield, if only out of consideration of common sense, morality itself being a field that is unavoidably controversial because it calls individuals to account, and subjects us to criticism insofar as we do not conform to commonly accepted standards of behavior. None of us enjoys being criticized, even when we are most conscious that every word uttered in condemnation of our conduct is entirely justified.

It is easy enough to point out that there never has been—and hence presumably never will be—a moral code accepted by all of the earth's cultures and societies. This is most clearly recognized when we consider the thousands of separate religious denominations. What may be perfectly permissible to members of one faith is often deeply detested by another. But the lack of unanimity on moral questions need not too deeply trouble us since what is of greater importance is that there is a large area of statistical concurrence among the religious and the secular as regards what makes sense, in terms of rightness and wrongness, and what does not. It is easy enough to observe, indeed to lament, that even those who most seriously defend the moral code they personally profess often are themselves not in conformity but in flat opposition with it. But there is still considerable security in the general recognition that not only are rules-of-the-road helpful but they are in fact a basic necessity in the total absence of which life on our already troubled planet would become literally intolerable.

It is a depressing realization, but some of the most outrageous crimes and offenses have their philosophical defenders. There is an actual organization, for example, consisting of men who think it is perfectly permissible to sexually abuse children. The fact that they have never convinced any outsiders of the wisdom of their views is evident, but so weak are reasoning faculties in the presence of emotional compulsions that these criminals—and that is indeed what they are—continue to believe that they are badly abused by a cruel world.

At the opposite pole from this is the admirable attitude of such groups as Alcoholics Anonymous—of which there are both religious and secular forms—that recovery for the alcoholic is either unlikely or impossible until the moment when he can look himself in the eye and admit, publicly, that he is indeed an alcoholic.

Is there any hope, in the present morass, that the perpetrators of vile public talk and behavior might begin to suspect that they are mistaken, that there is in fact something wrong with them? We do not know, though we can hope. In the total absence of evidence of contrition or reform, however, we must persist in our effort to protect not only America's children but also the sensitivities of our perhaps dwindling numbers of ladies and gentlemen.

VULGARIANS AT THE GATE

MEDIA ADVISORS

A company called Media Advisors International serves as consultant to various television and radio stations. When this came to my attention I sent the following letter to the CEO of Media Advisors, William W. Taylor:

> Dear Mr. Taylor:
>
> Having read about your work in the current issue of *Emmy* magazine I would appreciate it if you could provide either a personal answer—or some relevant literature—to the following simple question: To what extent have your representatives become aware of the problem of the increasingly loud protests about the degree of vulgarity now so typical of much of modern television— and, of course, the Howard Sternization of American radio?
>
> I ask not out of idle curiosity, but in connection with a book I am doing on the subject.
>
> Thank you in advance for whatever response you are able to supply.
>
> Cordially,
> Steve Allen

DENIAL OF RESPONSIBILITY

I found Mr. Taylor's response more interesting than my own message. He regretted that he could not assist me, and informed me that any client information he is privy to is proprietary in nature.

Taylor's reply may represent nothing more than fact and the terms of his work contracts. However, his response also leaves open the possibility that his clients do consult with him about the problem we have been discussing, but that he does not want to go on the public record with any of the embarrassing details.

THE SUBURBANIZATION OF TELEVISION

It has been widely noted that for at least two decades the three major television networks have been experiencing a significant erosion of their audience. What is happening might be referred to as the suburbanization of television. The more discerning viewers are going off to the Public Broadcasting System (PBS), the Discovery Channel, Arts & Entertainment (A&E), the History Channel, and many other news, business, and entertainment cable channels which, by and large, present superior programs that appeal to more discriminating viewers. So far so good. But there is a negative aspect to the equation and this is that, as the brighter viewers for the most part give up on network television, the networks' programmers feel they must continue to present shows that appeal to such viewers as they have, which inevitably adds to the general dumbing-down process that is now so troubling.

In an effort to make this point clear, let's back up a bit. Early on in their development, the vast majority of new cable television channels attempted to carve out a proverbial niche for themselves that was distinctly different from the offerings of the original broadcast networks (ABC, CBS, NBC, and PBS). While some of the aforementioned education- and arts-related channels took a high-brow approach, others (MTV, Comedy Central, FX, etc.) took a decidedly low-brow approach. Unfortunately, as the higher brow channels began to siphon off some of the viewers more interested in quality, the broadcast networks chose to go after the lower brow audience. This, in turn, led the "edgier" alternative channels to lower their standards even further and resort to ever more outrageous programming and self-promotion in a desperate attempt to protect their chosen niches at the bottom of the entertainment marketplace. The foul-mouthed cartoon *South Park* on Comedy Central, the crude and sophomoric *Tom Green Show* and the disgusting and downright dangerous *Jackass* on MTV, as well as the flagrantly boorish *Man Show* on Comedy Central and *X Show* on the FX channel are but a few of the embarrassing examples of what television programmers will resort to in an effort to protect their already tiny market shares from dwindling further.

As a result of this heated competition to dominate the low end of the television marketplace, I am doubtful we have yet seen the depths to which television is capable of plunging.

And how are the radio stations in major markets conducting themselves in the so-far losing battle against sleaze and verbal garbage? As of November 1994, Los Angeles station KLOS had a full-scale billboard campaign that used the slogan "We suck less," while station KFI, in a similar campaign, proudly stated "We cut through the crap."

SEXUAL HARASSMENT

It's a promising factor that our society is becoming increasingly sensitive to cases of sexual harassment, and such offenses are not limited to actual physical contact. The habitual employment of vulgar language in school or the workplace is considered cause for concern. So why don't women's organizations accuse Howard Stern and the other foul-mouths of our industry of sexual harassment on the grounds that they clearly use language that would get them sued in any business establishment in the country?

ADVERTISERS ARE PART OF THE PROBLEM

Although those not so afflicted may find it difficult to believe, there actually are certain individuals who, far from being disgusted by the presence of human waste products, as nature itself provides by marking them with foul and nauseating odors, actually find both the contemplation and the physical presence of fecal matter and urine erotically stimulating. Although the percentage of such emotionally disturbed creatures is presumably small, it is apparently one contributing factor to not the mere toleration but the actual relish with which some in today's society employ language of the most incredible ugliness. This relates to one sub-branch of the present foulness of media language that is associated with references to flatulence. In this case, too, nature has contrived to make us revolted by the associated odors. But there are those who make such unpleasant subject matter a subject of jokes. Parenthetically, it might be an interesting psychological experiment to subject such individuals to an experiment with aversion therapy since I pay them the compliment of assuming that there is at least some final point at which they are capable of feelings of revulsion and disgust.

But given this background you can imagine my astonishment when, in 1995, I saw, in prime-time, an expensive network television commercial for Grey Poupon mustard that commented on the sound a plastic, squeeze-bottle dispenser sometimes makes. Naturally I was moved to communicate with the gentleman who bore the ultimate buck-stops-here responsibility.

23 May 1995

Mr. H. John Greeniaus, CEO
Nabisco Foods, Inc.
Corporate Headquarters

Dear Mr. Greeniaus:

At a recent dinner party a number of guests—most of whom work in the entertainment industry—were talking about the degree of truly disgusting material that is now a matter of daily annoyance on television, radio, and in motion pictures. I emphasize that this was no meeting of the Moral Majority but involved just plain show-biz folks, most of whom—I assure you—are revolted by a good deal of what we presently see on the air or film.

Someone present asked me if I'd seen the latest Grey Poupon commercial in which the "humor" was based solely on the factor of breaking wind. Given that nature herself has provided a means by which the normal human response to this phenomenon is disgust, I take it the point does not have to be debated. I actually thought they were joking when they mentioned that the Grey Poupon brand of mustard had a new commercial guilty of such a lapse of taste.

To my astonishment I saw the commercial last evening.

In connection with a commentary on the matter that I'm planning to do, I'm writing to give you the opportunity to comment. Was the decision to produce and subsequently telecast this particular commercial something that was brought to your personal attention and approved by you? If not, does it nevertheless now strike you that the commercial was a perfectly marvelous idea?

I welcome any comments on the subject
that you might care to make.

Cordially,
Steve Allen

On July 17, 1995, I received a brief but polite
letter of response from Mr. Greeniaus, from which I
quote with permission of Nabisco. Though he did
not directly answer either of my questions, he did say,
"I've checked with our marketing people and our
advertising agency regarding the Grey Poupon commercial. The test scores for the commercial don't
seem to support your belief." He then supplied me
with several test scores indicating general approval of
the commercial among the test audience, but closed
by saying "I know that these test scores do not affirm
the correctness or rectitude of our commercial. However, I do hope that you'll view them as underscoring
our concern about the possibility of offending our
consumers."

Shortly thereafter a scholar of my acquaintance
also wrote a letter of protest.

VULGARIANS AT THE GATE

20 July 1995
Mr. H. John Grenniaus, CEO
Nabisco Foods, Inc.

Dear Mr. Grenniaus:

A commercial for Grey Poupon mustard has been playing on news programs in this area. It is a commercial which simulates the sound and circumstances of flatulence.

I thought the earlier commercials for this product were brilliant. They linked the product to wealth and class, and given the fact that Grey Poupon was not expensive it gave people the illusion of luxury without their spending much money. These were classy commercials.

Now your advertising agency has decided to link the product with flatulence. Incredible! I am astounded that anyone who knows anything about advertising could think that such disgusting bad taste has marketing value. Is your agency trying to tell us that your mustard causes flatulence, or do they simply think that bathroom humor sells food products? Either way, it's a loser, and I suggest you switch to an agency that has a better understanding of the demographics.

DENIAL OF RESPONSIBILITY

Or is this ad reflective of the type of conversation to which CEOs are accustomed at dinner parties?

Sincerely yours,
Marshall Windmiller
Professor Emeritus
International Relations
San Francisco State University

Professor Windmiller also soon received a brief but polite response, this time from a "consumer representative" at Nabisco who assured him "we make every effort to see that all of our television advertising campaigns are prepared and carried out with high quality and *good taste* in mind" (italics added).

MISPLACED INDUSTRY CONCERN

As of September 1999, the entertainment industry was still complaining not about the basic problem but about the wave of criticism that was, by that date, literally daily inundating it, in this case specifically the proposal by Sen. Sam Brownback (R-Kansas) to create a special committee to broadly examine U.S. culture. The Special Committee on American Culture, to be chaired by Brownback, would examine aspects of popular entertainment in the context of such other important social concerns as sexual behavior and family structure. Jennifer Bendall, senior vice president of government relations for the Recording Industry Association of America, said "Obviously, we are very concerned about a committee that would focus principally on the entertainment industry."

It's nice to know that Ms. Bendall and her colleagues would be concerned, but one would think that the fact that the new proposal, combined with the recent investigations by the Federal Trade Commission, would lead the recording industry to at least entertain the remote possibility that its representatives and officers have been, quite literally, doing something wrong, committing quite specific offenses, which of course is what has occasioned the wave of critical attention in the first place. Ms. Bendall, to be sure, is a lobbyist, and is not personally responsible for the more dangerous and disgusting recordings made in recent years. Nevertheless there must be moments when she examines her own conscience concerning her defense of instances of the most revolting forms of recorded entertainment ever produced.

In the absence of such sober consideration entertainment spokespersons begin to sound as if they are morally blind in the same way that the American Association of Bank-Robbers, or the National Foundation for the Rights of Rapists—instead of considering that perhaps they should begin to put a damper on all the bank-robbing and raping—attack both law-abiding citizens and police agencies for what the criminals choose to perceive as infringements on their freedom.

Any hopes that, despite present excesses, there still might be some large reservoir of moral sentiment in the entertainment industry were further weakened when early in the year 2000, policy makers in the White House Office of National Drug Control Policy were resoundingly and negatively criticized by entertainment spokesmen for simply trying to insert occasional antidrug messages into some television programs.

Hollywood was given a second opportunity to demonstrate its true colors when in mid-July of that year the White House released a new statement by former drug czar Gen. Barry McCaffrey, who said, "As powerful as television is, some experts believe that movies have an even stronger impact on young people."

Again, the entertainment industry's chief reactions were defensive and uncooperative. Consider what this means. The industry doesn't seem to give a damn about its daily flood of sleaze and schlock but suddenly takes a very high-minded posture at the actually quite modest suggestion that perhaps it might consider doing something to slow the present deluge of drugs. Please remember that the FBI's Uniform Crime Reports indicate that more than 1.5 *million* arrests are made in this country each year for drug abuse violations.

Defenders of the entertainment industry will rightly point out that television networks and individual stations occasionally provide antidrug and a wide variety of other prosocial messages in the form of public service announcements (PSAs). But I trust that no one would go on to argue that these brief (10–15 second) spots have the same effect on the behavior of young people as the messages carefully embedded in the dramatic content of a popular television series or movie. Put another way, does anyone really believe that teenagers would be successfully influenced by a PSA touting abstinence or "safe sex" when it appears in a lineup of weekly comedy and drama series regularly glamorizing casual and consequence-free sexual relations?

DENIAL OF RESPONSIBILITY

SEN. JOE LIEBERMAN

Another example of the entertainment industry's "Who me?" response to even the mildest forms of criticism came in early August 2000 in response to the Democratic Party including in its National Platform Committee Report a "Responsible Entertainment" provision calling on the entertainment industry to take more responsibility for its actions. Motion Picture Association president Jack Valenti called it "political pandering at its worst," and described the language in the platform report as "shameless and offensive." The next day, when Vice President Al Gore announced his selection of Democratic Sen. Joe Lieberman of Connecticut, a courageous critic of media violence and vulgarity, as his vice-presidential running mate, the Hollywood rhetoric continued. In the press coverage of the response to his selection, it naturally was not possible for any one of us to be aware of all of the defensive statements that were so hastily made in defense of show-business interests. But an August 8, *Los Angeles Times* article entitled "Hollywood Winces at Selection of a Critic" described the reaction of the Hollywood community using words like "disappointed," "anger," and "frustration." The Associated Press reported that *Basic Instinct* screenwriter Joe Eszterhas wrote an open letter to Hollywood urging colleagues to withhold donations to the Gore/Lieberman presidential campaign until their "veiled threats" of censorship could be clarified. In his open letter, published in *Daily Variety*, Eszterhas reportedly said "Joe Lieberman frightens me." These statements and others I encountered might have made sense if the entertainment conglomerates were literally innocent of all charges. But they are not. It is much closer to the truth to say that they were guilty of all charges.

If there were anything that could accurately be referred to as an element of dumbth in the industry's protests it was the statement by Jack Valenti, a paid lobbyist for the entertainment world and, incidentally, a gentleman for whom I have great personal respect, that "We don't deserve to be made a target of."

To the extent, Jack, that you are representative of our industry, your client *does* deserve to be made a target of.

3
THE AUDIENCE FOR GARBAGE

Those who corrupt the public mind are just as evil as those who steal from the public purse.
—Adlai Stevenson,
former Presidential Candidate and
former Ambassador to the United Nations

The Grateful Dead cannot be held accountable for the character of all their fans, but Jerry Garcia and the band were pleased to be thought of as keepers of the flame of the '60s. The band's music may have been grand, but the band has promoted much more than music. Around it has hung an aroma of disdain for inhibitions and recreational uses of drugs and sex. During the band's nearly thirty-year life the costs of "liberation" from such inhibitions have been made manifest in millions of shattered lives and miles of devastated cities.
—George Will, author,
columnist for the *Chicago Sun Times*
and television commentator

VULGARIANS AT THE GATE

THE YOUNG

Almost every one of the scores of radio, TV, and print-media interviewers who have spoken to me about the vulgarity-and-violence problem have pointed to the scary fact that, like it or not, there *is* an audience "for even the worst offenses," as one of my interviewers put it. Of course there is. But there's also an audience, which is to say a market, for heroin, cocaine, prostitution, child pornography, and various other socially destructive products. There is even a market in this country, among others, for murder-by-hire. This is quite literally the case. If the reader would like to have someone killed, such a thing is possible. There are criminals who will accept such assignments if their price is met. It follows that the simple existence of a marketplace settles nothing whatever of a moral or ethical nature.

New York Times business reporters Bill Carter and Lawrie Mifflin reported on July 19, 1999, that "The main buyers, the audience at the center of this wave of what the industry calls gross-out entertainment, are boys and men under 25. Not only has this group established itself as the most loyal to Hollywood movies—because of a desire to be the first to see the hip new film and a willingness to go back and see it several more times—it is the group favored by a long list of television advertisers." They go on to quote Gene DeWitt, chairman of DeWitt Media, a firm that buys advertising on television, as explaining that the advertisers' interest stems from the fact that the young male audience is also willing to spend "a lot of disposable income" on entertainment.

The fact, however, that the audience for sleaze consists chiefly of young males needs to be additionally considered. The fifteen-to-thirty age bracket is precisely that in which physical nature itself places sexual appetites at their highest peak. The instinctual urge obviously does not turn off when one reaches thirty, and it is not totally unknown to children fourteen and under. But it is among the youth that sexual appetite is combined with that general human goofiness to a degree that is clearly not the same among more mature adults. Even Princeton, Michigan, Stanford, and Purdue, all respected universities, enjoy no immunity from the particularly dumb forms of behavior associated with the young. For years Princeton has had an annual Winter Nude Run. In January 1999 the school called for an end to the always nonsensical practice after several of its participants had to be treated for alcohol poisoning. Purdue has succeeded in putting an end to its Nude Olympics, and Stanford was able to close down its annual Exotic Erotic Ball, while the University of Michigan is reportedly still struggling with its Nude Mile Run. My point here is that this is the sort of mass-madness with which one correctly associates young people. If the participants were in their fifties it would be man-bites-dog news.

In the July 21, 1997, *U.S. News & World Report*, social critic John Leo referred to the phenomenon in another context:

> In thirty years of college teaching, Prof. Robert Simon has never met a student who denied that the Holocaust happened. *What he sees increasingly, though, is worse: students who acknowledge the fact of the Holocaust but can't bring themselves to say that killing millions of people is wrong.* (Italics added.)

Think of it: Over forty million people were killed in World War II, presumably in defense of certain moral principles. What Hitler and his Nazis did was among the supreme atrocities of history, and Jews were by no means their only victims. Among the victims were the elderly and infirm, gypsies, homosexuals, intellectuals, artists, and others. But despite the massive suffering and sacrifice of the war against Hitler and his axis, and despite the fact that the concept of democracy itself is a moral idea designed to make less likely the monstrous evil inflicted, over thousands of years, by countless emperors, kings, dictators, and—especially tragic to say—religious leaders, we now have a generation of young Americans who apparently take a lackadaisical attitude toward not just evil but one of the supreme evils of recorded history. Leo continues:

> Simon, who teaches philosophy at Hamilton College, says that 10 to 20 percent of his students are reluctant to make moral judgments—in some cases even about the Holocaust. While these students may deplore what the Nazis did, their disapproval is expressed as a matter of taste or personal preference, not moral judgment. "Of course I dislike the Nazis," one student told him, "but who is to say they are morally wrong?"
>
> Overdosing on nonjudgmentalism is a growing problem in our schools. Christina Hoff Sommers, author and professor at Clark University, says that many students

come to college "committed to a moral relativism that offers them no grounds to think about cheating, stealing, and other moral issues."

While Professor Sommers refers to the now common inability to think about moral issues, readers of my book *Dumbth, the Lost Art of Thinking—and 101 Ways to Reason Better and Improve Your Mind*, published by Prometheus Books, will know of my assumption that millions of us now don't seem to really know how to think about anything. If that is the case then our muddle-headedness would obviously involve being guilty of dumbth about moral and ethical questions as well.

It is, then, this problem of larger scope that lends popular support to the "anything goes" school of social philosophy, thus benefiting Madonna, Howard Stern, Jerry Springer, MTV, and other disturbers of the peace and common sanity.

But perhaps the most depressing fact about the young male audience for tasteless vulgarity is that this is precisely the segment of our society from which our young women—our daughters, nieces, and young school girls—will shortly begin selecting their boyfriends and, soon thereafter, their husbands. In other words these same young pleasure mongers will be the husbands and fathers of the next generation. It is horrifying to even contemplate the question as to what kinds of husbands and fathers they will make.

CHILDREN'S PROGRAMMING

As of 1998, although almost 70 percent of children's programming is aimed at children in elementary school, these shows were even more likely to contain violence and vile language than those aimed at toddlers or teens. In addition, 46 percent of children's shows lack any educational content, according to researchers with the Annenberg Public Policy Center of the University of Pennsylvania.

Many parents hold low opinions of children's programming, say Amy Jordan and her colleagues who issued "The 1998 State of Children's Programming Television Report: Programming for Children over Broadcast and Cable Television." The researchers found PBS an exception, giving that network their highest ranking. According to the Philadelphia study, the best shows for educational content are science programs such as *Bill Nye the Science Guy*, *Beakman's World*, and *Science Court*.

The researchers also found that just 16.5 percent

of parents expressed a positive opinion about children's educational shows. Only one in ten agreed that there were "a lot" of good programs for kids. Nevertheless, television commands the "single biggest use of time by children in the home," the study reports. Kids average one hour of homework but more than two and a half hours of TV viewing per day.

The researchers were looking for the effects of a new rule from the Federal Communications Commission (FCC) regarding children's programming. The FCC requires commercial broadcasters who want speedy license renewals to air at least three hours a week of "educational and informational" (E/I), programming for children between 7 A.M. and 10 P.M. Broadcasters must identify such "E/I programming" for TV listings.

In reviewing the E/I choices in Philadelphia, the researchers found that

- The E/I ratings were not well known or reliable: 25 percent of E/I shows were of "minimal educational value."
- Families with cable TV access can choose from 25 stations and 247 children's shows; children without cable access lose half these choices.
- Less than 10 percent of children's shows air during the 7 P.M. to 10 P.M. "prime time."

THE AUDIENCE FOR GARBAGE

Among the survey's other findings,

- Programming for the five- to eleven-year-old audience is "abundant, but much of it is not enriching"; 44 percent of shows targeted to this audience have "a lot" of violence—meaning "intentional and malicious" violence in three or more scenes.
- Shows for teens also have the most sexual innuendo with "a lot" of such references in 19.2 percent of programs.
- Seventy-five percent of the shows that contain violence fail to carry the "FV" (fantasy violence) warning label.

ONLY SOME AUDIENCES WANT SMUT

One thing that at least some young comedians who work in a rough style apparently do *not* realize is that they are actually limiting their prospects for employment. The reason is quite simple. There are many audiences that do not want to be subjected to entertainment that is vulgar. The average audience will put up with a sprinkling of it but today, for the first time, we have entertainers who do practically nothing else.

I'm reminded in this connection of an instance, about twenty years back, when I reported to a southern city where I was scheduled to entertain a convention audience. The man who picked me up at the airport explained as he drove me to my hotel, "One of the reasons we booked you is that you work clean."

I had never before heard such a thing. Jokingly, I said to him, "I thought you hired me because I was funny."

"Of course," he said, "but there are a lot of funny guys around. My audience wouldn't touch most of them with a ten-foot pole because they do too much filth." His point was that such comedians make a serious mistake if they think that just because certain kinds of material are acceptable in Las Vegas or at a Friars Club Roast they are for all groups.

In another relevant case I was booked on an ocean cruise. As soon as my wife, Jayne, and I boarded the ship a uniformed attendant approached me and said "Mr. Allen, the cruise director wants to see you immediately."

"Fine," I said, "bring him to me as soon as possible."

THE AUDIENCE FOR GARBAGE

In a few minutes the gentleman approached, in a state of nervous agitation, and asked, "You work clean, don't you?"

"Yes," I said, having no idea why he should ask such a question. "What's the problem?"

"Well," he said, "I've just been through two weeks of pure hell."

He mentioned the names of two popular and certainly funny comedians, both now no longer with us. "I told them," he said, "that my audiences definitely do not like vulgarity. But they wouldn't listen to me. Instead they got angry and said that they didn't need any advice at this stage of their careers, that they knew how to make audiences laugh, etc. "

Perhaps the reader should be reminded of the old joke that the average age of the passengers on some round-the-world cruises is *deceased,* by which I mean that there is a great preponderance of people in their sixties, seventies, and eighties—in other words, people to whom the vulgarity and violent language characteristic of today's comedy is anathema. Nevertheless the two entertainers in question proceeded to do a certain amount of off-color material. According to the cruise director, the results were disastrous. People walked out during their acts, they got a generally cold reception, very few laughs, and were even socially ostracized after their performances. In the case of one of the poor fellows, the cruise director told him that there would be no necessity to do his second show because of the great number of complaints about his first.

In any event, it was clear why the director was so concerned that my own act be kept pristine. There was no problem about that, as far as I was concerned, since at least 98 percent of my act could be performed at the average church picnic. But when it comes to vulgarity, one man's meat is another man's whatever. In any event, when introduced for the first show, I walked out with a hotel front desk type call-bell in each hand, and two more in my jacket pockets, and while the applause and play-on music were still continuing I walked about the club floor and began to place the bells at various tables. "Ladies and gentlemen," I said, when the music had stopped, "your cruise director has brought to my attention the unfortunate difficulties in which my two predecessors who entertained you on this cruise recently found themselves. I understand that some of you were incensed at what you considered the vulgarity of their language, and I would naturally hope not to similarly offend you. Unfortunately, there is no possibility of unanimity as regards such judgments. In other words,

I might do a joke that I consider perfectly inoffensive, and yet some of you might regard as objectionable. I have therefore placed these attention-getting bells on several of your tables, and I want you to feel free to use them the moment you hear me say anything you consider the least bit offensive."

Well, naturally, the people were hysterical immediately. They began to ring the damned bells at almost anything I said. Within a few minutes, their mood had become such that some of them actually wanted me to do something at least moderately in poor taste, just so they could have the pleasure of calling me to account with the call-bells. The routine was so wonderfully successful that I've always been saddened by the fact that I could never do it again. It was perfect for that moment and that situation, but those particular circumstances are unlikely to be repeated.

4
THE OFFENDERS
A Closer Look
at One Teen Idol

Popular culture is the glue that holds a nation together.

> —Robert Thompson,
> The Center for the
> Study of Popular Television

Recently I paid my first visit to the west in a dozen years, and I was appalled by what I saw . . . I kept thinking of A. E. Housman's lines:

> *"Some could watch and not be sick
> But I could never learn the trick"*
> —Arthur C. Clarke,
> noted scientist and science fiction writer

VULGARIANS AT THE GATE

MADONNA

One reader of the manuscript for this volume has suggested that since Madonna has now been so heavily criticized, and for such a long period of time, the extended reference to her here may no longer be necessary. But I have decided to retain this discussion because of the tragic fact that made me prepare it in the first place. The woman in question was at a point in the not-distant past, reportedly the number-one role model for American girls from the age of eleven to eighteen, among the most impressionable years. And, to judge by her recent record sales and airplay on MTV, it appears she continues to be very popular with that age group.

As has been widely observed, and from all possible points of the political and philosophical compass, it is more difficult to raise children to be ladies and gentlemen in this day and age than in any earlier stage of our national history. One reason is that we have so many bad examples who, because they work in the popular media, are inevitably models for the behavior of American boys and girls. It should be instructive therefore to review the reasons for Madonna's great success in the marketplace. I believe the kind of behavior that accompanied her ascension to wide popularity would in earlier decades have led other entertainers to scandal, disgrace, and the loss of many work opportunities. That we live now in very different cultural times is painfully obvious.

The saddest aspect of the present situation is not that she herself is the problem, any more than the once-popular Andrew Dice Clay was the problem. It is that she, Clay, and the scores like them who market not beauty, the traditional province of the artist, but ugliness, are received by our society not as objects of contempt, as they might be in a more civilized culture, but rather are embraced by millions as icons of American pop culture itself and richly rewarded in the entertainment marketplace.

Mr. Clay, at least as of several years ago, was able to fill New York City's famed Madison Square Garden, something that probably no other comedian, however gifted, could do at that time. Just so, Madonna's services are even now more in demand than those of other popular singers or entertainers who far surpass her in talent, a fact that speaks volumes about our social predicament.

There is one point, of crucial moral importance, that appears not to have impressed itself upon either the public consciousness or the circle of professional critics. No one assumes that there was ever a Golden Age of personal rectitude among creative people. The statistics about alcoholism, drug addiction, sexual promiscuity, and emotional instability in the general population are tragic enough. They have always been higher in the arts, and particularly so in the creative art known as show business. When, therefore, we say the present degree of moral turpitude is shocking, we are not naïve enough to compare it to some sort of moral never-never-land in which entertainers were as righteous and heroic as the roles they played or the public images they manufactured.

But the sinners and offenders of earlier times at least attempted to keep their transgressions private, if only for selfish reasons. It has now become almost impossible to shame our public figures. In the American past there was always, under the combined facade and reality of the sort of happy home depicted in the old MGM Andy Hardy films, a strain of social and moral illness, but formerly sexual perverts, sadists, masochists, and the like at least scurried for cover when the lights were turned on. Today, by way of contrast, the offenders, though they may become the butt of a few random jokes by late-night television hosts, are promptly surrounded and defended by those who stand to make money from their professional activities, and we are quickly told that even the most vile onstage excesses are permissible because they are protected by the rights specified by the First Amendment in that most noble of documents, the American Constitution.

I do not take lightly the question of creative rights, and I'm certainly no abstract philosopher viewing the question from an impartial distance. I am myself the creator of a large body of music, poetry, and prose. But it would never occur to me to argue that simply because of my creativity I am entitled to introduce into the marketplace literally anything at all, however revolting.

The point here again is not that the present flood-tide carrying us all into the sewer is to be fairly contrasted with a state of moral perfection. Even Shakespeare occasionally inserted a bawdy comment or joke into his magnificent plays. Indeed, much poetry has included an erotic component, and the Old Testament's Song of Solomon is renowned for its sensuality.

The fundamental question as to the proper place of sex within the context of an even remotely civilized society is simply one of those ongoing dilemmas about which the ablest philosophers continue to differ. Relations between the creative community and the state, which through its laws is somehow supposed to represent the will of the people, have always been uneasy. But I deliberately return to the point that we are by no means presently faced with one of those historic balancing-acts. In the past no artist has ever argued that literally *anything* is permissible. Even the sexually frank novelist Henry Miller was not a complete moral anarchist. Today, however, *anything goes* seems to be the operative principle.

Am I exaggerating here? It is of crucial importance to understand that I am not. The marketing of the most depraved and disgusting material is now not only permitted—which would be bad enough—it is dominant in the commercial marketplace and philo-sophically defended there. Millions of Americans have died, in various wars, presumably not on the classic justification that our borders needed to be defended. That those millions of American deaths were justified as a defense of our economic system—which practically all Americans prefer—is part of the problem. As noted earlier, major national and inter-national corporations are now making no distinction whatever between a dollar earned by marketing vio-lence or vulgarity and one made by marketing fashion or food products.

When, in the past, at least a segment of the public became aware that some of its favored entertainers left a great deal to be desired as human beings, it could at least respond, "Well, I wouldn't want my daughter to marry the fellow, but I like his singing (clarinet playing, acting, or what have you) so much that I'll just turn a deaf ear to his personal faults." And indeed, this may be a reasonable attitude as regards individuals possessed of true artistic talent.

Although I understand the reasons behind the U.S. government's campaign to ban Bach, Beethoven, and other great German composers from our airwaves during our wars against Germany, it was always my private opinion that there was something dumb in the practice. It is, after all, possible to thrill to the music of a German genius while still despising the Nazis, or to enjoy an Italian opera while still loathing Mussolini and his Fascists.

But such equations do not apply to our present predicament, and this is nowhere so clearly illustrated as in the case of Madonna, for the simple reason that her talents are relatively modest. Many performers achieve success because of their remarkable gifts. Barbra Streisand, Meryl Streep, Robert de Niro, Tom Hanks, Al Pacino, and Robert Duvall come to mind in such a connection. Madonna does not. She has succeeded for a reason that reflects no credit upon the rest of us. She has succeeded because of what I believe to be a moral weakness and willingness to prostitute herself for fame and money. She is not, like the rest of us, simply someone who almost daily falls short of the moral standards we sincerely profess. She does not hide but rather flaunts her disdain for those standards. No doubt there are other women on this planet who behave similarly, but *they are not role models to millions of impressionable teenagers.*

In this general connection I am reminded of the evening, some years ago, when at a small dinner party in her apartment in New York, former congresswoman and social critic Clare Booth Luce, who was an admirer of *Meeting of Minds*, a television show I had created for the PBS network, recommended that I consider booking the Marquis de Sade as a guest. (*Meeting of Minds* was a television talk show, though scripted and rehearsed, in which important figures of history came together to engage in philosophical debate.) For a moment I thought that Ms. Luce was joking. "Oh, no," she said. "I'm quite serious. Sade was the most despicable person imaginable, but his views are very influential in today's society."

Ms. Luce was quite right, needless to say, and our two episodes in which Sade was permitted to advocate his depraved ideas were both stimulating and sobering. In more recent years, Madonna may have been the Marquis's ablest and most influential modern defender.

One clue to the profound seriousness of our present predicament concerns the term *deviant behavior*. The concept, which for centuries has had legitimate application among social philosophers, is obviously based on moral distinctions between more-or-less common modes of behavior, not all of them necessarily highly virtuous, and other forms of conduct that represent dangers to society. But that classic and common-sense distinction is not, in the public consciousness, as clear-cut as it formerly was. Indeed, many of those guilty of blatantly deviant behavior are now unapologetic, often defiant, and if they happen to be celebrities, their very fame seems to provide at least a degree of immunity from public criticism. Some such criticism is there, of course, though largely because there is an unappealing public appetite for scandal. But there is now so much of this deviant behavior, such a daily flood, in fact, and the public's attention-span is now apparently so short, that there is not only little likelihood that the offenders will suffer professional harm, it is quite likely that they will profit by rather than suffer from their escapades. Although it would not matter to me in the least if I were the only person in the entire entertainment field to express such views, the important thing is that I am not.

There has never been any such thing as a universally popular entertainer. The only American who came close was the brilliant and naturally lovable Will Rogers. It is therefore not particularly noteworthy that Madonna has her detractors; we all do. But it is instructive to consider what it is, very specifically, that makes her offensive to so many. A few examples:

On the night after a throat ailment caused her to cancel a concert, she announced to an audience in the Washington, D.C., area, "I don't care what anyone says, I'm f---ing hot tonight."

In the presence of a performer dressed as a Catholic priest, Madonna not only starts to disrobe but smashes to the ground a crucifix, the most sacred of symbols to hundreds of millions of Christians. Asked why she chose to use a sacred religious symbol as a trademark/logo, she reportedly replied, "Crucifixes are sexy because there's a naked man on them."

After nude pictures of her were published in *Playboy* and *Penthouse*, she explained, "It was like when you're a little girl at school and some nun comes and lifts your dress up in front of everybody and you get really embarrassed." Were there no journalists present to ask for the identity of the nun and the name of the school where the alleged incident took place?

A concert in Texas included one number about sadomasochistic spankings and another in which masturbation was feigned. Another number featured several cross-dressed male dancers wearing brassieres.

In 1993, Yves Saint Laurent, one of the world's true authorities on fashion, in deploring the state of contemporary couture was specifically dismissive of Madonna in an interview in *W* magazine. His comment: "she's not fashion; she just shows her ass."

Not long before Saint Laurent's assessment of the Material Girl, Madonna had released a sexually explicit book which *Vanity Fair* magazine, hardly a conservative publication, had dubbed "the dirtiest coffee table book every published." The publication of *Sex*, the photo book *Time* magazine called "shot-to-shock" led the famous news weekly to label Madonna a "purveyor of plain ole porn."

Given that few other entertainers in modern history have consciously conveyed so many destructive and perverted messages, is it perhaps possible that the young woman's own intentions are virtuous but that she has fallen under the influence of some evil guru or a cult? Not likely, as her close associate, songwriter Stephen Bray, has put it, "This is a woman who is in complete charge of her life. She calls her own shots." This is perhaps the one point about her that is not a subject of controversy.

Despite the entertainer's success, which is formidable, her eager willingness—or apparent determination—to shock does occasionally affect ticket sales. When she appeared in Italy in the summer of 1990, *Newsweek* reported sales were low, and one performance in Rome was canceled after Catholic spokesmen, quite correctly, termed her show blasphemous. When Madonna arrived in Buenos Aires, Argentina, in January 1996, her reputation had preceded her, leading to what *Entertainment Weekly* magazine referred to as a "less-than-stellar welcome." Some Argentines sent her graffiti messages. "Viva Evita! Fuera Madonna!" (Long live Evita, go away, Madonna!) And according to *Entertainment Weekly*, a former aide to Juan Peron publicly threatened to kill her.

It might be instructive for America Online executives—who have shown an admirable commitment to helping parents control what their children can access on the Internet, but who will be distributing Madonna's records through their merger with Time-Warner—to consider a few of the audience-segments she has alienated:

Eighty percent of Americans report being affiliated

with one Christian denomination or another. Many Catholics, in particular, despise her because she has directly attacked the church and its symbols. She was quoted in the *Detroit Free Press* in 1991 as having told the gay news magazine the *Advocate* that Catholicism is "a really mean religion and it's incredibly hypocritical."

And Protestants too strongly disapprove of her. Explains Christian columnist John Lofton, "The opening excerpt from the video ["Justify My Love"] shows some scum-bag, of indeterminate sex, sucking on the face of a blonde woman. And this androgynous something mounts this woman and as sexual intercourse is simulated we see, fleetingly, pressed between these two writhing bodies, a cross with a crucified Christ on it. . . . What we're seeing here is plain, old fashioned, blasphemous sacrilege. . . . Just how bad is this video? Well, it's so bad, so slimy and sleazy, that it's been banned by MTV—the cable network that, twenty-four hours-a-day, is already an open sewer."

I take it that any reader concerned about the present problem within contemporary entertainment is familiar with the fact that one of the most blatant purveyors of sexually suggestive material is MTV. Consequently, many television people photocopied and sent to each other a brilliant 1990 cartoon (reprinted here with permission) by Walt Handelsman of the *New Orleans Times Picayune*, in which a goofy-looking MTV television host is saying "and the management here at MTV feels the new Madonna video goes beyond the limits of tastefulness." After which the same spokesman says, "Okay. Up next, Satanic Blood Pimps' hot new video, 'Torch Your Teacher!' "

Since the Jewish community has historically had relatively elevated cultural tastes and has distinguished itself by its support of the true arts, the Jews have understandably not been conspicuous among the members of Madonna fan-clubs. As long ago as January 1991 Rabbi Abraham Cooper, associate dean of the world-famous Simon Wiesenthal Center in Los Angeles, described a track of Madonna's *Justify My Love* CD as "dangerous and an insult to every Jew." The passage in question, from the Revelation of St. John, is commonly translated as "and the slander of those who say they are Jews, but they are not, they are a synagogue of Satan."

"The notion," Rabbi Cooper said, "that an icon of American pop culture should, for whatever reason, zero in on the most notorious anti-Semitic quote in the Bible is totally unacceptable. . . . The idea of the synagogue of Satan was a very powerful weapon used

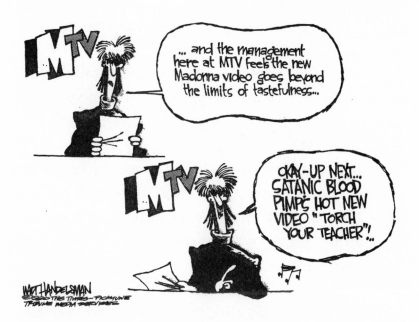

against Jews in the middle ages, and the Nazis depicted Jews with horns in the image of the devil."

The Anti-Defamation League (ADL) , commenting on the case shortly thereafter, said that lyrics of the song and anti-Semitic slurs spray-painted on three California synagogues in December bear a "painful resemblance." In a letter to an executive of Warner Brothers Records, which released the CD, the ADL expressed the "hope that the influence that you and your company have on the shaping of American youth can be used to impart a more positive and hopeful message."

I would not advise that any of us hold our breaths

until the record industry starts to take that recommendation seriously.

In the 1950s and 1960s there were hundreds of music critics in their middle years who had no doubts whatever that Cole Porter, let's say, was vastly superior at the song writing art to Mick Jagger, for instance. Why, then, did they so rarely say as much? I submit that the reason was a sort of social cowardice. The critics, though they knew better, held their tongues because they did not want to seem unhip.

I make a distinction here between middle-aged, generally well-informed critics and the teenage fans then attending rock concerts. The young people could be forgiven on the classic grounds that they simply didn't know any better. They were not consciously rejecting Porter, Ellington, Gershwin, and the other representatives of the glorious Golden Age; they simply had never consciously heard them before. Eventually a small minority of the younger generation who happened to be, for the usual mysterious and genetic reasons, gifted with the ability to write, used the ability to express their taste as modern entertainment critics.

The point is that even many of these modern critics have turned against Madonna. But she seems not to understand the essential message her detractors are now transmitting. When asked by *Today* show host Bryant Gumbel on April 29, 1996, about the barrage of public criticism to which she had been subjected, Madonna referred only to "bad reviews," showing that she either entirely missed Gumbel's point—or pretended to do so.

By the time of the release of her film *Body of Evidence*, in January 1993, quite a distinct phase of Madonna's career had been entered upon. Even the usually tolerant popular media had begun to treat her not so much as a femme fatale socially dangerous because of her willful assault on conventional morals, but as a laughing stock. *People* magazine, though a Time-Warner subsidiary, unwilling even to take the film seriously, ran a feature headed "Madonna's Movie Misadventure," in which it was pointed out that film critic Roger Ebert gave the picture *half* a star, Susan Stark of the *Detroit News* called it "trash," and in Peoria, Illinois, "52 people gathered in a 237-seat theater and giggled." At a Loews theater in Cambridge, Massachusetts, the audience reaction was "belly laughs that dwindled to snorts and cackles." An audience in New York City, according to the feature, applauded when Anne Archer's character called Madonna a "coke-head slut." It is important to grasp that audiences all over the country were not so derisive simply because the film was of such low quality; scores of pictures every year may be so described. What audiences were contemptuously rejecting, even with laughter, was precisely the merchandise that is Madonna's stock-in-trade.

In its important September 5, 1993, issue—it's sixty-third anniversary issue—the *Hollywood Reporter* carried a feature by Joshua Mooney in which the reporter observed, "The year's biggest sex-themed movies failed to satisfy at the box office. *Body of Evidence*, the *Basic Instinct* knock-off meant to keep the erotic flame burning, struck audiences as a crass commercial calculation, notable primarily for providing firm evidence that Madonna had dissipated whatever shock value she once had as a sexual-agent provocateur."

No society can long endure that has abandoned its ideals. Granted that ideals are by definition rarely achieved, they are nevertheless vitally important compass points. It might even be argued that in a society of liars, truth and honesty are needed more than ever. The relevance of this to Madonna's unhappy story is that for a very long time, and by no means only in Western nations, one purpose of social education was to prepare young people to assume the status of lady or gentleman. Granted that there has never been any shortage of sluts and rakes, it was nevertheless considered important that a society produce as many actual ladies and gentlemen as surrounding circumstances permitted. Madonna runs precisely counter to such an honorable tradition.

In August 1993 *Mademoiselle* magazine featured a piece in which Madonna interviewed her good friend, comedy actress Rosie O'Donnell. Here are a few excerpts that illustrate what kind of a woman we are dealing with:

M: What do you find more annoying: getting your period every month or watching *Sally Jessy Raphael*?

M: If you could have your choice, who would you pick to father your child: Denzel Washington, Damon Wayans, or Charles Barkley? . . . Charles Barkley is God. Denzel Washington is married, and you know what? I think Charles is probably married. See, all the good ones are taken . . . but that doesn't mean they can't father your children!

M: Do you pick your nose when people aren't looking? . . . I pick my nose sometimes, even when people *are* looking.

M: Have you ever farted and blamed it on someone else? . . . I think it's easier to fart and blame it on someone else when you live in an urban area.

M: But I don't take shit from anybody!

Classy stuff, right? Needless to say it cannot be argued, in *Mademoiselle*'s defense, that they were shocked by the result of their invitation. They knew exactly what they would get and I have seen no evidence that they were the least bit apologetic about the revolting results.

Perhaps none of Ms. Ciccone's adventures have attracted more criticism than her appearance on the David Letterman show on March 31, 1994. It's instructive to study portions of the transcript:

DAVE: Our first guest tonight is one of the biggest stars in the world. In the past ten years she has sold over 80 million albums, starred in countless films, and slept with some of the biggest names in the entertainment industry.

PAUL
(the show's
music
director):

She's your guest!

DAVE:

It's right there on her bio, for heaven's sake . . . Okay. Ladies and gentlemen, here she is . . . Madonna! [Madonna comes out and hands Dave her panties.]

DAVE:

How are you doing?

MADONNA:

I'm only here cause there isn't a Knicks game. Don't get excited.

DAVE:

Oh, come on. Let's go kiss a guy in the audience. Why don't you go kiss a guy in the audience?

MADONNA:

Why are you so obsessed with my sex life?

DAVE:

As we all know, I have none of my own.

MADONNA:

Well, um . . .

DAVE:

Go kiss the guy in the audience, it would knock him out. Look at that guy [pointing him out]. Just like, on the forehead, just on the forehead—

MADONNA: I can't. He's not tall enough.

DAVE: I like that, she said "I can't." Lots of people would cave in to the pressure and say, "Oh, all right." They'd go out and kiss him and get it over with.

MADONNA: Yeah, well, I've never succumbed to peer pressure.

DAVE: Well, good for you. That's what we love about you, Madonna.

MADONNA: Yeah.

DAVE: What brings you to—?

MADONNA: Incidentally, you are a sick fuck. [CHEERING, MUSIC] I don't know why I get so much shit.

DAVE: You realize this is being broadcast, don't you?

MADONNA: Yeah.

DAVE: Well, you can't be talking like that.

MADONNA: What? [Having handed him a pair of women's underpants] Wait a minute. Aren't you going to smell them? I gave them to you for a reason.

DAVE: Let's see what I'm doing at my house right now, ladies and gentlemen—[a running gag that evening]

MADONNA: No, no, no, no, no!

DAVE: I'll take care of that later, it's a lovely—

MADONNA: I gave him my, come on, I gave him my underpants and he won't smell. [Letterman stuffs the underpants in a drawer in his desk.] That's not where they go!

DAVE: No, believe me, that's where the underwear goes. See, look. Here's where I keep my socks, here's where I keep my panties.

MADONNA: No. That's where you keep *my* panties.

DAVE: [Shortly thereafter, attempting to change the subject.] So you like basketball a great deal. Where's your interest in basketball?

VULGARIANS AT THE GATE

MADONNA: [Looking up at boom mike] That microphone is really long. Speaking of the NBA . . . [Dave gives her a look.]

DAVE: So now let's talk about your interest in the NBA. You go to a lot of games. You were friends with Charles Barkley.

MADONNA: I wouldn't go that far.

DAVE: You weren't friends with Charles Barkley?

MADONNA: I don't think he understands the meaning of friendship.

DAVE: Oh, really. He seems like he might be a hothead, that guy.

MADONNA: Mmm-hmm.

DAVE: Did you know him at all?

MADONNA: Mmm, hmmm.

DAVE: Yeah?

MADONNA: Yeah.

DAVE: Did it hurt when you had that thing put in your nose? [referring to her nose ring.]

MADONNA: [Laughs.] I thought you were going to ask me if it hurt something else, but I . . . [crowd groans] thought you were going to continue the Charles Barkley line of questioning. . . .

DAVE: You're a lovely young woman.

MADONNA: Yes.

DAVE: But, you have like, a nose ring there.

MADONNA: Yes. Both questions. Yes.

DAVE: What happens when you take that out, will you ever—?

MADONNA: What happens when you take it out?

DAVE: Yeah.

MADONNA: Both questions?

DAVE: Oh, come on, what [exasperated] What, am I speakin' Chinese here?

MADONNA: Listen, all you do is talk about my sex life on your show, so now you don't want to talk about my sex life when I'm on your show.

VULGARIANS AT THE GATE

DAVE: Now what do you mean? Do you mean because we periodically, we make jokes?

MADONNA: Periodically?

DAVE: Yeah.

MADONNA: You can't get through a show without talking about me . . . or thinking about me.

DAVE: Well, but do you mind that? Is that a problem for you?

MADONNA: It's never a problem.

DAVE: All right. I'll tell you what. Let's do, let's do a commercial.

[After a few more awkward moments, Dave went to a commercial. Shortly after returning from that break, Madonna is puffing on a large cigar.]

DAVE: Are you enjoying that smoke, there?

MADONNA: It's just the right size.

DAVE: What are you, uh—now, when you leave here tonight what are you gonna do? Are you gonna go out, you gonna go—

MADONNA: Don't fuck with me, Dave.

DAVE: Oh, please—

MADONNA: Aren't there any other segments? That's it?

DAVE: Do we have more tape for Madonna?

MADONNA: I like the way you say my name, by the way.

DAVE: It sounds to me like somebody might be—hmm-hmming with you.

MADONNA: Somebody fucked up.

DAVE: [Laughing nervously.] Oh, God.

MADONNA: It's okay.

DAVE: I want to thank you folks for coming out for this run-through show. . . . This, of course, will never see the light of day. . . .

MADONNA: There seems to be a lot of confusion right now.

DAVE: Yeah. Guess why.

MADONNA: *Because I've been saying "fuck."*

VULGARIANS AT THE GATE

DAVE: You can't—

MADONNA: *Speak the truth and shame the devil, baby.*

DAVE: No, you can't be comin' on here—This is American television. You can't be talkin' like that.

MADONNA: Why?

DAVE: Because people don't want that in their own homes at 11:30 at night.

MADONNA: They don't? [Applause.] No. Wait a minute, wait a minute.

DAVE: Yeah! Yes, sir!

MADONNA: Wait a minute. Wait a minute. People don't want to hear the *word* fuck, or people—

DAVE: Oh, stop it! Will you stop?! Ladies and gentlemen, turn down your volume.

MADONNA: Wait a minute. What ab—

DAVE: Turn the volume down immediately. She can't be stopped. There's something wrong with her.

[After a bit more "dialogue," Letterman went to another commercial break. We pick up the transcript midway through the next segment.]

DAVE: Have you ever seen the show?

MADONNA: Well, actually I have seen the show, but I've never—I mean, *I've always been doing something while I was watching the show.*

DAVE: Oh, I know. I've heard. I've heard all about you.

MADONNA: Exactly. So I don't really—it's not funny. Forget it.

DAVE: Well, now what the hell are we gonna—

MADONNA: *Oh, fuck it.*

DAVE: No. Come on. Will you—you know—

MADONNA: We're going to have to deal with each other.

DAVE: Now, let's don't do that.

MADONNA: No holds barred.

MORTY
(the show's
producer):　Tape.

DAVE:　We have tape? Tape of what?

MADONNA:　Tape? Why can't we just talk to each other? Why do we have to have all of this contrived bullshit? You know? *Fuck the tape. Fuck the list.* Everything. You know what I'm saying?

DAVE:　Oh, man.

MADONNA:　I think we should get—don't you want to show everybody the underwear?

DAVE:　Well, uh, I think most everybody has seen underwear.

MADONNA:　They haven't seen mine.

DAVE:　Oh, now, that's not true. [Laughter.]

MADONNA:　No. They saw me *out* of my underwear. They haven't seen me *in* my underwear. . . .

DAVE:　Do you have a boyfriend?

MADONNA: *Why don't you ask me if I have a girl-friend?*

DAVE: Are you currently interested in someone?

MADONNA: Mm-hmmm.

DAVE: Really? What's his name?

MADONNA: Dave.

DAVE: Oh, no, no, no, not . . . former mayor of New York Dave Dinkins? Good night, everybody! [Laughter.] We have to say goodbye now.

MADONNA: Why?

DAVE: Because we have other guests.

MADONNA: Why?

DAVE: Probably not anymore . . .

MADONNA: Can't this just go on and on?

DAVE: Oh, it seems like it has. But we want to get, uh, the Counting Crows out here, and we want to get the bagger.

MADONNA: Why?

DAVE: Well, we want to hear their song. You know? They have a little song they've planned for us, so we'd like to hear that, and the grocery bagger—you don't want to break his heart, do you? No, no. Look at this. Okay. So—

MADONNA: It's not really this late, anyway. This is all a fantasy. . . . Don't fuck with me, Dave.

DAVE: I know.

MADONNA: Don't make me act a fool. Wait a minute! I just want to ask you one more question. Have you ever smoked Indo?

DAVE: I'm sorry?

MADONNA: Have you ever smoked Indo?

DAVE: I have no idea what you're talking about.

MADONNA: *You're a goddamned liar.*

DAVE: I don't know what you're talking about.

MADONNA: Well, you should.

DAVE: All right. Well, I'll put that on my list of things to do. Smoke some Indo. Okay.

MADONNA: *And, pee in the shower.*

DAVE: Pee in the shower. . . . Get those panties cleaned . . . okay, all right, Madonna, well—

MADONNA: Don't tell me you haven't peed in the shower. Everybody pees in the shower and *everybody picks their nose.* [Audience member yells "Get off!"]

DAVE: That's right. All right. Okay. Now, um—

MADONNA: Why do we have to be—why do you keep flashing that card?

DAVE: Because we—

MADONNA: Can't we just break the rules? [a shout from the crowd, "NO!"] Who said that?

DAVE: Oh, no—that's the guy you wouldn't kiss earlier. The guy out there. You irritated him. All right. Okay. Now—

MADONNA: Is the show almost over?

DAVE: The show is nearly over, yeah. We have
             to say goodbye now. . . .

David Letterman's producer, Robert "Morty" Morton, was quoted shortly thereafter in *W* magazine as saying of Madonna's appearance, "It was a disaster, it was embarrassing, it was not the kind of television we all got into the business to do. She was obscene, offensive. I'm not proud of presenting obscene and offensive people in the hour of television we're in control of. None of us felt particularly good that day."

Commented *Time* magazine, in its year-end 1994 issue, "The Material Girl, rapidly running out of material, tried pouty intransigence and four-letter words on David Letterman's *Late Show*, an appearance that proved you *can* turn your head away from a train wreck. By the end of her bleepathon even the studio audience was hooting her off the stage."

Traditionally, theatrical criticism relates to specifics— singing, dancing, acting, playing an instrument, or, at the more creative level, writing, composing, directing. It is important to understand, in this context, that no performer ever lived who was not occasionally negatively criticized. In any event, such traditional considerations have nothing to do with the barrage of criticism to which Madonna has been subjected. What outrages millions is not the quality of her singing, dancing, or acting. This particular young woman is criticized because she has made a conscious, calculated decision to debase herself.

STATEMENT TO TIME-WARNER

A brilliant example of literary sarcasm was a 1992 release distributed by a group of concerned New Yorkers as a letter to the Board of Directors of Time-Warner. I'm pleased to quote it here with permission:

> Ladies and Gentlemen:
>
> We are here today to commend the board of directors and chief executives of Time-Warner for providing America with a kind of "Family Dignity Packet." On every front Time-Warner is an uplifting encouragement to children and to parents who are trying to raise their families with a sense of dignity and moral responsibility. We are impressed that Time-Warner is enriching our children and families through such noteworthy entertainment as "Cop Killer" by Warner recording artist Ice-T. We are also impressed

with some of the wonderful incest lyrics of Prince and the charming influence of Madonna, who not only has had our children wearing their underwear on the outside but is now evidently trying to get them to wear their skin on the outside (when they are not wearing S&M leather). The recording "Cop Killer" is a special blessing to police officers who are risking their lives to maintain civility and safety among our people. The song helps equip our children to face such new phenomena as random, drive-by shootings.

We also commend Warner Pictures for their plethora of R-rated movies. They are just what the American teenager needs—more films celebrating kinky sex, big-time violence, anarchy, and charming four-letter words.

Time-Warner has also given us bright, happy movies like *Batman Returns* promoted in millions of McDonald's Happy Meals to six- and eight-year-olds. Kids came in droves to the theaters to witness Danny De Vito as the Penguin Man [*sic*] biting people's noses off and calling on the underground Penguin empire to kill children in their cribs. Also, the tender, lovely tones of Catwoman in her attempts to support male dignity through emasculation are just the images that our fatherless children need.

We also commend Time-Warner's awarding of Prince and Madonna with $100 million and $62 million contracts so that the enriching lyrics and music of two of our children's most admirable role models can be expertly marketed into our children's hearts and minds. Kids are enriched by the lyrics of a recent recording by Prince celebrating incest with his sister or another great song that depicted a girl masturbating with a magazine in a hotel lobby ("Darlin' Nicky" [sic]).

We commend Warner Books for their brilliant cooperation in providing America's coffee tables with 500,000 hardbound Madonna Sex books in which one of our children's favorite rock stars displays her body in bestiality poses, group sex poses, and sadomasochistic bondage poses. There is an especially constructive photo of Madonna sitting on an old man's lap while he fondles her breasts.

Time-Warner should also be especially commended for artistic pioneering in the photo where Madonna has her nose in a man's bare anus while biting his scrotum with her teeth. These images and messages are just exactly what America's youth needs at this time—a sort of vision of dignity and hope for the future. Our youth are facing new heights of self-worth through the admirable priorities and noble concerns of Time-Warner's leadership.

It's creative and praiseworthy of the Time-Warner board to have the vision to present one of our children's favorite rock stars with a dog nuzzling her G-stringed crotch while she smiles as if to enjoy bestiality. It attests to American corporate ingenuity at its best.

As we approach a new millennium, we can rest confident that Time-Warner is looking out for our families and our children, doing everything possible to uphold the finest heritage of free speech and responsible leadership. The artistically composed photo of Madonna in the nude between a man who from the front fondles her vagina and a woman who from behind fondles her breasts while giving her a large French kiss over the shoulder attests to Time-Warner's sensitivity and commitment to dignified family life.

We applaud Time-Warner's creative genius in working with Madonna to further strengthen America's youth, to give them a dignified vision of themselves and reassuring hope for the future. What more could America's children and the American family ask than to see its major communications-news complexes displaying such responsible and innovative leadership at a time in our history when teen suicide, teen sexually transmitted disease, AIDS, divorce, school drop-outs, and school violence are at record proportions?

The new Madonna *Sex* book just fits the needs of children to a T. Our hats are off to a truly responsible executive leadership and board of directors. We recognize the noble thoughts that will be nurtured in the hearts of our children and their parents as they enjoy this fine new book. It just gives one a deep-down feeling of happiness and good will for Time-Warner's corporate leadership. The board of directors can be proud of having had a role in passing on to their grandchildren these noble images of America's finest and best.

5
SHOCK JOCKS
AND
CONFRONTATION TV
Howard Stern
and Jerry Springer

The effects of overemphasis on sex motives, of the destruction of reticence and normal shame of the malodorous realism which claims superior candor and novelty for its rediscovery that man is an animal—what are the effects? Nothing at all that the eye can see; nothing but the slow unbalancing of emotion in the accepting mind, the disintegration of personality, the decay of taste, the gradual confirmation in the individual case of the hypothesis put before him that man is an animal—and nothing else.

—William Hocking, philosopher

The crudeness, cursing, profanity, vice, and violence we tolerate on our TV screens will be the crudeness, cursing, profanity, vice, and violence that we will be forced to endure for our real lives in the years ahead. By the current tolerance of this diminution

> *of taste and values on TV, we are teaching our chil-*
> *dren that the basest level of human behavior is the*
> *accepted norm.*
>
> —U.S. Sen. Robert C. Byrd

HOWARD STERN

To say that what Howard Stern does on his daily radio show is disgusting is not, strictly speaking, to express a formally critical judgment but merely to make a written record of what is the common assessment not only among Mr. Stern's detractors—which would only be expected—but even among his admirers. The point is that they admire him *because* he is disgusting. While driving to and from downtown Los Angeles not long ago I happened to recognize Stern's voice on the radio and stayed with the program for a while, just to see if my earlier negative impressions might perhaps require revision. They do. The program I heard in December 1997, as it happens, was even more revolting than what I had earlier been exposed to. Within the space of about fifteen minutes Stern three times used the phrase "bust my balls" and twice ran a mock public-service announcement which referred to "worms in your feces," among other things.

220

SHOCK JOCKS AND CONFRONTATION TV

On the day in question Stern also chose to deal with a particularly grave subject matter, the trial of Nelson Mandela's former wife, Winnie Mandela, in South Africa on charges of having arranged to have her political opponents—all black—brutalized, a charge she denied. Believe it or not Stern construed such tragic raw material as grist for flippant, morning-drive-time type "fun." We are not speaking here of bitterly satirical humor of the sort that can sometimes be mined out of tragic soil. There was nothing the least bit clever or, for that matter, even funny about the routine. It was all simply disrespectful horsing around of the sort that might appeal to poorly brought up twelve-year-olds. How it would be received by Stern's African American listeners is a separate question that deserves research. But again I don't see how Stern could possibly object to anything I am saying here. It is, we must constantly remind ourselves, his *intention* to be outrageously disgusting. He *deliberately* indulges in the poorest possible taste. According to *USA Today*, he told the National Association of Television Program Executives, "I'm the guy who put the sin back in syndication." It is his plan of life itself, apparently, to indulge in vulgarity for vulgarity's sake. Such laughter as he may elicit from those who constitute the bulk of his audience is what professional comedians call "shock laughs."

VULGARIANS AT THE GATE

And it is, after all, Stern's admirers who are the target of my concern. For Howard himself, I wish good health and personal happiness. Naturally I cannot wish him continued commercial success because I feel that his affect on the American consciousness—which those of his listeners who are children will suffer most seriously—is inflicting deep psychological and moral wounds on an already disturbed public.

The absurd attempt is sometimes made to defend Stern and others of the toilet talk fraternity on the same grounds that were quite legitimately employed on behalf of comedian Lenny Bruce. The crucial difference, of course, was that Bruce was a satirist, a brilliantly talented and original comic thinker who used the device of stand-up comedy to make often penetrating philosophical observations. The same cannot be said of most of the present vulgarity specialists.

Although young people may find it difficult to believe, there was a time, not terribly many years ago, when very real concern about Federal Communication Commission (FCC) reaction would have led the country-clubbers who own most of America's radio stations to promptly fire any radio announcer or disc jockey who used such language. Today, by way of a contrast that I find alarming, such behavior is more likely to lead to success and fame rather than to failure and obscurity.

In 1985, shortly after having been fired by WNBC radio, Howard Stern was recruited to bring his daily broadcast of filth to Infinity Broadcasting Corporation. According to J. Max Robins, writing in *TV Guide*, "As head of the Infinity radio network, [Mel] Karmazin made Stern his star, a partnership that helped Karmazin as well. After selling Infinity to CBS in 1997, Karmazin joined the Tiffany network and rose quickly through its ranks. So closely tied are the two men's fortunes that Stern recently bragged of being 'The Edgar Bergen who works Mel,' a reference to the famous ventriloquist."

It might be thought that because so much of Mr. Karmazin's career has been spent marketing in radio as well as television the most objectionable program in the history of entertainment, that of Howard Stern, he would personally be in somewhat bad odor among professional associates. To some extent he is. But that fact pales in importance with another commented on in the September 4, 1999, issue of the *Los Angeles Times*, about the then pending merger between CBS and Viacom. Presumably the reader is familiar with CBS, but not as many may know that the CEO of Viacom is the aforementioned Sumner

Redstone, whose company owns Blockbuster Video, Paramount Pictures, and a cable group that includes MTV, VH1, Nickelodeon, and half ownership of Comedy Central. The key factor in the *Times* story and the reality behind it is the comment that "Karmazin has become Wall Street's favorite media mogul in recent years because of the company's steady financial improvements."

So here we have the now widely recognized culture war in a nutshell. On one side of the confrontation we have millions of Americans who on time-honored moral grounds are outraged by what Karmazin and others of his kind are doing, while Wall Street—which means the nation's financial power centers—is cheering on Karmazin, Redstone, Rupert Murdoch, and the other major offenders. Being neither an economist nor a professional philosopher I am content, for the moment anyway, to toss this particular ball to the conservative intellectual community, for which I have a great deal more respect than I do for those guilty of cultural pollution.

I recently had the honor of being invited to sign a public appeal to the conscience—such as it is—of the entertainment community. (The letter is included at the beginning of chapter 1 of this volume.) That statement and similar appeals, even some emanating from within the entertainment media, held out not government restraint, but industry self-restraint as at least a partial solution to the undeniably real problem that confronts the nation. For whatever the point may be worth, the disgust-factor in modern entertainment has in recent years become considerably worse than at any time in the past. Logically speaking it does not necessarily follow that self-censorship is therefore an utterly hopeless ultimate solution, though it clearly is at present. It is said that when Americans are polled on the question over 90 percent state that they hold some sort of religious belief or affiliation. We know, furthermore, that in the nonreligious community there are also many individuals of high ethical and moral standards. A disinterested observer might think that such statistics alone would eventually lead to a triumph of virtue as regards the current "the public-be-damned" situation, but the majority force will never carry the day unless it is buttressed by some sort of publicly expressed sentiment by those who hold the real power in America, the power of money. Unless the leaders of Wall Street and corporate America begin to take an interest in this general question, there is likely to be no happy resolution, just a continuing worsening of an already morally deplorable situation.

VULGARIANS AT THE GATE

I have earlier mentioned "the little, local Howard Sterns" that have sprung up all over the country. An example is KQRS-FM's Tom Barnard and his "Morning Show" gang who, according to Noel Holston, TV and radio critic for the *Star Tribune* in Minneapolis, recently were talking about going in for a prostate exam and hoping that the proctologist "didn't have fingers like kielbasas."

The following portions of Holston's August 27, 1998, story, which ran under the headline "KQ 'Morning Crude': Cruel and Usual Punishment," provides yet one more piece of evidence that radio broadcast standards are declining rapidly throughout the country.

> Rectal humor is definitely a step up from some of their callous and irresponsible recent attempts to get laughs. Then I discovered that I was listening to a rerun—a "best of the KQRS Morning Show." . . . And it made me wonder if KQ might also pop in a tape of a sketch I heard several months ago during another "best of" broadcast.
>
> It concerned an Asian chef who goes ballistic when his customers send dishes back to the kitchen for additional cooking or seasoning. Angrily sputtering pidgin Eng-

lish, he takes his revenge in a variety of ways: He spits on some orders before sending them back. He drips armpit sweat in the sweet-and-sour sauce. He has a dog urinate in the teakettle. For his *piece de resistance*, he asks a waitress to remove her "female apparatus" and serves it up as a side dish, smothered in gravy and noodles, to an unsuspecting diner. . . .

Several hundred people, not all of them Asian-Americans, marched in St. Paul on Saturday to call attention to what they consider racist anti-immigrant comments by Barnard and other regulars on his show. Although the protesters contend that the KQ show has a long history of mocking Asian-Americans and other immigrants of color, a specific broadcast led to Saturday's rally and to demands for printed apologies and for free air time so that Hmong representatives could educate KQ listeners about their culture.

On June 9, the "Morning Show" cast did comic riffs on a *St. Paul Pioneer Press* article about a thirteen-year-old Hmong girl in Eau Claire, Wisconsin, accused of killing her newborn son after giving birth alone in a YMCA restroom. The girl apparently feared that her mother would beat her if she learned of the pregnancy. The [baby's] father was reportedly a twelve-year-old cousin.

There is nothing remotely funny about this story. It is a tragedy involving children that the *Pioneer Press* reported with appropriate seriousness and restraint.

But that didn't stop Barnard and Company—who often find their material in other people's misfortunes—from interjecting jokes as well as expressions of horror and indignation as Barnard read the news story aloud.

After noting that the girl could be fined $10,000 Barnard joked that she had responded, "$10,000? That's a lot of egg rolls." Graphically describing how the tiny girl had been ripped bloody while delivering the eight-pound baby, Barnard posed a question to listeners: "Which would you rather have—your mom slapping you or a torn vagina?"

A moment later, he answered the question for one crew member. "Brycee said he would rather have a torn vagina," Barnard said.

"He is a torn vagina," sidekick Terri Traen chimed in.

"Yes, he is," Barnard added. "He's a complete torn vagina." . . .

But forget racism for a second. Let's talk basic decency. Would anybody with a shred of it treat this sort of story as a comic possibility? Who are the real barbarians here?

KQ station manager Amy Waggoner steadfastly contends that it's fair for Barnard and his crew to insult anyone, regardless of race, color, creed, etc., because they insult *everyone*. . . .

Waggoner insists that KQ does care, but she is adamant that no group will dictate what the "Morning Show" crew can or cannot say on the air.

She shouldn't have to listen to any group. Listening to her conscience should be enough.

As you ponder the impact of this disgusting exchange on its many young listeners, assume you are married and have a teen-aged daughter. She is a sweet, bright, attractive young girl. As such she naturally attracts boys. Two in particular, in her social circle, appear to be quite interested in her. One is a straight-arrow kid; the other is a daily listener to Howard Stern, and thinks the *Jerry Springer Show* is about as good as TV talk gets. So there you have a simple, clear-cut choice regarding a boyfriend for your darling daughter. The choice is between a gentleman and a jerk. To extend the point a bit further, after years of being influenced by Stern's on-air celebrations of depravity and misogyny, what kind of eventual *husband* do you think the jerk might make for your daughter? How about as a *father* to your grandchildren?

In mid-June 1998 Canadian broadcaster CHUM, Ltd. proudly announced its intention to begin telecasting the *Howard Stern Show* over its Toronto TV station. A news story in the *Hollywood Reporter* on June 17 said that a CHUM executive "predicted controversy surrounding the *Howard Stern Show*." This was like the last passenger on the Titanic predicting ice.

As the Hollywood trade paper reported, "Toronto radio station Q-107 in Montreal, station CHUM-FM, which has aired the morning radio show since September, has already been forced to hire extra staff and new digital equipment to clean up the shock jock's radio broadcasts."

CHUM-TV executives explained that the Stern program would be recorded early in the evening on Saturday nights, "allowing time to bring the program into line with stringent Canadian broadcasting industry codes of taste and conduct."

It is small wonder that the Canadian broadcasters were so revolted by what they had wrought. On Stern's program of August 29 one of the features was an extended interview and allegedly comic sketch at the apparent expense of some pathetically handicapped individuals of the sort ordinarily honored by the Special Olympics programs.

Another feature—which was returned to several times during the program—consisted of an endless display of flatulence. Then there were several tragic young women who Stern deliberately humiliated by asking them to disrobe, which they did without hesitation.

As of September 2000 the Canadian television industry was not only willing to use the word *censor* but to control the content of programs it telecasts. The Canadian Broadcast Standards Council, still seething at the ugliness of Howard Stern's programs, said Stern was wrong to have insisted, on a recent broadcast, that most "retards" listen to his show, and to have referred to himself as "king of the retards."

It is surprising enough that the once-respected CBS, the longtime home of Edward R. Murrow and Walter Cronkite, *Mary Tyler Moore*, and *M*A*S*H*, made the conscious decision to put Stern on its television stations. What is even more surprising is that some of America's leading corporations, which at least in recent years have become so image-conscious, decided to support CBS's shocking decision with millions of dollars in sponsorship funds.

In trying to understand this decision, which is obviously bizarre on its own terms, I learned about an organization called the Media Access Project, based in Washington, D.C. According to its executive director, Andrew Schwartzman, "sponsors want a certain demographic and they leave it to the ad agency's computer models to pick where their ads go." If we interpret his comment strictly then it is the fault of no human being that depravity is now so extensively underwritten by sponsors. It is all just a matter of "computer models." But, as one who has worked quite happily with sponsors, advertising agencies, and television networks for some half a century, I can assure you there is always conscious human involvement with decisions, both wise and unwise. All that computer models can do is point, usually accurately enough, to information about the types of people—age, social status, race, and so on—who, at least by and large, watch particular programs. It can by no means guarantee that all viewers approve of what they see, but that is a subsidiary question.

In December 1998 my wife, Jayne, and I attended a simple but fascinating program at the Museum of Television and Radio in Los Angeles in which the museum's director, Steve Bell, interviewed—for just over an hour—Leslie Moonves, chief programmer for CBS television. Following the formal interview there was another half-hour or so during which Mr. Moonves responded to questions from the audience. His answers were forthright, reasonable, and instructive. Because of my special interest in the coarseness-and-sleaze problem I was most interested in his response to a woman who wanted to know what the network rationale was for having decided to air Howard Stern's program. Mr. Moonves could hardly wait for the woman to finish her question before clarifying, with emphasis, that the *network* was, in fact, *not* telecasting the program to all of its affiliates but instead only to its owned-and-operated *stations*—about a dozen in number. (Other stations were apparently offerred the show by the syndication arm of CBS, Eyemark, but not required to broadcast it as network affiliated.) This was not a Clintonian hair-splitting distinction. From his answer, it occurred to me that Mr. Moonves was not fully in favor of the decision that had been made by Mel Karmazin.

Howard Stern's syndicated television show hit a new ratings low, according to Nielsen statistics, in mid-1999. The bright side was the fact that Stern's ratings were low to start with, and quickly got worse. For the week ending June 13, 1999, a rerun of the program fell 25 percent from the preceding week, to a 0.9 rating (less than one percent of the nation's 99.4 million homes with access to television at that time). Compared with its heavily publicized opening episode in August 1998 the show had fallen 67 percent. According to the *New York Post*, more than 20 of the 79 stations that had carried the show on its premiere had dropped it during the first year.

Has Stern ever been reprimanded for his indiscretions? Yes. Certainly by the Federal Communications Commission he has. In 1992, about a year after his radio program was picked up by Los Angeles radio station KLSX-FM, "the FCC came down hard on Stern," according to the *Los Angeles Times*, imposing a fine of $105,000 on the L.A. station's owner, a subsidiary of Greater Media, Inc., for twelve indecent comments made by Stern in late 1991. According to *Daily Variety*, an FCC indecency violation typically prompts a fine of no more than $12,500, but the FCC said that "the egregious nature of the material, as well as the substantial number of days on which such indecent material was broadcast severely aggravate the violation."

In December 1992, the *Los Angeles Times* reported that the FCC was "also considering fines of up to $900,000 against Infinity Broadcasting, which broadcasts Stern's programs in the East." The *Times* reported that "Stern's repertoire includes talk of rape, masturbation, and sex organs; he has been accused of being racist, sexist, and homophobic."

By 1995, the Associated Press reported that Infinity Broadcasting, "the company that produces and broadcasts" Stern's radio show, had decided to "settle several indecency charges" levied by the FCC and agreed to pay $1.7 million to do so.

In the case of those comedians who, though talented, choose to emphasize vulgarity and shock, at least they have an alternative in that some of them would still have the power to amuse if they worked clean. The same certainly cannot be said of Stern, who to my mind has no discernable talent. I doubt the world would ever have taken any particular notice of him had he not long ago decided to specialize in verbal ugliness.

Incredibly, Stern personally placed into the hands

of his potential and eventually actual critics a remarkably effective weapon. Having apparently learned nothing from the serious mistake made by Arsenio Hall who, when given his own late night talk show, not only publicly announced that he was going to attract more viewers than the *Tonight* show, which had been a TV institution for decades, but predicted that he was going to "whip Jay Leno's ass." Not only did he fail to deliver on his boast but the *Tonight* show is still on the air, with impressive ratings, whereas Hall's program as of late 2000 was long gone. Stern's error was similar in that he predicted he would make short work of another popular television institution of long standing, namely, *Saturday Night Live*. Needless to say, nothing of the sort ever happened. The self-proclaimed "king of all media" not only ran well behind *SNL*, but by September 1999 his ratings were even below those of *Mad TV* (Fox).

It may at first seem a self-contradiction that, while I urge responsible citizens displeased by the current wave of cultural sludge to articulate the specifics of their complaints in letters to the chief executives responsible for the marketing of such fare, I do not also urge others to communicate directly with the Howard Sterns in the media. But the distinction I draw is intentional, not a matter of careless thinking.

SHOCK JOCKS AND CONFRONTATION TV

I believe that people like Stern—and his name is just shorthand for dozens who are perpetrating the same kind of harm—are very close to morally hopeless.

I am not saying that we should forgive him on the grounds that he doesn't seem to perceive the true harm he is doing; my point is rather that to lecture such poor souls directly is likely to be about as effective as scolding a narcotics addict. The more important fact is that Stern would not be in a position to do any harm whatever were it not for the fact that there are those quite willing to employ him. They are the people who are ultimately at fault on the simplest, most common-sense moral grounds. They are not under Stern's personal compulsion. Some of them, I have little doubt, would not dream of exposing their own children to such reprehensible programming. They do what they do for the buck.

Very little I'm saying will come as news to those television executives who appear to have come down clearly on one side of the present debate and that is, sadly, the amoral side.

Because my own position in the dialogue has long been known I occasionally receive copies of letters addressed to TV's leaders. The following message, from an important television veteran, Dan Jenkins, I include here because it is typical of its kind.

VULGARIANS AT THE GATE

16 May 2000

Dear Mr. Karmazin:

As a former TV editor and columnist for the *Hollywood Reporter* and for ten years *TV Guide*'s first Los Angeles bureau chief, not to mention twenty-five years as a publicist, let me put it this way:

You already have given us Howard Stern. If now you bring "WWF Smackdown" to your network, I give you my word I will no longer watch a single minute of CBS-TV until all three of you are out of there.

I am reminded of a step my old friend Grant Tinker (I was his PR director at MTM Enterprises for three years) took very shortly after becoming president of NBC. He turned his radio on one afternoon and found himself listening to someone called Howard Stern. Mr. Stern was fired *that day*. I believe the word is integrity, moral integrity. You could look it up.

I remember some great bygone names at CBS: William Paley, Frank Stanton, Howard Meighan (I still correspond with his widow), Harry Ackerman, Ed Murrow, Charles Collingwood, Hubbell Robinson, Perry Lafferty. You simply are not in their

league. And then there was Jack Benny. In
this thirty-odd years on radio and TV for
CBS Jack Benny never once used a four-
letter word. He didn't need it.

Why do you?

Sincerely,
Daniel Jenkins

JERRY SPRINGER

Another television production that has attracted an
incredible but well-deserved barrage of angry criticism
is the syndicated *Jerry Springer Show*, carried by most
stations during the daytime hours, and at least in Los
Angeles in October 2000 is scheduled at 9 A.M.,
directly following the children's series *Beakman's
World*. The format of Springer's program is similar to
that of other daytime talk shows in recent years,
involving the discussion of controversial subject
matter and often inviting questions from a live audience. But, unlike the illuminating, insightful, and frequently inspiring discussions led by Phil Donahue in
his early days or Oprah Winfrey today, Springer and
his producers deliberately concentrate on sleazy and
often tragic subject matter. Examples of episode titles

include "I'm Sleeping with My 13-Year-Old's Ex" and "I'm Pregnant by My Brother." Dysfunctional families are featured and are encouraged not only to bare their innermost personal secrets but to be deliberately rude and combative in their on-camera confrontations. Consequently it should come as no surprise that no less an authority than former NBC chairman Grant Tinker told delegates to the National Association of Television Program Executives who convened in late January 1998 that Springer's program "sets a new low for TV." Oprah Winfrey has called it a "vulgarity circus" and an August 16, 1999, *Newsweek* headline called Springer himself a "smutmeister."

As journalist Jefferson Graham explained in *USA Today*, Springer has deliberately booked "the most outrageous guests on TV," as a way of attracting attention while competing against the *Geraldo* and *Jenny Jones* shows. The key question, of course is this: Has Springer suffered as a result of his apparent lack of taste and discrimination? On the contrary, his ratings rose even higher than they were in 1997, passing those of the heavily promoted but more prosocial *Rosie O'Donnell Show*.

Even more depressing is that *Too Hot for TV*, a video-cassette of the *most* objectionable portions of Springer's shows, complete with uncensored four-letter words and breast-bearing women, has sold well.

SHOCK JOCKS AND CONFRONTATION TV

And yet, outside the world of *entertainment* television, Springer has not fared as well. I assume the reader is aware because the matter was so highly publicized that in May 1997, when Springer was hired to do news commentary for WMAQ, the NBC network's station in Chicago, newswoman Carol Marin resigned in protest, a move for which she was nationally cheered, especially by many news-media coworkers.

As an example of what sort of station policy the FCC might eventually take a look at, consider the reaction of some stations that had already indicated their lack of respect for their own communities by carrying the Springer show. Note what happened when Springer's production company, Studios USA, decided *not* to telecast some of the series' more revolting and, reportedly, occasionally staged misbehavior. Were the station managers and owners relieved that a difficult decision had, in effect, been made for them? No. An undetermined number of them actually complained at being deprived of episodes that had become an embarrassment even to the relatively tolerant USA Network company. Any FCC official—regardless of his own philosophical/political leaning—who did not give careful consideration to such management behavior should himself be subjected to sharp scrutiny and, it follows, criticism.

For the few readers of this report who may assume that the station programmers involved are themselves so irresponsible that they actually want to use their facilities to telecast sewer-pipe fare, the truth isn't quite that interesting. As Cynthia Littleton, a reporter for *Daily Variety*, explained at the time, the station people were simply aware of the obvious, that since the only reason for Springer's popularity in the first place was his shock-and-schlock, the stations no doubt correctly predicted that his toned-down programming would suffer in the ratings.

One more relevant thought does occur. There was a day when the Federal Communications Commission would have come down hard, and promptly, on any television station that broadcast such vulgarity. We owe to former President Ronald Reagan the unhappy fact that the FCC no longer much exercises such power. As part of his much-publicized effort to "get government off people's backs." Reagan deliberately removed the teeth from the FCC, apparently under the bizarre assumption that the broadcast media was fully capable of policing and censoring itself. To state the point in the simplest possible terms: as of the year 2000 it was not.

6
POPULAR MUSIC
AND RECORDINGS

In terms of what certain media outlets show you, it's very one-dimensional. It's not just hip-hop music—TV and movies in general are very narrow. Sex, violence, the underbelly, with junkies, prostitutes, alcoholics, gamblers. The new trend today is depravity.

Mos Def, 26,
gold-album selling rapper

When a guy like Mos Def thinks the culture's getting out of hand, you've got to wonder if all this election year posturing might actually be about something after all.

Newsweek, October 9, 2000

n the year 2000 it seems much of what passes for popular music is actually rap. In late September, six of the week's top twenty albums in America were rap records and all of them had parental-advisory stickers. A *Newsweek* poll, conducted about that same time, and reported in the October 9, 2000, issue of the magazine, found that almost two-thirds of its respondents said rap music has too much violence. Sixty-three percent said they believe it has a bad attitude toward women, and a substantial majority said it contains too much sex.

Since the great majority of American observers are obviously critical of rap music there is nothing particularly newsworthy about its low repute. It is even disdained by millions of African Americans. But what attracted *Newsweek*'s attention, and which I shall deal with later in this chapter, is that recently even some of rap's most successful performers and producers are publicly acknowledging the problem.

But first let's review the cultural and moral case against rap as summed up by Mark Steyn in his dazzling commentary on popular music culture, *Broadway Babies, Say Goodnight*. When discussing Charles K. Harris, the writer of song hits early in the twentieth century, Steyn mentions that the composers and lyricists of that day sometimes "took tabloid news stories of human interest and turned them into hit songs."

POPULAR MUSIC AND RECORDINGS

A century on, we've reversed the process: the guys with the hit songs turn themselves into tabloid news stories, and "Hit Parade" now means a bunch of gangsta rappers getting together and showing off their gunshot wounds. In 1994, while on bail for a sexual assault charge, Tupac Shakur was pumped full of bullets and narrowly avoided being reduced to One-pac Shakur; one year and five minutes after Tupac's shooting, his comrade-in-rap Randy Walker, producer of "Strictly 4 My N.I.G.G.A.Z.," was shot dead; a few months later, Tupac himself was killed in a drive-by shooting; Ol' Dirty Bastard had his liver blown away by gun-totin' dirtier bastards; Slick Rick took preemptive action and, consequently, had to record his latest album while doing time for attempted murder; and Snoop Doggy Dogg's murder trial collapsed on technical grounds. This is the weird odyssey pop music has taken since the mid-fifties—from "How Much Is That Doggy in the Window?" to "How long is that Doggy in the gaolhouse [jailhouse]?"

Rap is the logical consequence of promoting social over musical content: the reduction of the tune to banal stationary backing track, the debasement of lyric-writing to a formless pneumatic laundry list of half-baked hoodlum exhibitionism. Forget all those bogus generalizations about "energy" and "drive"; musically, Ice Cube's "The Nigga Ya Love to Hate" isn't a patch on "Honeysuckle Rose," never mind "All the Things You Are." If Ice Cube wasn't rappin' about terminating an unwanted pregnancy by booting his woman in the belly, none of us would be the slightest bit interested. And even then, we're not *that* interested. This is one "authentic black experience" that doesn't travel beyond the ghetto.

For a very long time, starting not long after the beginning of the twentieth century, black music was also America's music. During the 1920s and 1930s jazz was considered something of cultural interest only to a minority of specialists. In a word, almost everybody loved it. And for every African-American admirer of black musicians, vocalists, and entertainers there were many more whites who enthusiastically seconded the motion.

There was some falling-off from this happy state of affairs when, in the early 1950s, white jazz-lovers first became familiar with the new approach to music designated by the terms *progressive, bop,* or *bebop,* which featured extremely fast tempos with non-singable melodies and were poorly suited for dancing. Two mutually contradictory currents immediately were evident. On the one hand jazz fans, long warmly disposed to appreciate the playing of their favorite musicians, black or white, tended to either suspend judgment or truly like the new mode they were hearing. But others—including some blacks—simply had trouble understanding, much less appreciating, certain examples of bop. It was not even theoretically possible to attribute the aloofness to white racism since the same critics had long been on record as worshippers of Louis Armstrong, Duke Ellington, Count Basie, Joe Williams, Ella Fitzgerald, Earl Hines, Art Tatum, Lionel Hampton, and scores of other gifted black artists. The lack of understanding, therefore, was cultural, rather than racial. It is also importantly relevant that certain white musicians were playing the new music.

But there was never much philosophical objection to progressive jazz; negative reaction was just a matter of taste. The same cannot be said, however, as regards rap. First of all, whether one favors or dislikes it, the genre, properly speaking, cannot be referred to as music at all, given that music has always been defined as involving melody and harmony. Rap is pure rhythm, in its basic appeal. Even the "lyric" is spoken rhythmically, rather than being sung.

Is there anything good about rap entertainment? Certainly. Some of the dancing associated with its presentation is both original and inventive. The rhythms are infectious, even when, as often is the case, they do not involve actual musical instruments. Entirely separate criteria, however, are called into play to judge the content of rap lyrics. Some of them are innocuous, catchy, and occasionally even poetic or insightful. But a significant portion of rap lyrics are absolutely indefensible. It is an admirable thing to protest violence in the ghetto, but to transmit the opposite message, to approve of sadistic brutality, is quite another matter.

Consider, for example, the following lyric from the song "Mind of a Lunatic" by the Time-Warner distributed rap group the Geto Boys (illiterate misspellings are presumably to be taken as "hip"):

> Her body's beautiful, so I'm thinkin' rape
> Shouldn't have had her curtains open so
>   that's her fate
> Leavin' out her house, grabbed the bitch by
>   her mouth
> Drug her back in, slammed her down on
>   the couch

Whipped out my knife, said "If you scream,
    I'm cuttin'."
Opened her legs and commenced to fuckin;
She begged me not to kill her, I gave her a
    rose
Then slit her throat and watched her shake
    till her eyes closed.
Had sex with her corpse before I left her . . .

There has long been philosophical disagreement concerning what cultural fare is dangerous or destructive to a society's moral fabric. Since this is not a scientific question, it cannot be resolved with logical precision. In reasoning our way toward a just solution I take it that all camps can agree that there are indeed certain materials that cannot possibly be defended by any known moral standard. The debate, then, concerns where to draw the line between objectionable and acceptable fare.

A second factor on which there is almost universal agreement is that a legitimate distinction may be drawn between material that is acceptable for adults and that which is suitable for children. Even out-and-out pleasure seekers such as *Playboy* patriarch Hugh Hefner have never argued that the most blatant forms of pornography ought to be made available to the very young. This brings us to an argument that in the

VULGARIANS AT THE GATE

1980s and 1990s had assumed major proportions: The question is whether the lyrics on recordings by certain rap groups are, according to almost any sensible standard, suitable for the ears of children and young teenagers. Again I stress that this is by no means a black versus white issue. Large numbers of African Americans are just as revolted by the content of some rap lyrics as are members of all the other races represented in the American population.

Inevitably a certain percentage of the readers of this book, whether black or white, will not have been exposed to the actual lyrics that are so widely condemned. On the assumption that there will be no children among my readers, I feel it is important to include at least a few all-too-typical examples of the genre so that there can be no doubt as to what is at issue. As a lyric writer myself I hesitate to identify such material as lyrics at all, given the noble tradition through the years of such true artists of the trade as Johnny Mercer, Ira Gershwin, Dorothy Fields, Stephen Sondheim, Joni Mitchell, and scores of others, including Stevie Wonder and many other talented black lyricists who have provided clever, touching, and insightful lyric-messages for American popular music during most of the twentieth century. Today's purposely offensive material is much closer to men's room graffiti than to the art practiced by America's best song-poets. In studying the following examples, I suggest readers consider whether they would purposely bring these words to the attention of children in their own family.

2 LIVE CREW

From the 1991 CD
Sports Weekend: As Nasty as They Wanna Be (Lil Joe Records)

"Pop That Pussy"

Hot damn. Shit. Look at the ass on that bitch. Look at the titties . . . All you ladies are 'hos [whores]. . . . I like big booty and big old titties. Bitch, you know you've been fucked by many. Come and be my private dancer. I've got some money if that's what gets you off, and if you can't fuck that day, baby, just lay back and open your mouth. 'Cause I have never met a girl that I loved in the whole wide world . . .

VULGARIANS AT THE GATE

From the 1989 CD As Nasty as They Wanna Be
(Lil Joe Records)

"Dirty Nursery Rhymes"

My mama and your mama was talking little
    shit
My mama called your mama a bulldagging
    ass bitch
I know your sister, and the bitch ain't shit
She slayed me and all the boys
And even sucked our dicks. . . .
Abraham Lincoln was a good old man
He hopped out the window with his dick in
    his hand
Said "excuse me lady, I'm doing my duty
So pull down your pants and give me some
    booty." . . .
Little Jack Horner sat in the corner
Fuckin' this cutie pie
Stuck in his thumb, made the bitch cum
Said "helluva Nigga am I."

POPULAR MUSIC AND RECORDINGS

TUPAC SHAKUR

From the 1993 CD *Strictly 4 My N.I.G.G.A.Z.* (Death Row Records–Universal–Interscope)

"Strugglin"

I'd rather use my gun 'cause I get the money quicker . . . got 'em in the frame—Bang! Bang! . . . blowin' muthafuckers to the moon.

From the 1991 CD *2pacalypse Now* (Death Row Records–Universal–Interscope)

"Tha Lunatic"

Oh, shit! Jumped on my man's dick. Heard he had a 12-inch, now the bitch is lovesick. Who's to blame? The guy or the groupie . . . now she wants to do me. Hoo-wee, this is the life—new bitch every night.

I'm also including a few excerpts of some lyrics from the biggest selling *white* rapper of the year 2000, Marshall Mathers, who goes by the stage name Eminem, to demonstrate that record companies are color blind when it comes to distributing depravity to our children. Actually, the case of Eminem is even more insidious. The October 2000 issue of *Details* magazine featured a story titled "Funkateer: The Cult of Eminem—How Dr. Dre Took a White Punk from Detroit and Created the New Teen Idol." The article's author, David Samuels, suggests that Eminem is essentially a product created by rap producer Andre Young, better known by the stage name Dr. Dre. In fact Samuels suggests Eminem may be "the most daring teen idol since Elvis" and points out that "it would be wrong to not also recognize his creator."

Comparing Dr. Dre's influence on Eminem's career to that of Sun Records owner Sam Phillips's role in making Elvis a star, Samuels explains, "Dr. Dre has proved himself to be not only the greatest rap producer of the decade but also a pop wizard capable of seeing through to the heart of the genre: stereotypes of criminal blackness have made Gangsta Rap the chosen music of suburbia." The rest of the article makes eminently clear that the target audience for Eminem's music is not suburbia in general, but rather suburban teens in particular. Keep that in mind as you review the following excerpts from three songs on Eminem's *Marshall Mathers LP*, which is obviously reaching a great many in its target audience as the

POPULAR MUSIC AND RECORDINGS

October 2000 issue of *Details* magazine declared it "the best selling record in America."

EMINEM

**From the 2000 CD *The Marshall Mathers LP*
(Aftermath/Interscope Records–Universal)**

"Amityville"

I fucked my cousin in his asshole, slit my
    mother's throat
(*AHHH!*) Guess who Slim Shady just
    signed to Interscope?
My little sister's birthday, she'll remember
    me
For a gift I had ten of my boys take her
    virginity
(*Mm mm mm!*) And bitches know me as
    a horny ass freak
Their mother wasn't raped, I ate her pussy
    while she was 'sleep
Pissy-drunk, throwin' up in the urinal
(YOU FUCKIN' HOMO!)
That's what I said at my dad's funeral

VULGARIANS AT THE GATE

"Criminal"

If I ever gave a fuck, I'd shave my nuts
tuck my dick in between my legs and cluck
You motherfuckin' chickens ain't brave
    enough
to say the stuff I say, so this tape is shut.
Shit, half the shit I say, I just make it up
To make you mad so kiss my white naked ass
And if it's not a rapper that I make it as
I'm a be a fuckin rapist in a Jason mask
You know why?
Cuz I'm a
CRIMINAL
CRIMINAL
You goddamn right
I'm a CRIMINAL
Yeah, I'm a CRIMINAL

"Drug Ballad"

Then in a couple of minutes that bottle of
    Guinness is finished
You are now allowed to officially slap bitches
You have the right to remain violent and
    start wilin'
Start a fight with the same guy that was
    smart eyein' you

POPULAR MUSIC AND RECORDINGS

Get in your car, start it, and start drivin'
Over the island and cause a 42 car pile-up.

Critic Richard Goldstein, writing in the tolerant *Village Voice* as far back as October 16, 1990, assembled a few phrases of revoltingly vile and barbaric rap lyrics apparently from one of the first rap groups to test the limits of obscenity:

2 LIVE CREW

Suck my dick, bitch
And make it puke . . .
Lick my ass up and down
Lick it till your tongue turn doo-do
    brown . . .
I'll break you down
And dick you long
I'll bust your pussy
Cause me so horny

Goldstein goes on to comment:

This anthology of musings by 2 Live Crew is also part of the new sex "'tude." If Madonna represents the secretly submissive babe,

257

they signify the strutting sado-stud. His rage, his rectitude, his revenge have suddenly become a form of vaudeville. The airwaves bristle with the sexual "dis" of shock-jocks, stand-up sociopaths, metal marauders, and rough rappers. The word *bitch* has become a male mantra. (Ice Cube used it fifty-seven times on his last album.) The most memorable films I've seen this year—*GoodFellas, Cook/Thief, Henry Serial Killer*—are sermons on the wages of macho that lavish attention on every threat and thrust. In the wake of the Geto Boys, Rob Lowe is beginning to seem avuncular.

We're assured—mostly by progressives—that this stuff is "only rock 'n roll," not to be confused with power relations in real life. Women who link the rape-rap of the Geto Boys and the art of wilding [marauding attacks on women in public places] are called hypersensitive, as are gays who see a connection between Audio 2's invitation to punch a faggot in the face and the fact that it happens so frequently.

Not only are the blunt terms shocking enough, in the context of popular music heard on records, CDs and tapes, and on the radio, but the messages conveyed are even more chilling. Violent rape and out-right murder, for example, are not only described but condoned, recommended, glamorized.

Perhaps the only thing more inherently disgusting than the lyrics themselves are the defensive references to First Amendment rights made by those who earn large amounts of money marketing this garbage to our youth.

In my book *Dumbth: The Lost Art of Thinking* I deal with the collapse of general intelligence in our society. An appropriate example of dumbth was the decision made some years ago to market such vile recordings with a special "warning label." First of all, most parents do not buy these recordings for their children. Children buy them themselves, and those who have already developed an appetite for such garbage are likely grateful to the labelers since they will have even less trouble locating the most offensive examples of the form. The warning label approach would work only if the offensive merchandise was sold only in sections of record stores not accessible to children, or with proof of identification as an adult required to purchase them.

Again we must recognize that there are large num-bers of blacks in the country who are also deeply offended by such depravity.

VULGARIANS AT THE GATE

Witness the following 1995 exchange between the chair of the National Political Congress of Black Women, Dr. C. Delores Tucker, and former U.S. Secretary of Education William Bennett on an evening news program.

DT: That's what gangster rap is doing to our children, turning them into gangsters.

WB: I joined with Delores Tucker because I was very taken with her—first of all, her moral power.

Rapper: I got whores, bitches, and sluts.

DT: That's as offensive as calling us niggers. That's an offensive word.

WB: These things are so degrading, and so stupid and so violent.

DT: If we did not speak up to the youths saying that to us, who would stop it? We would have been in arms long ago.

WB: She's a liberal Democrat, I am a conservative Republican. We wanted to take politics off the table on this issue.

POPULAR MUSIC AND RECORDINGS

DT: The corporations should have had some social responsibility. When they glamorize and produce this kind of music, it shows that they are profiting and pimping off young children.

WB: Time-Warner is the biggest entertainment company in the world. They *say* they're very concerned about violence, about the degradation of women, about rape, and about our social problems, and then they sell music to kids which glorifies all of those things, and worse. They need to be stopped.

DT: I've been picketing these stores and going to jail myself to stop it, because it's not right. Children need a positive message, not this filthy stuff.

WB: I'm not interested in legislation; I'm not interested in regulation; I'm not interested in starting a boycott. I just want them to stop.

DT: Women are protected, men are protected. Our children must be protected.

Of all the "justifications" for such cultural garbage, the worst is the argument that goes, "Well, sure, this is shocking, but these young boys are writing out of their misery and desperation." What is most appalling about this argument is its stupidity. If Jack the Ripper, Attila the Hun, Al Capone, or Charles Manson told us of their personal torment, while on stage or not, would that lead us to approve of a single one of either their offenses or the drivel that describes them?

Again the argument boils down to the effect of unremitting exposure to such sordid fare on children and young teenagers. My own grandchildren, understandably attracted by the catchy rhythms and often brilliant choreography exhibited on videos, have often been exposed to it, even in their preteen years. When I occasionally watch television with them I order them to switch to another channel if blatantly offensive material is shown. But few if any children have parents or grandparents who can monitor what they watch or listen to at *all* times.

It is no wonder that serious discussions have begun, in Congress and elsewhere, about forcing broadcasters to have MTV removed from the most *basic* cable channel packages and transferred to a tier of additional channels for which viewers have to request and pay a special fee. Doing so would at least make such material less available to children and allow parents to make a conscious choice as to whether to receive it in their homes.

Ms. Tucker, a courageous leader of the African-American community, was one of many who was finally able to induce Time-Warner Inc. executives to feel a twinge of guilt. In one public exposition of her views, she held up a poster depicting degrading and violent actions against women which, she reported, was part of the album/CD package recorded by rap artist Snoop Doggy Dogg.

"Time-Warner produces this pornographic smut, which black children embrace as role models," Tucker said. "Children want to dress like them, walk like them, talk like them, and use language that you wouldn't believe. This is the filth that children are buying. . . . This is pornography, and every kid is saying these words now."

Unfortunately, when in 1995 Time-Warner eventually saw the light and cut its ties to the Interscope record label that produced most of this filth, the Universal Music Group quickly stepped in to purchase Time-Warner's 50 percent share in the label for $200 million, according to the *Los Angeles Times*. As of the year 2000, Interscope and Universal were together responsible for distributing millions of copies of the horrific lyrics of Eminem to America's young people.

VULGARIANS AT THE GATE

It is important to understand that this is not an issue that divides religious believers from secular humanists, atheists, or agnostics. I know of no American freethinker, black or white, who is not just as repulsed by such lyrics as is the most outspoken fundamentalist, whether Christian, Islamic, or any other.

When considering offensive rap lyrics, of course, there is an additional problematic complexity in that we are dealing with cultural differences so deep that it is almost impossible to agree on the proper use of normative terms. Consider, by way of evidence, the following transcript from the *Conan O'Brien Show* of March 31, 1998, in which O'Brien was interviewing recording artist Ice-T.

CONAN: Charlton Heston, he got you fired from your record company, didn't he?

ICE-T: He attempted to, back in the days when we were going through the Cop Killer controversy. . . . The man had never heard my record before. [He was] like a hired gun that they use, try to put me out of business. . . . I don't even know Charlton Heston. I don't tend to spend a lot of time speakin' on people I don't know. . . . He came out and went after me like he knew me or something.

POPULAR MUSIC AND RECORDINGS

CONAN: . . . I heard that you were stuck in traffic, and you looked over in the next car, and Charlton Heston [was there], and you saw each other.

ICE-T: We was in traffic, and I was in the Range Rover and I looked out. [Heston] was sittin' in a black 'Vette and I had two guys sittin' in the back seat that really he didn't wanna meet, and they were lookin' into the car, and they were like "yo, Ice, that fool right there." See, you gotta remember, when you dealin' with rappers, it's a lot of people I'm takin' care of. My career is really their livelihood. My friends wasn't really happy about Charlton Heston sittin' right there. They wanted to see if he could really walk on water at that point. Even though, with all the hate and the anger he had toward me, Charlton Heston, I saved your life that day by pulling off, and you should thank me for that.

CONAN: Now, did he see you?

ICE-T: Naw, we had tinted windows. It was one of those type of things where it could have just went down real quick.

VULGARIANS AT THE GATE

CONAN: Oh, my God. So what would happen if I ran into you, say, on the freeway?

ICE-T: I ain't got no beef with you. I'm, like civilized, you know what I'm sayin'? I'm not mad at Charlton Heston. I'm just sayin', you gotta know that people like me, my friends. . . . It's like this, OK. All these guys behind the cameras . . . everybody's down with Conan O'Brien. If somebody came out to try to take you out of business, these guys would have an attitude about it.

It is easy enough to look at such material critically; a nine-year-old child could do that much, but we are talking about true horror here. Consider: a prominent entertainer is discussing, with the utmost casualness, the fact that some of his close companions were literally willing to assassinate film star Charlton Heston. But then, far from apologizing for keeping bad company, he adopts a ridiculous semiheroic pose by suggesting that Heston's brains would indeed have been splattered all over his car if Ice-T himself had not intervened to discourage the murderous intentions of two of his associates.

It is even more depressing to see how weakly Ice-T appears to reason. He seems to believe that no one is entitled to criticize his recordings unless they have somehow encountered him personally. I have never met Joseph Stalin, Adolf Hitler, or Charles Manson, to mention only three monsters among the thousands who could be cited in this connection, but certainly that cannot be taken to mean that I have no right to speak critically of them and their notorious crimes.

If only white critics had condemned rappers for chanting their points it might be well-grounded but would be largely ignored by the black community. To turn from fantasy to reality, there have been many black spokespersons who have criticized rap, much of which—again—is inexpressibly vulgar, cruel, and in flat opposition to long-accepted moral standards, whether Jewish, Christian, Islamic, or secular. But Michael Eric Dyson, professor of American Civilization and African-American Studies at Brown University, in his brilliant work *Reflecting Black* (University of Minnesota Press) refers to a rap about African-American history. This points to an admirable solution to the problem that rap represents. Given that it is obvious that the basic appeal of such performances lies in their wonderfully infectious rhythms, why not do away with the morally hideous messages that many rappers convey and replace them with more noble and uplifting thoughts reflecting the higher aspirations of urban youth?

VULGARIANS AT THE GATE

While on a work-visit to New York in October 1999, I happened to tune in to a few random minutes of MTV entertainment. The number being featured was an R&B tune (from the *Blue Streak* movie soundtrack) called "Criminal Mind." It would obviously be possible to write a lyric with that title which taught a valuable moral and social lesson since presumably there is a consensus that disapproves of criminality. This being MTV, however, no such luck. The cast consisted of a number of remarkably talented dancers and singers, the choreography was top-notch, and the camera and editing work had the usual professional polish characteristic of the more highly budgeted MTV music videos. Unfortunately, the philosophical point of the production seemed not to be a condemnation but a celebration of criminality.

MUSIC AND VIOLENCE

It has taken a discouragingly long time for the national consciousness to concede the obvious fact that there is a direct cause-and-effect relationship between (a) violent attacks on women and (b) some popular music.

For those coming to this now widely acknowledged connection for the first time I'll explain that that narrow aspect of the debate has already been settled. I am not blind to the fact that there are those who deny the relationship, but the rest of us should waste no further time on them because they consist of two general types—dunces and those who simply don't want to rock the financial boat, given that the worst music in cultural history currently generates billions of dollars in revenues each year.

One would certainly not suggest that the abuse of girls and women is an unprecedented social phenomenon, its roots are traceable throughout history; but in that true Golden Age of popular music—the 1920s, '30s, and '40s—neither the Hit Parade's momentary best-sellers nor the songs that because of their rich beauty became timeless standards ever featured women-hating or violent lyrics.

Part of the overall problem all this poses is that many of those who would react with proper horror if they had the situation in clear focus simply do not listen to today's music, unless perhaps they are occasionally forced to do so by the ear-splitting volume of tapes played in passing cars. Understandably they may perceive that suggesting they become informed on what is obviously a social problem of enormous importance is like asking them personally to wade knee-deep into a festering waste-dump to become personally familiar with garbage.

Nevertheless, the time has come for them to put on their intellectual wading-boots and jump right in. In early June 2000 fifty-three women in New York City's Central Park were assaulted by groups of men who, according to witnesses, were singing women-hating lyrics. One of the many disgusting aspects of that national embarrassment was that the offenders were shaking beer bottles and squirting foam all over the helpless women. What has that to do with popular music? Precisely that outrage is part of the action of the recent *Next Episode* video by Dr. Dre, Eminem's producer and a highly influential rapper who is often referred to as the godfather of one of rap's most violent subsets, Gangsta Rap. Was such revolting fare perhaps a quickly passing oddity? Would that it were so. The video in question, as of late June 2000, was the second most played on MTV.

The reader might be forgiven for thinking that MTV executives would at least feel twinges of guilt about this, but apparently they do not. If you'll pardon the cliché, they're undoubtedly laughing all the way to the bank.

Several years ago Dr. C. Delores Tucker and William Bennett were able to use the energy created

POPULAR MUSIC AND RECORDINGS

by public shock over rappers' justifications—glorifications is more like it—of rape and antipolice violence to persuade Time-Warner to stop distributing such vile products. But by the year 2000 such moral garbage had become so popular with young people that it was increasingly perceived as normal, par for the course. Alisa Valdes-Rodriguez, a writer for the *Los Angeles Times*, contributed an admirable and insightful essay on the problem, "Is Music Issuing a Call to Violence?" (June 26, 2000):

> While the media have searched for answers in the Central Park assaults via race and class, using code words such as "inner city" and "urban" (read: black/brown), I have a very different theory: The young men in Central Park were simply imitating their idols, as have many generations of insecure pop music fans.
>
> While "pimps" are certainly responsible for the assaults, so too are the record executives who continue to sign and promote only the lowest and most moronic and stereotypical of "artists," wholesaling misogyny in the name of profit.
>
> If sex and violence sell, their line goes, then sexual violence sells the most.
>
> Perhaps. But sales at what cost?

VULGARIANS AT THE GATE

As Valdes-Rodriguez and other surveyors of America's tragic social scene have noted, we are not talking here about a one-time phenomenon. Atlanta's Freaknik celebration (an annual spring break street party of mostly black college students) and the numerous actual rapes—as well as examples of public intercourse—that were part of the 1999 Woodstock concert involved men chanting lyrics *while they were committing their felonious assaults.*

But do not think for a minute that this sad news relates only to blacks and Latinos. White males buy more copies of the vulgar rap and rock music and also commit many of the most hateful crimes.

Because of the heavy media coverage of the two white punks who committed the Columbine High School massacre it was widely recognized that they were sick racists. It was not as well perceived that on the video tapes they left behind they also declared their hatred of women. And the two high school students who killed four girls and a female teacher in Jonesboro, Arkansas, also made clear that they had specifically targeted females.

Ms. Valdes-Rodriguez's involvement with the issue was first stimulated in 1993 after a chilling confrontation with a young thug on a New York subway platform. "He wore headphones, stared into my eyes, and rapped loudly to a song that called for men to slap women down if they 'act up.' He looked me up and down. When the train approached he pretended he was going to push me in front of it. Within weeks I read in the New York papers that a young woman had been raped, in a public swimming pool, by a group of young men who chanted the lyrics to another popular song that degraded women."

Is the United States alone, among the world's nations, in regard to the problem of violence against women? Of course not; it is still common in some nations of Asia for parents to kill their newborn babies if the little ones are girls. In Muslim cultures the suggestion that women have equal rights with men is considered a satanic idea. In some parts of the world if a poor woman is raped the whole society considers it the duty of the male members of her *family* to kill her to protect their *own* family honor.

But there's one crucial distinction between such savagery in other parts of the world and similar crimes that take place within our borders and that is that in Afghanistan, India, and China *popular music is in no way involved*. Realize what that means—a brutal evil exists in both camps but only in our own country is there a massive music recording and publishing industry that not only justifies but encourages and profits by such atrocities. As Valdes-Rodriguez says, "The idiots who ripped the clothes off the women in Central Park were *raised* on gangsta rap and aggrorock. It did not *reflect* their worldview, it *formed* it."

For the last several years I have been depressed by the fact that certain black intellectuals were exercising their formidable intelligence as lawyers for the defense of rap entertainers. Fortunately, in early October 2000 that unhappy factor began to change. A new attitude was signaled by the cover story in the *Newsweek* magazine of October 9, which described a best-selling rapper named Mos Def as having come to the conclusion that popular culture had gotten out of hand. *Newsweek* reported that this twenty-six-year-old rap star "blames the music industry for endlessly promoting the same tired, vacuous product without offering much in the way of alternatives."

Reginald Dennis, former editor of the hip-hop magazine *The Source*, said "Everything people hoped for came true, and everyone's miserable about it. It was a hollow dream." The magazine's feature refers to a number of rappers who became popular in the 1980s as lamenting the genre's recent directions, particularly those rappers now raising children of their own. Darryl McDaniel, a thirty-six-year-old member of the early rap trio Run D.M.C. said, "I have a six-year-old son. I don't want him thinking that drinking champagne and slapping bitches is what he has to do."

But by no means are all comfortable with the new criticism. Gangsta rapper Ice-T told *Newsweek*, "I listen to some of them rap now—I mean, c'mon, that shit is warp-factor-seven hip-hop. Hip-hop is like rock and roll. It's about wild men, scantily clad women, and fast living. This is the food of human beings."

Another example of unclear thinking comes from a young Philadelphia-based rapper named Eve. "I think if Biggie and Tupac were alive, you wouldn't hear so much bullshit like you do now. Guys would be ashamed to just put anything out, because Biggie and Tupac talked about something." Indeed they did, but all too frequently that something was socially and psychologically sick.

And yet, I am encouraged by the awakening of some in the rap community and by the courage and clarity with which Alisa Valdes-Rodriguez concluded her commentary in the *Los Angeles Times*, saying "If those who favor enlightenment and human rights are not vigilant, if we don't speak out, if we don't protest, the pull to barbarism can, and will, take hold. . . . The music industry needs to take responsibility for what it is teaching people about the roles of men and women. . . . And everyone with a conscience should be asking one very important question: Why all the woman-bashing *now?* . . . We need to change our musical direction. If not, we are literally destroying the lives of girls and women, and our society along with them."

7
VIOLENCE

Media offer entertainment, culture, news, sports, and education. They are an important part of our lives and have much to teach. But some of what they teach may not be what we want children to learn. Sometimes you can see the impact of media right away, such as when your child watches super-heroes fighting and then copies their moves during play. But most of the time the impact is not so immediate or obvious. It occurs slowly as children see and hear certain messages over and over, such as the following:

> *Fighting and other violence used as a way to "handle" conflict. Cigarettes and alcohol shown as cool and attractive, not unhealthy and deadly. Sexual action with no negative results, such as disease or unintended pregnancy.*
> —American Academy of Pediatrics

277

We now know that by the time the typical American child reaches the age of eighteen, he or she has seen 200,000 dramatized acts of violence, and 40,000 dramatized murders. Kids become attracted to it, and more numb to its consequences. As their exposure to violence grows, so, in some deeply troubling cases of particularly vulnerable children, does the taste for it. . . .

What the studies say, quite simply, is that the boundary between fantasy and reality violence, which is a clear line for most adults, can become very blurred for vulnerable children. Kids steeped in the culture of violence do become desensitized to it and more capable of committing it themselves.

That is why I have strongly urged people in the entertainment industry to consider the consequences of what they create and how they advertise it. One can value the First Amendment right to free speech and at the same time care for and act with restraint.

—Pres. Bill Clinton, June 1, 1999

THE PROBLEM OF VIOLENCE

The problem of violence in media is in that category of social dilemmas that have no simple answer. Among the complicated factors is that our country itself has been incredibly violent from its earliest days. We did not, of course, on arriving here from Europe, find a continent devoid of human inhabitants, and the abandon with which we killed massive numbers of indigenous animals was pretty much equaled by our treatment of those fellow humans who had gotten here first.

Then there's the fact of slavery, which we cannot consider simply a matter of social injustice. That it certainly was, but the institution was accompanied by daily acts of violent cruelty. That bastard offspring of the struggle to abolish slavery—the Civil War—was also characterized by incredible savagery, although I suppose one can say the same for all wars. But it is important to review these and similar ugly realities of our history, otherwise we run the risk of believing ourselves to be essentially sweet, civilized folk who are, only recently, being morally contaminated by the make-believe violence that is present in our motion pictures and television fare. Our films, parenthetically, have glamorized and romanticized the real history of the settling of the territories that now comprise our nation. Actors like Gary Cooper, Alan Ladd, Randolph Scott, and John Wayne gave us a sanitized portrayal of early Americans, many of whom, in reality, were considerably less admirable. The novels of Cormac McCarthy, *Blood Meridian*, for example, help to make up for the glamorized Hollywood version of the winning of the west.

To approach the problem from an even more basic level, whether the existence of our lonely planet was the creation of a conscious God or the blind, mysterious working of natural law, the results have been notoriously unsatisfactory. The noneducable animals, of which there are millions of species, survive largely by eating, sometimes alive, creatures more vulnerable than themselves. We human animals eat representatives of other species, too, but at least we kill them first, though this is more a matter of our own comfort and convenience than of tender concern for the lesser of earth's inhabitants.

Yet another complication is that there is a genetically implanted, partly instinctual and, therefore, perfectly natural aggressiveness in humans. It's degree, of course, varies—some of us are largely peaceable while others are natural bullies or sadists—but none of us is exempt from what some philosophers and poets have viewed as a tragic curse. All of this means that we have an interest—sometimes to the extreme of morbidity—in witnessing violence. Professional boxing, wrestling, and to some degree even football are obvious examples. We are, in this regard, probably in no essential way different from the mobs of ancient Rome who, while no doubt considering themselves generally civilized, nevertheless used to witness, and greet with applause and laughter, the spectacle of gladiators fighting to the death and terrified prisoners being torn to pieces by lions. Other cultures, too, have been guilty of similar social atrocities. In ancient China one method of execution was to enclose the unfortunate object of public wrath inside an enormous metal likeness of an animal. Fires would then be lighted under the bellies of the metal beasts and the crowd standing about would shortly be entertained by the pitiful shrieks of those who were so imprisoned. Whether we, as individuals, have risen very far above such savagery remains an open question.

At least one lesson can be learned from this otherwise depressing spectacle and that is that civilization itself—which I suspect most of us assume is set firmly in place—is, in fact, a fragile veneer that can easily be swept aside when mob passions are aroused.

Parenthetically, there are those who assume that our great protective bulwark against outbreaks of uncontrolled violence is religion. No historian would make such an astonishing mistake. For thousands of years our religious denominations have not only failed to abolish violence, rather they have distinguished themselves at the other extreme. In the present day one marvels at how casually we can employ, in conversation, a phrase such as "burning at the stake," usually accompanied by emotionally blank facial expressions, which reveal that we scarcely know what we're talking about. Nor are we limited only to the record of history in our consideration of relevant evidence; our daily news media provide more than enough examples of religious fanatics gunning each other down, blasting airplanes out of the sky, bombing public facilities and abortion clinics, with all of the above accompanied by the slaughter of innocent by-standers.

The good news is that the religions can still play a constructive role in the campaigns for moral reform that are now so necessary. My point is merely that they should do so with all due humility. If we assume there is a God, it is highly unlikely that he is much concerned with rituals, dietary laws, and the props and schticks commonly associated with religion. Religion is more properly concerned with human behavior, which is to say with moral and ethical questions. Such observations are not to be interpreted as digressions from our theme. In fact, they bear directly on campaigns to find a reasonable resolution to the

problem of violence in films, television programming, and recordings.

There never was a great deal of sense to the debate
as to whether excessive violence on television and
films affects the consciousness of children. Of course it
does; the only sensible relevant question is to what
extent? For at least twenty years violence in the entertainment media has frequently been mentioned by
those who attend my concerts or night-club performances, a fact which leads to an incident worth
describing here. In the 1980s I was hired to entertain a
gathering of about nine hundred women in the charming seaside community of La Jolla, California. One of
the questions ran as follows: "Mr. Allen, what do you
think of the degree of really sickening violence that is
so common these days in television and movies?"

Since my purpose at that moment was to amuse
rather than inform, though the two are not mutually
exclusive, I put on a mock-serious face and said, "I
happen to share the emotion that motivated the
writing of this question. In fact I would go so far as to
say that any television or motion picture producer,
director—any TV writer, actor, or stunt man—who
deliberately crams unnecessary, sadistic violence into
a theatrical production (*dramatic pause*)—ought to be
taken out and beaten to a pulp."

VULGARIANS AT THE GATE

I was totally surprised that only about twenty percent of the audience laughed at what I had said,
which would of course be the rational response. The
majority assumed that I had spoken in all seriousness
and gave me a rousing, foot-stamping roar of affirmation, of the sort that would, a few years thereafter,
be associated with the flag-waving sentiments expressed by Oliver North.

Fortunately I was able to mask my shock at the
fact that the ovation went on so long, but its length
gave me a few moments to collect my thoughts, after
which I said, "Ladies, do you realize what you've just
done? You have suggested, by your cheers and
applause, that the solution to *imaginary* violence—is
real violence."

But the women's reaction, inappropriate as it was,
must at least be understood, and the explanation for
it, of course, is that these women were even in the
1980s at the limits of their patience with the sort of
barbaric violence that had become so common in TV
and films.

There is in the minds of many of us—and perhaps
all of us—at least an occasional temptation to suc-
cumb to the vigilante impulse. We witness outrageous instances of crime, corruption, even the hon-
oring of men known to be murderers, and we want to

do something about it. Law enforcement people, for the most part, are largely immune to such fantasies for the obvious reason that they *are* doing something about it, although perhaps the temptation is represented by a form of Dirty Harryism in which it at least enters their mind that in certain contexts it might be convenient if one could go beyond what the written law allows.

I had a relevant experience recently which was so bizarre it may sound like fiction but I assure you that the incident did in fact take place.

I had been entertaining and lecturing in a western state and was flying back to Los Angeles after I had completed my assignment. My seat was 1B, front row, aisle. As soon as I sat down I opened a bag and withdrew a collection of work-papers which I studiously attacked at once, reading and underlining certain passages. Despite the obvious fact of my busyness, the fellow on my left, a short man in his mid-fifties, began to talk to me. He did not have the usual excuse that I had been recognized and the poor fellow simply wanted to communicate with a celebrity. I have had many such pleasant conversations while traveling, but at no time during our conversation was this man aware of my identity. The situation worsened as he drank more liquor, which the stewardess continued to pour him in what I thought was too generous a supply.

He seemed one of those nervous, jumpy, congenitally talkative types who indulge mostly in mind-numbing small talk. I treated him politely but kept my answers brief, and continued my reading and underlining.

As I became more annoyed at his persistence, however, I tried to think of a way in which, without taking an insulting tone, I might be able to say something that would induce him to withdraw from the conversation. The opportunity presented itself a few minutes later when he asked "What do you do for a living?"

"I'm a hit man," I said.

"A *hip* man?"

"No," I said "hit, h-i-t—a hit man."

"Wow," he said, softly.

If I had assumed that his acceptance of my absurd announcement would turn off his conversational tendencies I had guessed wrong. He began to ply me with more and more questions. What did I charge per job? Did I work for an organization? Did I personally know the people I was hired to kill?

A few minutes later in the conversation, to my astonishment, the man tried to hire me. He knew a certain woman, he said, one who had ruined him in his business, which I shall not publicly describe, but he obviously was extremely angry at the woman he said had treated him very unfairly and cruelly. She was ruthless. She was a bitch. In his mind she deserved to be killed, and—I repeat—the fellow wanted to know if I was interested in taking the assignment.

I told him that I was not. At one point he said, "Do you work alone?"

"Usually," I said, "but in some situations I have a partner."

At this point my professional involvement with humor came to the fore. As it happens my accompanist, a gifted pianist named Paul Smith, does not look at all like a professional musician but rather like an offensive lineman for a professional football team. He is about six-four, weighs about 250 pounds and looks, to use a simple word, tough.

When my new companion asked if my partner was flying with me I pointed to Mr. Smith and said "Yes. He's that fellow right over there."

My now semidrunk interrogator seemed suitably impressed. "Wow," he said. "He looks like one tough dude."

"He is." I said. "That's why I work with him."

The fellow then actually gave me his business card

and told me that he'd like to consult with me further about the possibility he had raised. Inasmuch as comedy is about tragedy it's easy enough to laugh at the sadly comic elements in this tale, but there is something deeply disturbing about the fact that a businessman who probably considers himself law-abiding would so casually attempt to arrange for a contract killing. It is all part, I'm afraid, of the increasing lawlessness of American society.

STATISTICS

Presumably all American adults are aware that children are now committing murders. If nothing else, the school shootings in various parts of the country, because they were so widely reported, have raised our consciousness about such tragedies. But the reader might be interested in an entirely unofficial poll I have taken about the problem. It involved my having said to about twenty friends and acquaintances, "We all know now about the terrible school shootings and other murders committed by kids in our country. I doubt that even many experts have the correct, up-to-date arithmetic but, just making a guess, how many killings of this sort do you think are taking place in our country each year?"

I confess that I myself would have answered that there might have been fifty or sixty such crimes in any recent year. Other estimates I've heard range from a couple of dozen to perhaps a hundred. The fact is that *child-murderers have risen to claim nearly 1,000 victims per year in the United States,* according to author Michael Newton in his book *Killer Kids.*

Unfortunately behind these alarming statistics there are additional troubling factors. We have long known that being raised in degraded, poverty-stricken circumstances and exposed to violence in the home or on the streets at an early age can lead young people to commit physically aggressive crimes, including murder. But that classic explanation does not apply to some recent outrages. Some of today's young killers are the products of so-called good families. Newton's book provides important information for those who want to learn more about this tragic development.

EVADING RESPONSIBILITY

Recently I saw, on C-SPAN television, a discussion about the effects on society of violence portrayed in the media. To my astonishment, the various entertainment-world representatives, although obviously concerned, as citizens, with the problem of violence—who isn't?—seemed more interested in asking for stricter gun control legislation. This is certainly a popular position to take; poll after poll clarifies that the majority of Americans do indeed want not only more antigun laws but stricter enforcement of such legislation as already exists. That much is a given. What was more newsworthy about the discussion was that there seemed little willingness on the part of the show-biz participants to accept any responsibility for creating a social climate in which guns and other weapons are more likely to be used.

Rather than continuing to debate this specific point it is now reasonable to say that the defenders of the entertainment field should simply knock off that "who, me?" approach. The news is out: The facts have been established. No one has ever argued that TV and films are the *sole* cause of violent behavior among our nation's children. But to suggest that they should not even be included on the list of causal factors is sheer nonsense. As Dr. Jerome Singer, psychology professor at Yale University, has put it, "If you came home and found a strange man teaching your kids to punch each other, or trying to sell them all kinds of products, you'd kick him right out of the house. But here you are—you come in and the TV is on—and you don't think twice about it."

Well, the American people now *are* thinking twice. And the more informed among them are simply no longer going to let the entertainment moguls get away with their traditional denials of guilt. The intellectual and professional medical community has spoken out repeatedly and forcefully. The American Medical Association, for example, said—and this was as early as 1976—"TV violence threatens the health and welfare of young Americans." In 1982 the National Institute of Mental Health issued an extensive report reviewing over 2,500 studies on the effects of television violence and concluded there was "a clear consensus among most researchers that television violence leads to aggressive behavior." The American Psychiatric Association, in 1986, stated that, "The evidence is overwhelming that violence in television programming can have a negative and severe behavioral impact on young people." In 1993 the American Psychological Association's Commission on Violence on Youth declared that there is "absolutely no doubt that higher levels of viewing violence on television are correlated with increased acceptance of aggressive attitudes and increased aggressive behavior."

VULGARIANS AT THE GATE

Peace activist Jan Arnow has made the point that the problem is not so much the absence of studies of violence but getting people in responsible positions to read the many studies that are available. All the major film and television studios—like the major publishing houses—have their own professional readers. If a given executive is literally too busy to read a full 127-page study then it might be helpful if he assigned one of his readers to give him a twelve-page synopsis of it so that he would then be at least familiar with the basic information.

STOP TEACHING
OUR KIDS TO KILL

Anyone interested in the connection between violence on television and films and violence in real life should read *Stop Teaching Our Kids to Kill: A Call to Action against TV, Movie and Video Game Violence* (Crown Publishers, 1999) by David Grossman, a retired army lieutenant colonel, and Gloria De-Gaetano, a media literacy consultant. At a time when spokespeople for the film and TV industry have the nerve to issue flat denials that there's a connection between their product and crime on the streets,

292

Grossman and DeGaetano deal with hard realities. In our country per capita aggravated assaults are up almost sixfold since 1957. In Canada the rate of the same assaults are up fivefold since 1964. The same general patterns have been discovered in Norway, Greece, Australia, New Zealand, and Sweden. Commented Grossman in a "Perspective on Violence" he wrote which was published in the *Los Angeles Times* in October 1999, "The major new factor responsible for this is the marketing of visual media violence to kids. I sat beside Surgeon General David Satcher on *Meet the Press* after the Columbine High School shootings in Littleton, Colorado. He was asked if he could do a report on the link between media violence and violence in our kids. 'Sure, I can do another Surgeon General's Report,' he said, 'but why don't they start by reading the 1972 Surgeon General's Report?'"

The nation owes a debt to Colonel Grossman for pointing out that the same Surgeon General who issued the now-famous report on the long-denied link between tobacco and cancer also issued a report on the link between media violence and violence in society. Getting right to the crux of the modern conflict, Grossman has pointed out that everyone now knows that for generations the tobacco industry lied about the link between its product and cancer, which continues to kill hundreds of thousands of Americans each year. Comments Grossman, "If you ask media executives about the link between their product and violent crime they will do exactly the same thing—and they control the public airwaves." He points out that a review of almost 1,000 studies, presented to the American College of Forensic Psychiatry in 1998,

> found that all but 18 demonstrated that screen violence leads to real violence, and 12 of those 18 were funded by the television industry.
>
> As recently as 1992 the American Psychological Association concluded that forty years of research on the link between TV and real life violence has been ignored, stating that the "scientific debate is over" and calling for federal policy to protect society.
>
> The American Academy of Pediatrics has said, in a January 5, 1999, formal report, "Children don't naturally kill. It is a learned skill and they learn it most pervasively, from violence as entertainment in television, the movies, and interactive video-games."

Concludes Grossman, bluntly,

Congress must provide what Americans have been pleading for: regulation to restrict the marketing of violence to children. Forget the Federal Communications Commission. It is a toothless watchdog, made up mostly of people with past associations with the electronic media. It is like having tobacco farmers in charge of the Food and Drug Administration.

• • •

A guest who appeared with me in a 1999 radio station KPFK interview in Los Angeles was William Link, who with his partner Richard Levinson, created and developed over a dozen television series, including *Columbo, Mannix,* and *Murder She Wrote,* as well as writing some of the finest television movies ever made, including *My Sweet Charlie, That Certain Summer, The Execution of Private Slovik,* and *Crisis at Central High.* In answer to a question about how TV became so objectionable Link said, "I think when cable came in the standards really deteriorated. The three networks, which were fairly clean up to that point, took a big hit, lost almost 50 percent share of the audience. And now, to compete, it's getting even worse. The vulgarity, what the soaps are up to, even during the day, it's outrageous."

VULGARIANS AT THE GATE

Asked why his shows were acceptable to families, Link said,

> I grew up reading detective novels of the 1930s which were very cerebral—the Ellery Queens, the John Dixon Carrs. . . . They were violenceless, most of them. And then I read people like Graham Greene and [J. D.] Salinger and Dostoevsky, and Tolstoy—all the greats. That really formed my sensibility.
>
> I am proud of the fact that Dick and I created probably the only nonviolent police show, *Columbo*. If you watch that show, Columbo hates guns, will not carry a gun . . . and there are no car chases. There's no violence in Columbo, except the murder that triggers the intellectual duel of wits between the protagonist and the antagonist. On everything else you're going to find violence in the shows. Even on *Law & Order* you're going to find violence. In my career I really try not to write the violence, and it's tougher because it's easy to throw in car chases and some guy being hit over the head. We did a show called *The Storyteller* that starred Marty Balsam, Patty Duke, and Doris Roberts about twenty years ago. It was about a television writer who writes a movie

of the week and in it a kid burns down a school. A child in Seattle sees the show, duplicates it and dies in the fire. And here's a writer who's written junk his entire career and has got his pool in Beverly Hills and suddenly looks deep into the well of his own conscience and says, "What have I been doing and what's so wrong about this?" and he goes on an odyssey up to Seattle to find out about what caused this, and to get a profile on this kid. And at the end he comes back and his wife is in bed and he crawls in. He's weary and she says, "Well?" and he says, "Well, he was disturbed. So I'm off the hook." He says, "I'm off the hook, but I'm not going to write violence any more. I'm not going to stop other people from doing it, you know the First Amendment, etc., but I'm not going to write it any more." And that is our statement. It's a show that should come out again now because it really is pertinent to what's going on.

When asked if young writers trying to get a start have more trouble writing cerebral stuff or avoiding violence, Link said,

VULGARIANS AT THE GATE

Before we wrote *The Storyteller* we interviewed dozens of writers, friends, people we
didn't know. And the majority of them said,
"Look, we're protected by the First Amendment. We write violence. It's a mirror of a
violent society. We live in a very violent
society. They cannot tell us as creative
people—the government or anyone else—
not to write what we see and to interpret
what we see. And if it's violent, so be it."
That seemed to be the majority opinion of
writers we interviewed. Right now money
rules. I've been forty years in this business.
I've never seen such a bottom-line industry
as it is now. Sponsors, the networks, the big
film studios, even the independents, everything is the buck. You have very talented
writers who will write violent junk; you
have *Lethal Weapon 1, 2, 3, 4*. There is a
handful of the top *action* writers—that's a
euphemism, that comes out of television—
for violence. They call it action but it's violence. . . . Some get a million dollars a
script, or more. There are some writers who
come in to patch up, to gun up the screen-
play. And some get $100,000 a week. Now
you've got to be very strong to turn down
that kind of money. And if you're going to

do a violent picture and you know it going in, then you're going to follow the dictates of the producer. And it sells because you have a kid audience now. This is the target audience, male kids under eighteen. These are kids who will see a *Lethal Weapon* three, four, five, six times. This is money again. Where does the money come from? Well, the parents. It goes back to the parents.

I go to Tower Records and I see kids in there with the baskets, and they've got all this rock stuff and rap. Now these are, with tax, nineteen dollars apiece, these CDs. Well, they've got three hundred dollars worth. Where is this money coming from? They are not earning this money. Again it's the parents. Get rid of the kid, give him the bucks.

Mr. Link is obviously right. Parents do have to accept responsibility for the access and resources they provide their children to consume this media violence. But at least he is one member of our entertainment industry who is conscious of his own responsibility as well.

A friend of mine, Rabbi Jacob Pressman, knowing of my interest in the problem of media violence and its relationship to violence in society, sent me a copy of an article he had written for the *Beverly Hills Courier* on May 21, 1999. There is considerable wisdom in what he had to say.

ALL MY SONS

As this century winds down, the shocking newspaper headlines remind me of what I and all of us have been methodically taught day after day by books, magazines, newspapers, motion pictures, television, and the computer Internet. From the days of the silent westerns with their title frames bragging, "And another Indian bit the dust," to today, when I can learn on the Internet how to build a nail-packed [anti] personnel bomb or even a primitive atom bomb, my education has been life-long. I learned how to poison an arrow, load and fire a cap pistol, a B.B. gun, a rifle, a 22, 38, 44 [*sic*] caliber handgun, automatic assault weapon, bazooka, or cannon. I learned how to use a bowie knife, slash a throat with a razor, garrote someone with a wire, strangle someone with a nylon stocking, smother someone with a pillow, crush a skull with an ax or a baseball bat, spray someone with acid, pepper, or mace. I have been taught how to pick a lock, use a plastic card to open a closed door, invade a chamber through the air conditioning ducts, kill someone in a bathtub by tossing in a live electric appliance, fool an alarm system, cut telephone or electric wires, substitute the fake for the genuine, print counterfeit bills, and create false IDs. I have learned the best places for mass murder: stores, fast-food restaurants, underground garages, schools, and churches. With all that I have learned I know that there are many more life-trashing techniques for which others were better students than I.

My parents didn't teach me these things, nor did my school teachers, nor my rabbis, nor television preachers, nor my friends at any age. Where did I and five generations learn these refinements of the murder weapons which were already around before this century began? It had to be the *books, magazines, newspapers, motion pictures, television, and the Internet.* But these are inanimate objects, incapable of moral judgment. So it has to be the bright, creative minds who dream up the mayhem to make a buck. Many are rethinking the necessity to drench us in blood to make that buck. Everything from laws to sermons is being suggested.

I, for one, have been haunted by the impact of a movie, *All My Sons*, I saw years ago about a man who got rich selling scrap iron to another nation which used it to make armaments which eventually were turned against us and cost him the life of his one, precious soldier son. I am in dread fear that by the law of averages, one day, one of those bright, artistic creative persons who saturate our lives with their violent entertainment will find him or herself standing at the graveside of a child murdered by one of those methods he has effectively taught. He will gaze in agony at the casket in which lie his dreams, his hope for immortality, and will ask, "Is it possible that in a roundabout way I am responsible for the death of my own child?" and from myriads of voices from beyond the grave will come the whisper, "Yes, you are."

8
CENSORSHIP

There is a moderate measure of things;
There are definite limits
Which sensible conduct should neither
Exceed nor fall short of.

—Horace,
as translated by Smith Palmer Bovie,
Professor of Classics, Rutgers University

[O]nly a deeply confused society is more concerned
about protecting lungs than minds, trout than black
women. We legislate against smoking in restau-
rants; singing "Me So Horny" is a constitutional
right. Secondary smoke is carcinogenic; celebration
of torn vaginas is "mere words."
—George Will, *Newsweek*, July 30, 1990

VULGARIANS AT THE GATE

Conventional wisdom—if the reader will pardon my opening with a cliché—has it that censorship is a dangerous evil, always and in every way to be opposed. The opinion is perfectly understandable, as every casual student of history knows. Censors have often abused their power, and in the days when religion and the state were united rather than separated, as the wisdom of our Founding Fathers has stipulated, censorship and tyranny often went hand-in-hand. In more modern times censorship is not as savage as it was centuries ago, but it has often been exercised in the pettiest and, if I may say, the dumbest ways.

Sidney Sheldon, the best-selling novelist and one of the true gentlemen of the entertainment industry, has created a number of successful television programs and written and produced several important films. He told me recently of an instance involving one of his pictures of the 1950s in which Cary Grant was addressing his leading lady about two decidedly minor characters in a scene. Looking at them Cary muttered, "It looks as if they want to be alone," at which he ushered his companion out of the room. When later he was told that the line would have to be deleted from the script he naturally asked the rational question, "Why?"

"Well," said the censor, "there are sexual overtones to the line about the two who want to be alone."

In the strict context of biological science the critic was absolutely correct. The problem was that the two characters being spoken about were goldfish in a bowl on a nearby table.

Believe it or not the line was actually deleted.

There are similar ridiculous stories about television censorship in the days when sponsors had the power to pass judgment on the content of the shows they were underwriting. Bob Finkel, at the time the producer of the *Dinah Shore Show*—a program of the wholesome, family entertainment sort that so many are presently yearning for—wanted to book Tennessee Ernie Ford, a country singer enormously popular at the time, as a guest. The word came down from on high that he would not be permitted to do so for the reason that Ms. Shore's program was sponsored by Chevrolet and the company—or at least someone presumably acting in the company's interest—did not want anyone on the show to say the word "Ford," the brand name of Chevrolet's chief rival.

Dinah insisted on the booking but with a combination of humor and Solomon-like wisdom resolved the problem by introducing her guest as "Tennessee Ernie Chevrolet." As Finkel chucklingly observed,

Ford ended up getting more publicity out of the situation than they ever would have otherwise.

My wife, actress Jayne Meadows, was for seven years a panelist on the popular CBS game-show *I've Got a Secret*, in the days when such programs were glamorous prime-time hits. Because the show was sponsored by Winston cigarettes the sponsors and their advertising agencies became a bit hysterical if either a panelist or a guest, in all accidental innocence, happened to use the word *lucky* in a phrase such as "Boy, that was a lucky guess." The allusion to a competing cigarette brand (Lucky Strike) was thought to be a suggestion to the public to buy the other brand. Who says we're not affected by what we see or hear on television? Certainly not advertisers who spend billions of dollars each year on television and radio in an effort to influence consumer behavior.

There is still more serious censorship of the dangerous sort, needless to say. In August 1999 the Kansas State Board of—you should pardon the expression—Education voted to make it impossible for Kansas students to be told of views which have been accepted for years by scientists the world over. Kansas's science or history text books may not make reference to the age of our planet or to the theory that animal life as we presently know it has evolved from older, simpler forms, a classic instance of dumbth that affected the teaching of astronomy, biology, and geology.

But despite mountains of such evidence very few who are understandably biased against censorship have arrived at their opinion by any careful exercise of critical thinking. I suggest, therefore, that the time has come for us to reason together in the hope that we can arrive at a broader consensus as to whether it is indeed the case that there is literally never the slightest justification for the imposition of censorship.

The great French social philosopher Voltaire is invariably invoked in such discussions since, as a lover of and courageous spokesman for political freedom, he is credited with having observed that, though he might personally and strongly disapprove of a given public statement, he would nevertheless defend to the death the proposition that the offender had a right to speak his mind. Parenthetically, although tens of millions of Americans are up in arms about the sexually offensive nature of much modern TV comedy and drama, and are, to their credit, demanding that something be done about it, many who defend the creative right to transmit actual pornography to our children are going only half-way in quoting Voltaire. They argue in favor of the creative right to market trash, but they often do not join the famous French philosopher in deploring the material under consideration.

Voltaire's line has a blood-warming second-act curtain ring to it. But does it, in fact, adequately resolve all specific questions of controversial speech? The answer to such a simple question is equally simple: No, it does not. What it was intended to assert—as do our constitutional freedoms—is the right to public political, philosophical, or scientific speculation and a denial of the right of any government or church to outlaw rival or unpopular expression.

It is obvious, however, that individuals, societies, cultures, and states make a simple and necessary distinction between purely political or philosophical rhetoric on one hand and expression that calls into question basic moral and ethical standards. (No doubt in their hearts extremists of the far right and far left would dearly love to silence each other, but they share the perception that in the United States they could never get away with it.)

Concerning the category of moral questions, the situation is by no means so clear. To the extent that we interpret the word *freedom* as a political term we will naturally be opposed to the great majority of limitations on it, and may even personally chafe under such restrictions as have been codified into law.

At this point I repeat an insight that I confess occurred to me rather late in life, namely, that every law ever enacted, however wise, or necessary, was—and is—an infringement on freedom. When, for example, we commonly agree that no one has the right—the freedom—to drive 75 miles per hour in a school zone there is not the slightest question but that we are indeed limiting the freedom of certain drivers. And in so agreeing we are saying, in effect, to hell with that particular freedom—it is more important that we protect the lives of innocent children.

I will next submit some specific instances in which censorship, in certain forms, is not only permitted but enthusiastically supported. Consider this: Every state in the United States requires that its residents who own automobiles purchase license plates for them. Each state also permits the purchase of personalized plates for a fee. Given that among the human inhabitants of our nation there is a percentage of those who apparently derive some sort of perverse pleasure from the inappropriate use of vulgar terms such as the proverbial four-letter words, the licensing authority, *with full popular support*, deliberately censors submitted license plate content that it deems to be offensive to good taste and decency. Again, there is no question but that what is involved is simple, dictionary-definition censorship. Are there those among us who will now step forward to try to end such censorship?

Maybe some would, but most would not.

Another area in which there is increasingly emotional demand for regulation—including censorship—is the national computer networks. Even the most casual familiarity with the less admirable aspects of human nature could have led us to predict that both professional pornographers and sexual weirdos—including child-molesters—would have moved into Internet territory at the first opportunity. Although I try to keep at least fairly well informed about most things, I learned only recently, from reading the transcript of a speech by Sen. John McCain, that according to *Wired* magazine *there are approximately 28,000 adult Web sites promoting hard- and soft-core pornography.* I have since been told that number has risen to over 100,000!

As McCain explains, "Together these sites register many millions of 'hits' by Web surfers each day. The sad fact is, included among these hits are children, who are either deliberately searching for this material or who accidentally stumble upon it." The senator is absolutely right in observing that the same Internet that can benefit our children is also capable of inflicting terrible damage on them.

In late September 1999, the Federal Trade Commission issued a special warning to parents about web sites that closely duplicate legitimate ones but lead children and others into an electronic maze of pornography. The agency called the custom "page-jacking" and described it as the most pernicious example it has discovered in the many cases of Internet deception investigated.

In another instance of actual censorship, in mid-December 1999 President Clinton signed into law a federal ban against the sale of one of the more revolting examples of creative license in an already sick culture. Both the President and Congress are attempting to forbid the sale of "crush" videos, in which mice and other small animals are actually stomped to death by women wearing high-heeled shoes.

•   •   •

Although television networks and studios are sometimes perceived as victims of actual or potential censorship, the fact is that all of them impose it themselves. Since the beginning of television the networks have asserted their right to blue-pencil certain portions of scripts submitted to them by writers who—it should be noted—as American citizens, were under the protection of our constitutional guarantees of freedom of speech. But occasionally a studio or network official would say, in effect, "You have the freedom to write what you want, but we have the freedom to decide whether or not we will release your work, unedited, into the marketplace under our auspices."

To deal with an actual case, when Madonna appeared on David Letterman's television program in 1994 she spoke in shockingly vulgar terms. Now it happened that many of her four-letter words were bleeped out of the program's audio track, although of course the viewer did not have to be an expert at lip-reading to tell what they were. In any event, the censorship was not only agreed to but insisted upon by the CBS Television Network, David Letterman's producers, and Mr. Letterman himself.

It is fascinating that at the same time that more and more demands are being made to oppose the current overemphasis on truly vile speech in popular entertainment a separate though somewhat parallel social trend is evident, an example being recent laws, company rules, and regulations intended to punish examples of political incorrectness in factories, offices, shops, and colleges. If, for example, I shared a workplace with a female reader of this volume, I assume that she would not at all agree that, perhaps from a desk position next to hers, I had the total freedom to address her in blatantly sexual terms, to make what used to be called indecent proposals, and all-in-all to speak to her in a manner that I would be personally uncomfortable in using even if she were a prostitute.

In the last few years there have been repeated and understandably strident attempts to rule out such boorish conduct—the term is sexual harassment—in public and private facilities. I support the development but in so doing I am clearly advocating censorship.

My friend, actor Dean Jones, having read an early draft of this essay, wrote "You have observed a truly unanswered question. Why do we exclude the 'F' word from a license plate but okay it a hundred times in a movie? Why can I not make inappropriate remarks to a woman, yet I can produce a TV show that speaks ten times worse to our children?" Why, indeed?

Certainly no society has ever become so thoroughly depraved, while claiming to respect freedom, that it preaches that there must be no limitations on freedom whatever. It is, after all, literally a crime to "incite to riot," or as Justice Oliver Wendell Holmes put it, "No one has a right to falsely shout *fire* in a crowded theater." We forbid such incitement and we punish those who commit such offenses. We are perfectly right in doing so, but—again—what is involved is certainly censorship.

We have laws against murder and we punish severely those who ignore such laws. Part of that highly virtuous process involves censoring those who seek—by speech—to solicit murder or encourage its commission.

It is also illegal to dispense false information about stocks, products, services, even health-care products. To protect the public the FTC and the FDA sharply limit what companies can say or print about their products; again, an instance of censorship firmly supported by the American people and their government.

It is a mistake therefore to assume that there must be no limits whatever to forms of speech. No one has the right to threaten others in the way that a former student of the Irvine campus of the University of California did in September 1996 when he sent an e-mail message to a group of Asian students. According to CNN, student Richard Machado, though he hid his identity, did not disguise his intentions. "I personally will make it my life career to find and kill every one of you, personally." Machado was eventually identified, tried, convicted, and sentenced to a prison term.

A similar threat was aimed at the Planned Parenthood organization and a number of doctors who provide abortions. The offending web site included "Wanted" posters featuring specific physicians including, in some cases, home addresses, phone numbers, automobile license numbers, and other personal details. Given that as of May 2000 seven abortion doctors had in fact been murdered in the United States since 1993, a jury rendered a $107 million judgment against the defendants, who had created and administered the site. U.S. Judge Robert E. Jones, who presided over the case, reaffirmed the verdict, issued an injunction against any further online threats and stated that the "Wanted" posters [and Web sites] were "blatant and illegal communications of true threats" against doctors. *USA Today* reported that he went on to say "I totally reject the defendants' attempts to justify their actions as an expression of opinion or as a legitimate and lawful exercise of free speech."

While there cannot be the slightest reasonable doubt that justice was served in the few instances I have cited, the point here is that in every such case it is clear that speech was being censored.

A relevant item in the "going too far file" led to a formal apology released to the press by the CBS network after its *Late Late Show with Craig Kilborn* superimposed the phrase, "Snipers Wanted" under video-taped footage of George W. Bush's acceptance speech at the Republican National Convention. Along with its apology for broadcasting an "inappropriate and regrettable" graphic, the network reported that it was conducting an internal review of the matter.

We may be reasonably certain, given the attendant circumstances, that some network official is going to say to one or more of the program's producers "Isn't there anybody on your staff with the minimum brains required to have cut this joke out of the script after one of your writers submitted it?" Obviously the joke never should have been aired given the climate of general political animosity and the prevalence of more than enough trigger-happy people in our society. But if, in a momentary fit of social wisdom, the joke had been cut out, what would have happened is another instance of *censorship*.

It follows that organizations opposed to literally *all* censorship must argue, by virtue of their basic position, that such material should be telecast.

This essay is hardly designed to resolve the issue one way or the other. At this early stage of what I hope will become a public dialogue I am chiefly concerned to encourage the clearest possible sort of thinking on such an admittedly complex question.

CENSORSHIP/HUMANISM

A perfectly fair question has been put to me recently as to whether there might be a conflict between my views as a humanist—a school of thought which absolutely depends on the ideal of free inquiry—and my feeling that current cultural outrages are so extreme that they may call for certain formal restrictions on public expression. The question, as I say, is legitimate; fortunately it is also easily answered. The International Academy of Humanism was founded in 1983, in part because that year was the 500th anniversary of the Spanish Inquisition and also the 350th anniversary of the trial of Galileo. The date was chosen, I assume, because it provided an excellent opportunity to refer to the sort of dangers that are always more likely to occur when free inquiry is not formally respected.

That most noble of documents, the Constitution of the United States, is itself, of course, an attempt to protect the freedom of study and thought in the absence of which societies are not free or democratic at all. What many do not realize is that the U.S. Constitution—like the Ten Commandments, the laws of the state of Kentucky, or any of the world's formal codes of conduct—does not—in fact, can never—communicate an obvious and inescapable meaning in all particulars. Such documents always require the organized existence of a body of interpreters and/or judges.

And even after such authorities issue their formal pronouncements these are practically never regarded, by the world jury, as settling the issue in some final and eternal sense. Many Supreme Court decisions, after all, are not unanimous but come about by the process of democratic vote among the concerned justices. But to return to a more central point, we should all attend, I argue, to the obvious-enough distinction between free philosophical or political inquiry on the one hand and the attempt to market the kind of literally sickening merchandise publicly dispensed by the likes of a Howard Stern or an Eminem. Legal authorities at whatever level—national, state, county, or local—often feel perfectly free to decide what is or is not acceptable as regards offensive sexual behavior and speech.

Consider, in this context, the depressing fact that there is an actual organization, formally constructed, with officers and concerned members, the purpose of which is to assert and defend the alleged rights of certain males—commonly referred to by the pejorative term *perverts* by everyone else—to have sexual access to children. Behavior that makes the blood of the average person run cold is actually defended and quoted as a "right" by people suffering from such a sexual compulsion. Now for a moment think of what is a suitable public response to such criminal license in the context of, say, the U.S. Constitution and its guarantees of freedom of speech. There is some complexity to related legal factors. But the consensus appears to be that the sexual miscreants involved do have the freedom to produce literature in support of their disgusting inclinations but absolutely do not have the freedom to act on the basis of their inclinations. In other words, if a child they molest (or even attempt to molest) happens to be the reader's son or daughter, he would have a natural and quite sensible desire to summon the police and have the molester arrested.

I submit that something like the same quite common-sense solution presents itself as regards those who market pornographic materials to children, whether the marketplace is that of commercial television or computer web site in cyberspace.

AN ANCIENT LEGAL PRINCIPLE

One of the most ancient of legal principles is this simple statement: Circumstances alter cases. This applies not only very narrowly to individual human dramas, which is obvious enough, but also to large societal contexts. Even if we perceive legal systems in ideal terms it is clear that nothing more complex than the inescapable evolution of human societies makes the evolution of law not only inevitable but necessarily so. The laws of the United States in, say, 1947, are not identical to the laws of Egypt in 1000 B.C. or, for that matter, those of the United States as of the year 2000.

What we are talking about here of course is the essential tension between two separate and noble political ideals—democracy and freedom. Should the masses of people have any say at all concerning the laws that govern them? Of course, but the problem is that most of us receive close to no education at all about the law and therefore must depend on specialists. This is either inevitable, or rationally necessary, as the case may be, because of the ever-present danger that the majority can easily be swayed in their judgments by angry passions. There have been numerous experiments made that involve putting certain questions to laypeople on some controversial subject matter and in case after case most of those taking the tests are surprised—and, one hopes, disconcerted—to learn that they have just voted against the guarantees of freedom found in their own national Constitution.

The Founding Fathers were, of course, familiar with all of this, and so are many in our own time. In any event humankind can never reach the point where all such questions have been settled once and for all. They will never be settled but must endlessly be considered, studied, attacked, defended, debated, and reconsidered.

It almost seems as if there is something unnatural about freedom. There is certainly precious little evidence of it in history. In the days of kings and emperors who were thought to wield absolute power we were stupid enough to believe in what was called the divine right of their authority. But we would be guilty of equal stupidity to assume that because the law has often been abused we should therefore dispense with it in its entirety. The grand tragic fact is that we are a troublesome species who—except for certain noble and high-minded individuals—cannot always be trusted.

It is hardly my purpose here to lay out what might be called a unified theory of law; I am merely putting on the table a few factors that are worthy of consideration in the context of the present debate.

One such—which I have not encountered heretofore in the public record—is that both the Founding Fathers and later wise jurists lived in times when there were no such things as television, radio, or the Internet. This leads immediately to the question: Is it reasonable to assume that laws established to preserve freedom of speech in the press also apply perfectly to the newer and long undreamed-of methods of communication?

I have never argued that there should be censorship of the written word, despite the fact that some ugly and horrifying things do get printed and published as a result of such freedom. But there is an important distinction between freedom of the press and freedom as it applies to the electronic media. No book or pamphlet has ever forced its way into our homes. On the other hand, if by turning on a radio or television set in the hope of hearing the morning news, a weather report, information of civic importance, or even casual entertainment, we and our children may be exposed to material for which there can be no moral and rational justification, then we should rethink the matter.

Again, making such observations by no means settles the issue; I am concerned here only to point out that a law that may reasonably apply to the printed word may not automatically be invoked to permit the broadcasting of pornography to children.

9
CONCLUSION

Pure tolerance thus has its limits, it cannot succeed unless it is accompanied at the same time by a commitment to raising the level of appreciation. Although we do not wish to legislate morality, this does not mean that we should not criticize the vulgar excesses of modern consumer-oriented culture. This should not be left to the conservative railing from the pulpits. We have an obvious obligation to encourage the finest cultural expressions, intellectual, aesthetic, and moral appreciation.
—Paul Kurtz, former president,
American Humanist Association

We have outlined and documented the problem. Now—what do we do? Where do we start?

Recently, while at the airport of a large Midwestern city, I picked up a copy of the local newspaper, the front page of which contained no international news and only one item of national significance. What was apparently important to the people of this city were local fires, local crimes, the election of a local beauty queen, and news of sports events. I didn't bother to check but I am reasonably sure that the same newspaper employs a television critic who from time to time laments that TV is not enlightening the masses.

He is correct of course. But perhaps we cannot expect to be greatly enlightened either by the American press or by American television. Perhaps the real task of education is something that each person must accomplish separately and then by some means hope to pass along to his children. As I have said before, it is a task for our entire culture and our society. Improve the popular taste and television, films, radio, and recorded music will follow.

And yet one hates to leave it at that. When will the popular taste become more refined? The answer may be never, unless television itself is equal to the task. We cannot be content with the observation that we must not confuse art with entertainment, that the public wants only froth and distraction. The statement is true enough as a descriptive commentary, but surely we cannot therefore relax and give up. Popular taste is for the most part deplorable, and probably always has been, but the commercial structure of television, radio, recorded music, and film may drive it to a lower level than civilized society has ever known. That we must resist.

Make no mistake, the fact that television is an advertising medium has led to some of the present difficulties. But is the solution to throw the sponsors out? Certainly not. To begin with, it's not possible. We should continue to work with the advertisers, but they must assume their responsibilities. They are as knowledgable and experienced regarding the use of media to influence human behavior as anyone involved in the debate.

Will advertisers have the discipline to sacrifice a certain part of their potential audience if this is the inevitable result of sponsoring programs of the better sort? It remains to be seen. Sadly some factors militate against the possibility. In most large companies, for example, there is really no one Mr. Big, although some leading executives may flatter themselves that this is not so. The people who look like the unqualified masters of all they survey are almost always at the mercy of boards of directors and major stockholders, those who hired them in the first place and can fire them or vote them out if their handling of company affairs leaves anything to be desired. So "the sponsor," in one sense doesn't even exist. There is no one person, ordinarily, who is the sponsor. There are usually several executives who have conferred on the decision to back a particular program and they rarely see eye-to-eye on all details of its production. Invariably there are those on the sponsor team who, from the first, snipe at the project and let it be known that the decision to endorse it was made without their consent or, in any event, against their better judgment.

In circumstances such as this the sponsor is a rare captain who can say, without fear of contradiction, "Yes, by God, I'll settle for program A, which is a fine show, even though it's audience is not as large as program B, which is not a very good program at all, but a popular one."

Let us hope there are a few such executives around. For actually, the future of the industry poses something of a challenge to the free-enterprise system. The question is whether the bare profit motive can continue without compromising cultural values that are important to the health of a well-rounded society. TV is not merely a matter of electronics or show-business. It is also a reflection of democracy in action, for better or for worse. Therefore, we must resist the daily temptation to take the narrow or selfish view. And we must not forget that stations and networks get their licenses because *they agree to provide programming in the public interest.*

Again, it is not merely television, it is our national ethic and structure that is on trial. All the 1950s talk about poor Charles Van Doren and rigged quiz-shows, about payola and dishonest commercials, about misleading statistics and the resort to the appeal of violence and trashy music—all of this has been brought about because of the temptation placed in the path of weak individuals by our economic system. Once a business person has sold a product to everyone who needs it he feels driven to sell it to those who do not need it, which involves the artificial stimulation of sales by psychological methods. The completely honest person is at a tremendous disadvantage in such an undertaking. When Jesus Christ said that it was more difficult for a rich person to get into heaven than it is for a camel to get through the eye of a needle he cannot have meant that wealth in itself was evil, as the army of wealthy Christians will no doubt attest. It seems to me that he meant simply that it is almost impossible to get rich by entirely ethical means. It can happen, of course. In show-business, for example, a garage mechanic with a beautiful voice may suddenly find himself earning thousands of dollars a week. An honest person may also hit oil, buy a winning lottery ticket, or enjoy some other sort of windfall. But businesspeople or broadcasters who simply climb up the ladder slowly, by traditional methods, making and selling, may occasionally find integrity an intolerable burden. The West must prove that economic competition in the free market need not of necessity cause us to debase our standards. We must join this fight on the side of our free-enterprise system. Its advantages are plain to see; but we must strengthen ourselves to resist its temptations.

And so we go around the circle again. Television offers the key to true universal education in great ideas and the many important debates of our day. Our best scholars and professors are currently speaking to classes of fifty or a hundred students. If they spoke to audiences of twenty million, we might enter upon a golden age the like of which can scarcely be conceived.

It is this exciting vision that forces us to hammer away at the problem. Television, considered in this sort of framework, may be a powerful force like nuclear power or a worldwide religion, beneficial or harmful not in and of itself, but in how it is employed.

THE PRINT MEDIA

As to the eventual outcome of the present cultural debate, a great deal hinges on the opinions expressed by the print media. Anyone hoping that the dominant journalistic voices would take an antiraunch position was disappointed by the 1999 critical accolades showered on *South Park: Bigger, Longer, and Uncut*, the feature-length movie version of the animated television series so popular with teenagers. The critic for *Time* magazine said the picture was "inspired comic rudeness." The publication also described the film as sick but the dominant message was that it was "ruthlessly funny."

Newsweek was equally complimentary, correctly referring to the film as "a raunchy assault on authority . . . tasteless, irreverent . . ." but nevertheless emphasized that the film has a "gag-to-laugh ratio even higher than the new Austin Powers." The magazine also reported that the film gets in a few digs at its critics, describing their arguments as "pious finger-pointing." The *Los Angeles Times* critic called the film "so gleefully vulgar, so eagerly offensive, it's tough not to get down on all fours and beg for more." The *Washington Post* also raved, though it also said the picture was "outrageously profane."

VULGARIANS AT THE GATE

That the *South Park* picture is funny is neither surprising nor to be interpreted as an eighth wonder of the world; the Hollywood community is full of writers who are able to produce funny material, but the newsworthy element in the story is that leading critics and editors seem no longer troubled much by rudeness, emotional sickness, tastelessness, irreverence, political incorrectness, and outrageous profanity, even when it involves a cast of third grade elementary school children as its lead characters. In other words, if a picture is funny such old-fashioned considerations as what effect it might have on the minds and hearts of America's children may simply be disregarded.

But if all this is so, could it be argued that the writing of a book such as this is itself largely a waste of time? Yes, sad to say, it could. Ten years down the line our popular culture may be even more degraded than it is at present. In that case ultimately my efforts here may be of interest chiefly to social historians.

An unexpected plot-twist in the ongoing saga of *South Park* was announced in one of the show business trade papers on July 19, 2000. According to Scott Hettrick of the *Hollywood Reporter*, "*South Park: Bigger, Longer and Uncut* may be too rough even for the cable network that spawned it. Comedy Central executives have expressed reluctance to try to obtain TV rights to the R-rated animated film being distributed by half-sister Paramount (Paramount parent Viacom owns half of Comedy Central)."

Hettrick continues:

> The abundance of rough language and offensive situations not only present dicey issues about how to show the film on TV and how to deal with advertisers, but executives say the movie is perhaps too drastic a departure from the outrageous and vulgarity-filled TV series and needs to be treated as a separate animal. Comedy Central has first dibs among basic cable networks for the broadcast window if the broadcast networks pass on it. (Fox is believed to be the only broadcast network that would even consider it for a run after its premium channel window on Showtime.)
>
> But Comedy Central president Larry Divney says about the only way he could make it work is to run it at midnight with one or two sponsors and limited commercial interruptions. Viacom-owned MTV is also a potential candidate, according to insiders, but so far none of the cable net-

works has even initiated talks for the cine-
matic hot potato.

The *Wall Street Journal*, commenting on the film,
could find no way to avoid reference to the details of
its offensiveness. Describing the picture as "a paean
to the f-word," the paper said, "The film clobbers the
viewer with it at the beginning and doesn't let up for
a second, continuing through skits featuring Saddam
Hussein's penis, a giant clitoris, and the de rigueur
insults to Jesus and Jewish mothers."

Referring, approvingly, to *The Simpsons* the journal
says that *South Park* is "crudely drawn and makes no
pretense to being well-written." The journal's editors
shared my fascination with the total surrender of
quality standards on the part of so many otherwise
intelligent critics, to the film's purposeful vulgarity, as
if that particular factor was of little or no importance.

We have come to a hell of a pass when our society
derides those who speak out for virtue and decency
but richly rewards those who practice vice. The issue,
of course, is not a totally one-sided matter. The massive edifice of the law is itself an attempt to punish
evil-doing, if not to reward virtuous behavior, but
what is by no means clear is that the general population always considers itself allied to law-and-order.

While it is true enough that we want ourselves and

our kind protected we are all too easily swayed, in our loyalty to righteous conduct, by other considerations. The criminal offender need only be a member of our own race, nationality, religion, or other social circle to be accorded treatment not so readily granted to those not so connected. Even the most monstrous terrorist, with his guns, bombs, and bullying threats, may be supported if we happen to share the philosophical biases that motivate his atrocities.

Representatives of our nation's many subcultures—the Sicilians, the Irish, the Jews, the Muslims, the blacks, the Latinos, and others—even if they are full-time professional criminals, far from being spat upon, as they would be in any truly moral society, are often accorded that degree of respect and admiration that if we were not so ethically irrational ought to be reserved for the truly virtuous.

There is a peculiar philosophical standoff at present in the ongoing debate as to what we can do in attempting to find a solution to the problem of the unremitting wave of media vulgarity. Actually the list of alternatives is lengthy, but most of them must be ruled out according to generally accepted standards of responsible social behavior. But inside this very dilemma there is a certain unfairness to which the defenders of moral society are subjected in that, by the very rules dictated by their own professed values, they are prohibited from the sort of extreme counter-tactics to which some on the political right do resort, the bombing of abortion clinics and assassination of abortion providers being one example. Also excluded, one would hope, are all instances of personal intimidation such as death threats, menacing phone calls in the middle of the night, stalking, more aggressive forms of picketing, and retaliatory invasions of privacy of the sort that have given some cult religious organizations such a bad name.

But those who are critical not of the offenders but of attempts to contradict the Madonnas and Howard Sterns of our society in the context of the public dialogue tend to use different language, different terms. People for the American Way, for example, a group with which I am in general sympathy, is properly concerned to defend constitutional liberties, but Arthur Kropp, president of the organization until his death in 1995, was quoted by the *Hollywood Reporter* in December 1990 as saying, "This controversy isn't about what's on Madonna's videotape, it's about freedom of expression in America." Mr. Kropp is only half right. The question of constitutional freedoms is obviously part of the issue, but to ignore the original provocation that gave rise to the argument is not likely to be productive of much progress.

In attacking specifically a Florida attorney named Jack Thompson, who in 1990 attempted to get Madonna's "Justify My Love" video banned from stores, Kropp said, "Thompson's goal is to intimidate the entire music industry into accepting his standards as national standards."

I've never met Mr. Thompson and, for all I know, he may be a member of the extreme right wing. My point is that even if he is, it is absurd to say that his actual *goal* is to intimidate the music industry and, by inference, popular culture itself. His goal, it is reasonable to assume, is to *do something helpful about a true problem*, the tidal wave of barbaric ugliness, both moral and aesthetic, that now dominates American culture.

What Mr. Thompson's critics seem to be saying is that, given the freedom of speech to which all Americans are indeed entitled by constitutional guarantee, there is literally nothing that can be done to protect our children from the two separate but cooperative groups that now assault them: (a) the often disgustingly depraved performers themselves and (b) the businesspeople who, though they may be morally inoffensive in their private lives, are quite happy to market cultural garbage so long as they can make a buck by doing so. And this is not a point to be lightly passed over since the profits in today's video and recording industry are truly astronomical.

The First Amendment right to free speech does trump many such concerns. But consider this counterargument: You have options: don't buy the music, don't buy a ticket to the film, forbid your children to watch this or that television program. So long as the speech is not inciting to riot or restraining your activities then maybe all we can do is don't look and don't listen. If enough people do that—decrease the demand—the supply *will* dwindle on its own.

Let's return to the qualifying phrase, "so long as the speech is not inciting to riot." The objection is obviously not intended to refer solely to the crime of riot. It would therefore improve the argument if the phrase were revised to "so long as the speech is not inciting to the commission of a crime." Well, some modern speech, it turns out, is leading certain impressionable viewers and film-goers to the commission of rape and murder. I refer the reader—again—to the book, *The War against Parents*, which provides a rich supply of consistent evidence.

PAX NETWORK

It is sometimes assumed that the TV networks and production studios, when criticized, operate on a circle-the-wagons mentality in which the relevant issues are dealt with on an us-against-them basis. While the assumption has a degree of validity, it by no means accurately represents the total picture. Some of the most effective criticism of television, in fact, comes from within the industry. It's hard to even imagine a more accurate description of the present problem than that expressed by Paxson Communications Corporation in ads for its new Pax TV Network. In a *Daily Variety* ad that ran on July 17, 1998, the Pax network stated:

> Once upon a time, there was a huge uproar about whether advertisers should be allowed to sell cereal and toys in children's programs. Nowadays, what the advertisers are selling our kids is the least of our worries. Some so-called creative people seem to be using what was once the family viewing hour to peddle every kind of alternative language and lifestyle to our kids. And anyone who doesn't share their sometimes bizarre and depressing views of family values gets

337

> vilified for being intolerant. . . . *Broadcasters
> are losing touch with the vast majority of Amer-
> icans. By attacking notions of decency and belit-
> tling the idea of virtue, television has alienated
> millions of informed, thinking, responsible par-
> ents.* (Italics added.)

THE FUNCTION OF A PARENT

We must also ask the basic question: What is the proper function of a parent? The first thing that comes to mind is that the individual, to assume the role of parent, must create offspring. There is nothing more complex at this stage than simple biology. Whether or not there is a conscious God who somehow brought about a beginning of all life and its millions of manifestations, everyone agrees that so far as observable reality is concerned each living generation physically creates the next generation of its species who will follow it. But once that primary function has been accomplished, a secondary obligation is incurred: A parent must also nurture and protect its offspring. With regard to very simple forms of life nature has made other arrangements, but as for the higher forms nurturing and protection are invariably required. It would obviously make no sense for women to bear children and then simply walk away from them, leaving them on the ground to die. The reason is that the new little humans are unable to tend to their own needs. Our particular species has obligations above and beyond those of all other living creatures in that we must also be concerned about the psychological well-being of our children. It is a tragic and all-too-evident fact that many of us who are parents do not distinguish ourselves in this regard, but our very failures make the necessity for proper nurturing all the more evident. It is then this basic biological requirement that underlies the seriousness of our concern about those elements in our society that are clearly having destructive influences on the hearts and minds of our children.

In 1987, the NBC Television network asked me to participate in a public service campaign of theirs called "NBC: Tuned in to America," a public forum the network had provided to stimulate commentary on the subject of television itself. Invited participants included consumer advocate and recent presidential candidate Ralph Nader, former astronaut James Irwin, and the president of the National Parent Teacher Association. My message was simple: "Occasionally, turn the damn set off."

VULGARIANS AT THE GATE

Ruth Koscielak, popular host of a radio call-in show on the RK Radio Network in the greater Minneapolis/St. Paul area, after putting some questions to me recently about the sleaziness of too much modern television, said, "I agree with you about that. Just the other night I was sitting with my son—he's thirteen—and we were watching the *Ally McBeal* show [on Fox]. After just a few minutes I realized that the program wasn't suitable for anyone my son's age, so we turned it off."

QUESTIONING VERSUS SIMPLY REJECTING AUTHORITY

Some observers may assume that the dim view I take of guiltless and clearly promiscuous sex, unrestricted drug use, and general disrespect for authority— almost regardless of what that authority teaches— grows out of nothing more than the fact that I am now old. Any such assumption is a mistake. My reservations about such behavior were formed during the 1960s when I was much younger.

A person with even moderate intelligence should have been able to recognize that such nuggets of wisdom as "Don't listen to anybody over thirty" may

340

accurately be described as stupid, as may the advice to "Do your own thing," without regard to whether that thing is wise, virtuous, or constructive on one hand or idiotically destructive on the other.

Authority may obviously always be questioned, in whatever forms it takes. We have perfect freedom to subject literally everything that authority says to common-sense critical analysis. We also have the freedom to subject authorities' dicta to moral criteria, but to simply reject authority a priori, on principle, is an example of what I call dumbth.

As regards one of the chief energizers of 1960s protest—the war in Vietnam—I was myself a critic of it from the first, not on pacifistic grounds, or on the absurd assumption that whatever the United States government does is always wrong, but on the entirely practical awareness that we could not possibly win such a war. I concluded this, some scholars of political rhetoric will be interested to learn, from reading an article published in the conservative journal *National Review*, in which a *French* general explained that to win a war of counterinsurgency the military of the dominant nation must outnumber its opponent by roughly ten to one.

Since the investment of so enormous an army of young Americans in a country most of them had never heard of was obviously not going to happen, I spoke out against our war in Southeast Asia and felt in no way revolutionary or radical for having done so. After all, the conservative and respected Catholic spokesman, Bishop Fulton J. Sheen—among many religious leaders—had done the same.

We must now place far greater emphasis on public campaigns of education about basic questions of right and wrong, which is to say morality and ethics. It is quite understandable that most of us are confused about the issue in that we are guilty of assuming that morality absolutely depends on religion. It does not, as we may observe simply by looking at the world's millions of atheists.

BERTRAND RUSSELL

Those religious believers who are themselves intellectuals—and may their tribe increase—ought to be wise enough to use the British philosopher Bertrand Russell as a whetstone against which to sharpen their own analytical knives, for faith that is never tested or never questioned is little more than that of the primitive savage or five-year-old child. Russell is obviously not the only challenger of orthodoxy whose arguments are worthy of serious attention, but because he is of the modern world and was personally aware of the tragedy of the history of the twentieth century, his arguments have a timely relevance that commands our respect.

I have elsewhere written that the world of religious faith already owes a deep debt to the freethinkers and Socratic questioners of—let us arbitrarily say—the last thousand years, for in helping to construct and articulate a secular conscience, which is to say one that is moral but not religious, they have provided a great service not only to humankind but to the churches themselves. In demonstrating what should have been obvious from the beginning—that morality has no *necessary* connection whatever with religion—though the two may be in certain contexts harmonious—the worldly philosophers have erected a standard against which the actual behavior of our planet's millions of believers may be measured. And it is precisely this service which has been so vitally essential to the advance of nothing less than civilization itself. There are numerous social atrocities which were, over a painfully long period of time, finally swept away not because the religious believers of the world demanded such social progress but because the secular conscience recognized such evils for what they were and forcefully demanded the application of the ideals of social justice, charity, and compassion to the millions who suffered, bled, and died under the ancient regimes.

When the churches literally ruled society, the human drama encompassed (a) slavery; (b) the cruel subjection of women; (c) the most savage forms of legal punishment; (d) the absurd belief that kings ruled by divine right; (e) the daily imposition of physical abuse; (f) cold heartlessness for the sufferings of the poor; as well as (g) assorted pogroms ("ethnic cleansing" wars) between rival religions, capital punishment for literally hundreds of offenses, and countless other daily imposed moral outrages. Again it was the free-thinking, challenging work by people of conscience, who almost invariably had to defy the religious and political status quo of their times, that brought us out of such darkness.

Religious believers of the world, you are free to continue to debate the simple, narrow question that divides you from atheists, but you have no right, in so doing, to treat the Humanists of the world with contempt. You owe them a deep debt of gratitude, for not only have they shed much light on a naturally dark world but they have very probably helped civilize your own specific religion.

NATIONAL PUBLIC RADIO

Whenever there are social conditions that are widely and rightly deplored it is easy enough to think of alternatives. In the present case, however, there's no requirement at all to exercise the imagination; we have only to turn to a shining example of a broadcasting medium that presents civilized discourse, an absolute minimum of garbage music, no vulgarity, no political hysteria or paranoia, and is, in fact, at the opposite extreme from the cesspool of much current commercial radio. I refer to public broadcasting, as exemplified by National Public Radio, home of such valuable programs as *All Things Considered* and *Talk of the Nation*. It has always been good, and well worth the attention of intelligent listeners. Now it stands as a true light in the darkness, a simple demonstration not only of how things could be but rather how they are.

Dennis Henigan, of the Center to Prevent Handgun Violence, made a marvelous comment when, discussing the recent rash of lawsuits against gun manufacturers, he said, "The goal is not to bring them to their knees. It is to bring them to their senses." *Precisely* the same point now applies to entertainment industry executives.

Our country will never do without its radio, television, films, and recordings. But it is certainly to be hoped that the present generation of sleaze-merchants can see that they have no moral right to contaminate the minds of America's children.

RESTRAINTS

It will perhaps enlarge the scope of our thinking if we approach the problem that concerns all of us, in one way or another, by asking if any restraints at all should be placed on television, film, radio, and recordings. Let us start by arbitrarily assuming that there is literally no living human who will answer this question in the negative. But this simple understanding leads directly to the question as to *what* barriers would be sensible. I can see the pure beauty of the ideal of anarchism, at least considered in the abstract, but it is a philosophical system remarkably unsuited for the human race as it has ever behaved or is likely to in the foreseeable future. We can, nevertheless, agree that self-restraint would be the best sort, and indeed most of the more outrageous comedians do from time to time, in certain settings, inhibit themselves. Even comics who work almost totally dirty in night clubs would not dream of doing precisely the same if they are fortunate enough to be booked as a guest on the *Tonight* show. The other side of that coin, however, is that comics who work chiefly in clubs quickly develop a certain insensitivity to standards of taste appropriate for television. This is particularly true of those performers whose biggest laughs come from their most shocking material.

It is a rare entertainer who willingly eliminates the parts of an act that elicit the loudest laughter. Up to a few years ago one could say the same thing about radio, but Howard Stern, all by himself, has not only trampled on standards that had worked out reasonably well for half a century but has done so with remarkable success, at least if the criteria are crassly commercial.

There was one entertainer before Stern who at least attracted the critical attention of network executives and advertisers and that was Arthur Godfrey. Since today's audiences have almost totally forgotten Godfrey, I should explain here that he was not only extremely successful in radio but was literally in his day the biggest thing in the medium and, simultaneously enormously popular on television as well. Although not, strictly speaking, a comedian, he nevertheless had a good sense of humor and a sort of jolly air about him that audiences found richly amusing. Needless to say, he never wallowed in the disgusting depths with which we are all today painfully familiar. Nevertheless, in the early 1950s, he did occasionally step beyond the customary boundaries. His example at least clarified one point, that you can get away with almost anything on television if you have impressive ratings. Network executives may wince—at least they used to—but because they make no pretense of being seriously interested in anything much except ratings, they would rather have a vulgar or politically offensive show with a Nielsen rating of 15 than a tasteful, inoffensive program with a rating of 10. A large audience constitutes an invisible protective shield that keeps network censors at bay. But of course, if your points drop then the censors and vice presidents may swarm all over you. In the early 1950s, Godfrey said almost anything that came to his mind but the CBS programmers were essentially powerless to rein him in because he brought in millions of advertising dollars each year.

Let me step back here to a point made a few moments earlier when I said that network executives are interested primarily—it sometimes seems solely—in ratings. This is true, although in their defense—and for many of them I have personal warm regard—they often wish it were not so. The reader may be surprised to discover that those who hire network programming executives do not do so in the hope that they will come up with hours of dazzling excellence. In fact if they thought any such thing they wouldn't hire many of these people in the first place since there is unfortunately an all too frequent correlation between (a) high quality and (b) low ratings. Also there is the fact that the majority of network executives have never personally created a program in their lives, but this is not a matter of much importance as long as they are in communication with the creative community. But the programmers' actual assignment is the simplest thing in the world—to schedule programs that will get higher ratings than those of the competition and thereby attract larger advertising dollars. Those executives who do not deliver the goods have no more security in the industry than do performers, who are dropped overboard every year in large numbers. Those who dismiss them are themselves cast aside without a moment's hesitation regardless of how many glowing reviews or Emmy awards the programs they commissioned have earned. It is very much like the philosophy that says if a football team isn't winning enough games, fire the coach. Oddly enough this makes a little more sense in football than it does in the arts since coaches usually have a specific track record to point to, whereas this is rarely the case among network or studio executives, where the Peter Principle—that workers tend to rise to the level of their incompetence—is more relevant.

SOCIAL UNREST AND DELINQUENCY

Now a few words about social unrest and delinquency among the young. I hope it will occur to you to wonder why I take up the subject with the young rather than the older generation. The reason is that the most serious long-term threat to law and order, to social stability, comes from the community of youth, not only in this country but around the world. The forces of law are invariably defenders of the status quo but it is precisely the status quo—the way things are—that is unacceptable to hundreds of millions of young people in today's world.

The older community, perhaps largely on an unconscious level, perceives that the ancient arguments that buttressed certain of our common social assumptions are not as self-evident to the new generation as they seemed to the old. Social evolution has always been somewhat alarming to the mature generation but now its pace has increased so rapidly that the older generation scarcely has time to create new ideas because it is so busy defending the old ones. This is not to say that all of the old ideas are bad. Two and two will continue to be four. Honesty will always be an important virtue, and compassionate love for the rest of humankind is, if anything, more necessary now than ever before. If there is a God—which I assume to be the case—it is reasonable to conclude that He will continue to exist. And if a God does not exist, it will certainly be beyond our power to create one. But on top of such eternal verities, if I may so arbitrarily describe them, we have erected an enormous mountain of other concepts, of varying degrees of probability and utility. This larger body of opinion and belief is now being challenged by young people and radical thinkers all over the world.

To be understood at all, even quite imperfectly, the present worldwide wave of unrest among the young must be studied in the context in which it exists, which is to say in which humankind is moving into a period of highly accelerated social evolution and revolution. We are moving into outer space, positioning communications satellites in orbit around the planet, controlling thermonuclear energy, automating industry, and integrating the use of electronic computers and high-speed communication into our daily lives.

In our day we are seeing concentrated certain results of various long-term historic trends. The intellectual awakening that characterized the Renaissance, the Reformation, the Age of Enlightenment, the invention of the printing press, the Industrial Revolution, radio, television, Capitalism, Socialism, and their subsequent modifications—all of these and other social forces have produced, and are producing today, profound changes in the human condition. Out of all this will come a certain amount of good. If humanity can modify its own conduct in our time, there is hope that it can make the blessings of our remarkable discoveries in science, technology, and psychology available for the welfare of the entire human race. But in the meantime it is inevitable that a great deal of unrest, sometimes even chaos, will result. We will make an absurd mistake if we seek the cause of our present turmoil in one source such as persons of color, the Communist apparatus, the Nazi or populist parties, or whatever social group we might disapprove of or fear. We must get it through our heads that we are all responsible, in varying degrees, for the present state of affairs.

CONCLUSION

We must beware of attributing social unrest to any one cause. There is no question but that poverty, for example, is one of the contributing causes of juvenile delinquency. But we also find juvenile delinquency and drug abuse in neighborhoods that are not poor. In Sweden, where practically nobody is poor, there is still a serious problem of delinquency among the young. The phenomenon of unrest among young people seems to have some connection with the industrialization of a culture because it is the highly industrialized nations such as the United States, Canada, Japan, and Germany that have very high rates of delinquency.

Another cause for the rebellious mood of the young, and the destructive ways in which the mood is sometimes expressed, is the condition of world affairs, the primary attribute of which is anarchy. We insist on law and order for individuals, for families, for communities, and for states or provinces within the nation. But *between* nations we have little or no effective law. Nations, therefore, behave selfishly and immorally. All of them. This must have some effect upon the popular mind, particularly the plastic mind of the growing young.

War, as Union general William Tecumseh Sherman said, is hell, but only in the sense that it is hell to live in fear, to sleep in mud and filth, to kill or maim perfect strangers—including perhaps innocent women and children. It is certainly hell to have an arm or leg blown off, to die alone and far from familiar ground before you have had the chance to really live. War is hell also because of the inevitable way in which it brutalizes the nations and peoples that participate in it, at home as well as on the battlefield, regardless of whether the war is just or unjust. In time of war and preparations for war there is a tremendous increase not only in crimes against property and people, but in divorces, broken homes, illegitimate births, prostitution, disease, narcotics addiction, alcoholic excess, political fanaticism, and social irresponsibility generally.

Disrespect for law, I repeat, does not grow in a vacuum. It occurs within a context of practical causes. Simple exhortations to virtue, therefore, are not enough. It is a remarkably virtuous young man or woman who will not be adversely affected by the general moral climate of today's world.

An aspect of the current collapse of standards is that although many of its causes are rooted in the 1960s the young generation of that period was at least interested in political and philosophical ideas. Only a few of the troublemakers of today can say as much. Indeed if we are talking about values perceived in an economic context, today's fifteen- to thirty-year-olds are quite traditional. They are extremely interested in money, possessions, luxuries, toys, and clearly less idealistic than the generation that matured in the 1960s.

Even in the case of young African Americans, who at least have a reasonably clear-cut and definable problem to address, an examination of such of the hip-hop and rap lyrics as might represent a form of social protest suggests they are remarkably devoid of specifics. Killing policemen and raping women, of whatever color, is obviously not an intelligible form of political protest. It is, in fact, a recipe for disaster.

DOVE FOUNDATION STUDY

In 1993, Ken Auletta, a member of the *New Yorker* magazine's editorial board, wrote a significant report summarizing the answers, from the film industry's leading executives, to the simple question as to whether they would want their own children to see some of the pictures they had commissioned. Most of those reading Auletta's feature would have assumed that it dealt simply with that ancient moral question concerning what should be done when one's sincerely held moral principles come into sharp, abrasive contact with one's assignment as an officer of a profit-making enterprise. But it now turns out, thanks to an astonishing new market survey, that it is perfectly possible for studio executives to gratify their stockholders while at the same time not further contaminating the marketplace with schlock-and-shock fare.

Based on data provided by prominent media research firm Kagan Media Appraisals, Inc., a team of university economists and statisticians carefully studied bottom-line statistics of more than two thousand theatrical films released from January 1, 1988, through December 31, 1997, and announced in January 1999 that G-rated movies showed the highest total profit per film, generating a 78 percent higher rate of return on investment than R-rated films. Pictures rated PG-13 and PG also made good economic sense.

Perhaps the most significant finding is that per-film earnings for G-rated films far outweigh those in the R-rated category. The study itself was commissioned by the Dove Foundation, a pro-family media advocacy organization based in Grand Rapids, Michigan, and grew out of the disturbing fact that, while there was a recent increase in the total number of pictures featuring sex and violence, there were apparently a limited number of motion pictures of the family-friendly sort produced. The study reported that while Hollywood produced 17 times more R-rated films during the period than G-rated films, the average G-rated film generated 8 times greater profit per film than its R-rated counterpart.

All these and other such happy facts are fully documented in the study itself. But now, of course, the moral question takes a new form. When it was generally assumed, as it has indeed been for quite some time, that the tastes of American filmgoers, even the most unedifying, must be catered to if studios are to show a profit, there was at least the economic "excuse" for marketing films that even many of their creators would not want their own children to see. But in an otherwise gloomy cultural landscape there is suddenly a brilliant ray of light cast by the Dove Foundation study. Will Hollywood's movers and shakers take advantage of the consequent opportunity to produce more wholesome films?

It may be argued however, that there is justification for producing pictures that, while definitely not suitable for children and the tender-hearted, are nevertheless of high quality. This is indeed the case, as *Schindler's List*, *Saving Private Ryan*, and even the *Godfather* trilogy—to mention only a few examples— clearly demonstrate. But for every such true work of art and social documentation there are now dozens of pictures that have no such aesthetic motivation. In other words, certain moral and ethical questions remain. It will be fascinating to see how the industry responds to them. But in the meantime—applause, applause!—there is this happy news that virtue is, if all too rarely, rewarded.

In May 2000, Dick Rolfe, president of the Dove Foundation, shared additional encouraging news. In announcing the home video release of the first family-edited version of a major motion picture by New Line Home Video, he said "the company has decided to bite the 'creative integrity' bullet in favor of profits, and release an edited version of the Warner Brothers 1994 hit movie, *The Mask*, starring comic Jim Carrey. New Line has toned down the rhetoric and the images in this sanitized version to test the market for family-edited films. . . . The edited version of *The Mask* has been awarded the Dove Seal for Family Audiences over age 12."

BETTER ALTERNATIVE

When discussing any problem it is always advisable to point to a better alternative. Since one obvious choice would be the kind of situation comedies that were popular in the 1950s, I must therefore hasten to explain that that is not what I would like to see. Oh, if all the shows could be as well-written and funny as *I Love Lucy*, the *Dick Van Dyke* show, and *The Honeymooners* that would obviously be marvelous news. But the great bulk of the comedies of earlier decades were lightweight fare that seemed to have been aimed—intentionally or not—at the fourteen-year-old mentality. *Dennis the Menace, Leave It to Beaver, Petticoat Junction, Gilligan's Island*, et al., were exactly what I meant in using the term "bubble-gum for the mind" in describing the dominant sort of fare of the earlier and in some ways more innocent period. It may surprise some of today's producers to know that I would like to see continuations of many of the better situation comedies of the last decade, but simply with less emphasis on bar-room language and anything-goes sex.

Is this asking for pie in the sky? Certainly not. At present it is common that motion pictures rented for exhibition on airplanes are subjected to a slight bit of editing. I don't care if you call it editing or censorship; we all know what we're talking about here. No one ever got off an airplane after seeing a good, exciting film, saying "Well, of course it was a very good picture but to tell the truth it could have used more words like s---, f---, and c---s-----."

Recently at a cocktail party at the Paramount Studios the gifted impressionist/comedian Fred Travelena told me of an experience he had had in doing what is called "looping" for actors Joe Pesci and Robert de Niro, whose voices he is able to reproduce with uncanny accuracy. The technical term is used when audio problems develop during the production of a motion picture and a given line either isn't recorded at all when it is supposed to be, or is perhaps obscured by some other source of sound. The film in question was *Casino*, in which my wife, Jayne, and I played cameo roles, acting as ourselves since we had performed in Las Vegas during the 1970s, the time setting of the film's true story about two organized crime associates, Anthony "Tony the Ant" Spilotro (played by Pesci), and Frank "Lefty" Rosenthal (played by de Niro).

Pesci had used the term *batshit* but the studio wanted the word eliminated for future television air play and also for the airline market. Travelena replaced it with a term he made up himself, *batso*, since the meaning was clearly the same as that of *crazy*, *bananas*, *nutso*, etc. This incident demonstrates how easily shocking language can be deleted from a film's soundtrack without in any way harming or weakening the film.

One added factor that would be required, however, to wean the youthful audience from its present addiction to sewer-pipe sludge is a certain amount of actual collusion among network and cable operators. Without such cooperation a renegade telecaster could simply refuse to reform and probably reap ratings benefits, and the most disgusting programs of recent years would continue to enjoy some popularity. The solution outlined here does not sound to me particularly utopian at all. I take it as a given that all participants in the debate would agree that the writers presently creating the kinds of vile scripts that are the essence of the problem facing us would also agree that any writer so talented—as at least some of them undoubtedly are—would be perfectly capable of writing good, strong, dramatic, or comedy material if they played by more conventional rules.

But is there the possibility that there might be at least a handful of writers simply incapable of reigning themselves in and providing scripts of the quality of, say, *Cheers, Frasier,* or *Cosby*? Yes. My solution? Advise them to take a few months away from the computer, during which they could watch the work of their superior peers who can entertain without indulging in toilet-paper humor or references to sadomasochism.

STRENGTHENING MORAL VALUES

As recently as 1996 in their General Assembly, American Presbyterians registered strong concerns about the media by approving an announcement that called for the General Assembly Council to "continue to develop and implement a plan of action . . . to bring the church's influence to bear so that the media will act to strengthen moral values."

I have the impression that millions of Americans would now be willing to settle for something far less. Many have become so cynical about the possibility of radio, television, films, and recordings doing anything whatever to strengthen moral values that they are willing to accept a *much more modest achievement, one which will greatly diminish assaults on morality.*

George W. Bush will have an unprecedented opportunity to use the bully pulpit of the White House as an effective weapon in the obviously necessary campaign for moral reform. To restate an earlier point, I am not deluded—nor should any of us be—that this means a simplistic "Back to God" campaign, which the leaders of a thousand-and-one quite distinct religions would inevitably interpret in terms of their own group's self-interest. What I refer to is an emphasis on social conduct guided by recognition of the fact that it is right to behave in some ways and wrong in others. One does not have to be a sophisticated theologian to perceive that there is a large body of opinion, on moral questions, which is shared now, as it has always been, by the majority of the human race.

It is obvious that there are honest differences of opinion on specific moral questions. A Catholic Christian, for example, may believe that birth control is a great evil while an equally devout Protestant Christian may hold not only that birth control has nothing whatever sinful about it but that the widespread practice of it is, in fact, absolutely necessary for human survival, as conservative Republican presidential nominee Barry Goldwater thought. But Christians have differed, occasionally violently, since their first appearance on earth, a social process characteristic of all other religions as well. Such differences, in any event, will always be evident and will work their tragic way through human history. We may therefore concentrate on those moral and ethical questions concerning which there is general agreement. We must understand from the outset, however, that promoting virtue and criticizing vice can never be totally a matter of sweetness-and-light. But then neither is life itself. If we are truly serious, however, in our dedication to that moral reform which is so necessary to the preservation of our nation itself we must be prepared to speak that degree of moral truth of which we are capable and therefore not at all surprised that our labors will occasionally force us to speak critically of some powerful forces and individuals in society. Certainly the present negative role of the mighty entertainment-media moguls is an example of precisely this sort of social drama.

While those of us who are not very well informed may think that the evil-doers, in this particular context, are easily identified, that is only partly true for, as I have suggested earlier, some of the worst offenders are themselves proud Republicans and conservatives. For critics who happen to carry these same two identity cards there will therefore be some discomfort in pointing the moral spotlight into certain corners.

Additional difficulties will present themselves as regards those would-be critics who are themselves part of the political process. The ancient saying that the man who pays the piper calls the tune has clear relevance here. Any idealistic young politician—of any party—who envisions himself the kind of imaginary but very appealing figure of the sort played by Jimmy Stewart in the famous Frank Capra film *Mr. Smith Goes to Washington*, will promptly run into serious problems when it comes to fund-raising.

And, if he is elected, he will also find that some who supported him when he was running will withdraw once he is in office simply because some of his most high-minded and virtuous social recommendations will inconvenience them personally in their capacities as corporate executives or even humble lower-level employees. Indeed they may be the first to subject their once-heroic young idealist to such epithets as "enemy of the people." In reality, of course, he will in no sense be an enemy of the people, but he will be an enemy of corporate polluters of our soil, air, water, and minds.

HUMANITAS PRIZE

Readers may be interested to learn of another organization that has long struggled to maintain and encourage respect for social standards, the Human Family Cultural Institute, which annually awards the Humanitas Prize for the specified purposes of encouraging, stimulating, and sustaining the nation's writers in their humanizing task, and to give them the recognition they deserve. As the group states in one of its brochures, "Only the human family itself surpasses the visual media in their capacity to communicate values, form consciences, and motivate human behavior. This means that the writers of American entertainment are people of great influence, for the values projected on the TV or theater screen begin in their minds, hearts, and psyches. Few educators, church leaders, or politicians possess the moral influence of the entertainment storyteller. This entails an awesome responsibility for writers. But it also provides a tremendous opportunity to enrich their fellow citizens."

THE POWER OF A LETTER

Never underestimate the power of a responsibly worded letter of complaint or criticism. Having worked in television and radio for over half a century I can assure you that while small numbers of complaints are unlikely to have much influence, the effect is quite the opposite if a sizable number of letters are received, all making the same general point.

CONCLUSION

Americans are, quite typically, joiners. Their response to perception of a social problem is to bring together like-minded citizens, largely on the quite sensible perception that in union there is strength. A good many organizations are created with quite specific agendas—to find a cure for AIDS, to favor or oppose abortion rights, the protection of minorities, and so on, but large numbers of Americans are already members of organizations such as religious denominations, the Rotarians, the Elks, the American Legion, and fan clubs. They should therefore work to move these various existing social groups to take a formal interest in the problem of gross cultural pollution. A television or studio executive receiving a letter from an individual will—all other things being equal—be somewhat less impressed than if he receives precisely the same letter, from the same individual, but printed on organizational stationery.

Also local civic and governmental boards and agencies may choose to pass resolutions critical of network or studio executives or others marketing violent or obscene programs or records in their communities.

VULGARIANS AT THE GATE

PICKETING AND BOYCOTTS

Picketing and other forms of public demonstration are also a time-honored and effective weapon. Oddly enough, the news branches of the broadcast media will often willingly give time to the sight of even a dozen or so people marching in front of city hall, a television station, music store or any other agency considered to bear responsibility for outrageous entertainment fare. Nothing is ever settled with finality by such means, but they do affect the public consciousness and perception of troublesome social issues.

Some critics of the more depraved forms of popular culture resort to organized boycotts of television networks, radio stations, motion picture studios, record companies, or corporate sponsors of such offensive products. As to whether such efforts are morally justified, they probably are in some cases and not in others. But they are usually considered a last resort and generally arise out of desperation, on the part of critics, that the offending powers will never otherwise become willing to give serious consideration to the observers' arguments. In the case of offensive programs that are underwritten—sponsored—by major corporations there is little doubt that threats of boycotts can be effective.

368

THE RELIGION SOLUTION

The school shootings that shocked the nation in 1999 did not take place in urban intellectual or humanist centers. The killing sprees happened in typically small-town American communities—Pearl, Mississippi; Jonesboro, Arkansas; West Paducah, Kentucky; Springfield, Oregon; Edinboro, Pennsylvania; and Littleton, Colorado. What they all have in common is that they are well-supplied with churches.

We should not, therefore, be misled by suggestions that all we need do to resolve the present impasse is display the Ten Commandments in school, encourage public prayer before football games, or "let God back into our schools," as if the power of the Creator could be in any way limited by the decisions of local government. As mentioned earlier, Germany, in the 1930s, was the most church-affiliated nation in Europe. The German people were almost entirely Catholic and Lutheran. Despite such factors they launched the Holocaust and World War II. In fact there are few pages of history which do not demonstrate that public prayer and ritual never inoculated people against mass-madness and cruelty. What is needed is emphasis on morality and manners.

VULGARIANS AT THE GATE

DISTRIBUTE LITERATURE

Another thing the reader concerned about American moral behavior can do is to distribute relevant literature. Many newspapers and magazines are now supporting the cause of both common sense and general decency. If you encounter such a feature, consider making copies of it and mailing, faxing, or e-mailing it out to friends and associates. It is possible to reach an impressive number of people by such a simple method.

KEEP FILES

Everyone concerned about this issue ought to develop files on it. You can use a standard file drawer with individual folders or, as some prefer, a three-ring notebook. When you come across a research report, news story or editorial you consider important, don't just read it and then—due to the weakness of human memory—shortly forget its details. Preserve the materials so you can refer to them again in the future when you choose.

JACK VALENTI ON TEACHING MORALITY IN SCHOOLS

It's encouraging to learn that Mr. Valenti has made the quite specific recommendation that our schools —both public and private—should now introduce, at the kindergarten or first-grade level, formal instruction in morality and ethics. The wisdom of our Founding Fathers has led us to prevent churches from controlling public education, as they did for centuries, but it by no means follows that we cannot instruct our little ones that some things are right and others are wrong. Since I have been making exactly the same recommendation for some years I am obviously pleased that my friend Jack agrees on the point, but I trust his recommendation will not come as a surprise to other influential members of the entertainment industry, for whom Jack is a paid spokesman and lobbyist. He is also, some will be surprised to learn, a former member of the advisory board of the Parents Television Council. It is fortunate that he is a gentleman, something that cannot be said of some of the sleaze-merchants now so dominant in the entertainment professions.

VULGARIANS AT THE GATE

FEDERAL TRADE COMMISSION

On September 11, 2000, the Federal Trade Commission issued a long-awaited report absolutely establishing—beyond question—that major entertainment companies have deliberately marketed violent and vulgar motion pictures, recordings, and video games to children, actually placing commercials for such products on cartoon shows and in comic books favored by the very young. In some cases film studios have even employed young teenagers to promote offensive productions to other children. It should not be assumed that this well-deserved criticism applies only to a late development. On the contrary, says the FTC, from 1995 to 1999 some 80 percent of R-rated films and 70 percent of electronic games with adult ratings were targeted specifically to children under seventeen.

The agency also criticized the film industry's audience-testing system, pointing out that children as young as ten have previewed films that the studios knew would receive an R-rating. An interesting passage of the report is the rhetorical question directed at parents and other concerned adults who might find it hard to believe that the entertainment industry could actually be so cynical. "Do the industries promote products they themselves know warrant parental caution, in venues where children make up a substantial percentage of the audience? And are these advertisements intended to attract children and teenagers?" For all three segments of the same industry the answers are plainly *yes*, the report concludes. In response, the *Los Angeles Times* quoted Congressman Edward Markey (D-Mass.) as saying, "It's analogous to beer companies putting on ads about how to drink responsibly, but then marketing intensively on college campuses."

Is it at least theoretically possible that the studios and production companies acted in some combination of ignorance and innocence? It is not. The FTC report stated that PG-13 films, which are given that rating to warn parents that some material might be unsuitable for children under thirteen, were consistently advertised to youngsters eleven years old and younger.

It is important to note that while lawyers and publicists are paid to defend even the worst criminals the public ought not to be deluded by arguments that attempt to excuse even the most sordid forms of entertainment.

According to *Daily Variety* of September 27, 2000, Jack Valenti said that the Motion Picture Association of America's plan [to address the FTC hearings] "proves that Hollywood is dedicated to rectifying any past digressions." Let's have full public discussion about the implications of that word *any*.

Incredibly enough, at least as of the fall season of 2000, those speaking for the entertainment industry seemed to be largely missing the point that increasing numbers of millions of concerned American adults have been trying to impress upon them. This is odd, to say the least, since the point is extremely simple. Massive numbers of American parents, teachers, and leaders in the professions and sciences strongly object to the fact that producers of films, television programs, and musical recordings have been marketing a veritable tidal-wave of cultural sleaze that is directly at odds with those common codes of moral conduct without which it is perfectly fair to ask whether any society can accurately call itself civilized.

The amount of apparent insensitivity to attendant realities manifested by industry spokespersons and executives is mind-boggling. Do they honestly think that their only critics, their only opponents, are a few Congressional leaders? If so, then it is sadly likely that in the future the studios, networks, and record companies are going to see a degree of public anger and criticism that will make the scoldings of recent months seem like a tea-party.

All the recent emphasis on the studios' attempts to market their worst garbage to children and young teenagers, while important, doesn't refer at all to the heart of the problem. The inappropriate marketing is bad enough but the essence of the argument concerns what appears to be an endless barrage of dirty movies and TV shows, to use the plainest possible language.

How about this for a helpful idea? We hire several buses to meet at a convenient location in the Beverly Hills/Bel Air area at a specified time. The one hundred leading studio executives agree to deliver their own children between the ages of ten and sixteen to the gathering-point, after which the kids are bused to nearby theaters, where they will be shown the most hideously vulgar and violent portions of recently released films that every knowledgeable person knows were created specifically for this teenage market.

Surely those entertainment executives who don't even perceive the reason for the present public outcry would welcome such an experiment, would they not? After all, if they think their pictures and programs are perfectly acceptable, then on what grounds could they possibly not want their own children to see them?

VULGARIANS AT THE GATE

Naturally no such experiment will take place, but there may be some value in entertaining the possibility as an instructive fantasy. Surely if by any chance a significant number of the executives would *not* want their own young children to be exposed to such rot then the American people would quickly deafen them by roaring, "By what right do you market to our children—by the millions—films and television shows that you wouldn't want your own to see?"

MORE GOOD NEWS

For several years a negative factor in the ongoing debate about America's cultural collapse was that critics for the mainstream print media seemed reluctant to employ ethical or moral standards, perhaps on the totally unsubstantiated assumption that to do so would make them seem square or—God forbid—in agreement with middle-aged critics of modern culture. I'm happy to observe that there has been a change for the better: starting in the year 2000 there have been more and more instances where professional journalists permitted their personal disgust with certain examples of popular entertainment to show. The thought occurs to me after having just seen local reviews of a revoltingly tasteless film called *Whipped*, a Destination Films release. Concerning the picture's three male characters reviewer Kevin Thomas of the *Los Angeles Times* says, "Their talk could scarcely be more crass, reveling in the grosser aspects of sex and bodily functions. . . . The way they hit on women is repellent. . . . *Whipped* leaves you with the feeling of having at last escaped a numbing experience, trapped in the company of people too pathetic to be amusing."

Bob Strauss, film critic for the Los Angeles *Daily News*, says of the same film, "The sleazoid Summer of '00 ends with the nadir of foul-mouthed shock movies. *Whipped's* only apparent ambition is to discover just how degradable the young male mindset can be. Pretty depraved, according to this. It fancies itself a comedy . . . in fact it's not off-base to call *Whipped* the Firestone recall of gross-out comedies."

The entertainment industry's own trade press agreed. Said the *Hollywood Reporter's* Michael Rechtshaffen, "While it may seem as if there's no end to the depths of distaste to which a movie will sink in pursuit of box office glory—witness the recent hits *Scary Movie* and *Road Trip*—not all gross-out comedies will outgross the competition. Take, for example . . . Destination's *Whipped*, a particularly noxious, achingly unfunny sex comedy." The *Reporter* placed the film in the category of "the most depraved of shock comedies," saying that the picture was "definitely one for the potty." The other main trade paper, *Daily Variety*, described *Whipped* as "grotesquely smutty and obnoxiously overbearing, . . . a pitiful excuse for a comedy."

These examples are chosen at random simply because they happened to have fallen on my office desk at the same time. I mention them only because as the quality of Hollywood product deteriorates, such reviews—which actually have been well-deserved for at least a decade—are finally bubbling to the surface. It's high time.

AND STILL MORE

Recently at a dinner party at the home of our friends, the Sidney Sheldons, a group of us saw the film *The Winslow Boy*, based on the play by Terence Ratigan, adapted as a motion picture by writer/director David Mamet, who is ironically a master of the employment of coarse language for dramatic effect in film and theater. Everyone present had a connection with the entertainment industry. The film struck all of us as an achievement of dazzling excellence. The reason I mention the matter here is that *The Winslow Boy* achieves its superb effects without resorting to so much as a second of coarse language, nudity, violence, or indeed any of the cheap tricks upon which so many of today's film-makers have come to depend. This beautiful accomplishment by Mr. Ratigan and Mr. Mamet stands all by itself as an inspiring rebuke to the modern vulgarians. Let us all be grateful for it.

THE POWER OF A STAR

My wife, Jayne, and I recently had the pleasure of spending about a week and a half filming an episode of Dick Van Dyke's popular series, *Diagnosis Murder*. Dick is not only a richly talented gentleman—as has been widely recognized for a good many years—but is delightful social company. Parenthetically Dick is one of those major talents who makes his work look so easy that he sometimes doesn't get all the credit he deserves. He sings, dances, and acts well, and is genuinely funny. The week and a half that Jayne and I spent in his company, along with a number of other old friends—Tom Poston, Tim Conway, Norm

Crosby, Ruth Buzzi, and Dick Martin—made for an extremely pleasant if all-too-brief tour of duty. For every minute on camera we spent at least an hour just hanging around telling stories and making each other laugh. At one point the subject of the over-emphasis on vulgarity came up and Dick shared an interesting bit of news.

"A couple of years back," he said, "although the network obviously liked our show—after all, they kept renewing it year after year—they apparently began to wish the ratings were a bit higher, so their solution was to call in some new writer-producer people. There's nothing wrong with that, as far as it goes, but almost immediately our scripts began to have more emphasis on sex and vulgar humor. So I asked one of the guys why they were doing that and they said they had gotten a go-ahead from the network. I said, 'Well, if you are really determined to go down that road, I'm sorry to tell you, you're gonna have to make the trip without me.'"

Dick's will prevailed and the show, as of the fall of 2000, was still on the air, marking its *eighth* successful season on prime-time television.

Alas, I fully recognize that Dick Van Dyke and I are members of an earlier generation than those who make up the vast majority of entertainment's creators or consumers today. To the reader, I offer the ideas in this book, as I have to audiences in my public remarks on this subject for many years, not out of concern for the sensitivities of my contemporaries raised in the early twentieth century, but rather out of genuine concern for the generations which are being raised right now in the early twenty-first century.

When my own children were growing up in the 1960s a highly regarded former FCC Chairman, Newton Minnow, declared television at that time to be a "vast wasteland." Recently, the still widely respected and quoted Mr. Minnow updated his assessment of television to describe what he sees today, and what my own eleven grandchildren are growing up watching, as a "vast *toxic* wasteland."

Since the time of his original assessment, I have been traveling regularly throughout this country, performing and lecturing in towns from coast to coast. I've taught at universities, addressed legislatures, and faced the prestigious Washington, D.C., Press Club. I've had the great good fortune to be able to talk personally to thousands upon thousands of hardworking Americans from all walks of life. I've exchanged opinions with conservative Southerners, liberal urbanites and high-minded New Englanders; with citizens of all ages, varied ethnic backgrounds, professions, and educational levels; with the wealthy and the needy. And everywhere I go I am asked the same question: Steve—when will they stop promoting vulgarity and violence in all forms of entertainment? When will it happen, and what can we do to make it happen?"

My answer is always the same: It won't stop—it will only increase, unless the American public, each one of us, individually, cares deeply enough about the alarming proliferation of such material into our lives and our homes to become actively involved.

This book is my own modest attempt to frame the problem and discuss potential solutions. Every time you and I buy a ticket to a violent or vulgar film, or purchase a CD laced with obscenity or even a product advertised on an offending television show we are directly contributing to the violence, sleaze, and vulgarity that is poisoning the minds of our children and blunting the moral sensibilities of all of us.

For the sake of our children and grandchildren, and the society they will inherit and pass on to the next generations, I implore you to let your own voice be heard on this important subject.

APPENDIX A
RESOURCE
ORGANIZATIONS

American Academy of Pediatrics (AAP)
141 Northwest Point Blvd.
Elk Grove Village, IL 60007-1098
Phone: (847) 434-4000
Fax: (847) 434-8000
Web site: www.aap.org
E-mail: Kidsdocs@aap.org

Washington, DC, Office:
Department of Federal Affairs
601 13th Street NW, Suite 400 North
Washington, DC 20005
Phone: (202) 347-8600
Fax: (202) 393-6137

The AAP was founded in June 1930 by thirty-five pediatricians who met in Detroit in response to the need for an independent pediatric forum to address children's needs. The AAP and its member pediatricians dedicate their efforts and resources to the health, safety, and well-being of infants, children, adolescents, and young adults. The AAP has approximately 55,000 members in the United States, Canada, and Latin America.

American Medical Association Chicago (AMA)
Headquarters
515 N. State Street
Chicago, IL 60610
Phone: (312) 464-5000
Fax: (312) 464-4184
Web site: www.ama-assn.org

Washington Office:
1101 Vermont Avenue NW
Washington, DC 20005
Phone: (202) 789-7400
Fax: (202) 789-7479

Physicians dedicated to the health of America. The AMA is the nation's leader in promoting professionalism in medicine and setting standards for medical education, practice, and ethics.

APPENDIX A: RESOURCE ORGANIZATIONS

American Psychiatric Association (APA)
1400 K Street NW
Washington, DC 20005
Phone: (888) 357-7924
Fax: (202) 682-6850
Web site: www.psych.org
E-mail: apa@psych.org

The APA is a medical specialty society recognized worldwide. Its 40,500 U.S. and international physicians specialize in the diagnosis and treatment of mental and emotional illnesses and substance use disorders.

American Psychological Association (APA)
750 First Street NE
Washington, DC 20002
Phone: (800) 374-2721 / (202) 336-5500
Fax: (202) 336-5723
Web site: www.apa.org
E-mail: publicinterest@apa.org

The APA is the largest scientific and professional organization representing psychology in the United States. With more than 159,000 members, the APA is also the largest association of psychologists worldwide. Providing information for parents, teens, the media, and others about parenting, healthcare, depression, and more.

Better Business Bureau
Children's Advertising Review Unit (CARU)
845 3rd Avenue
New York, NY 10022
Phone: (212) 705-0111
Fax: (212) 308-4743
Web site: www.bbb.org/advertising/childrens
            monitor.asp
E-mail: info@bbb.org

The bureau reviews advertising and promotional material directed at children in all media. When advertising is found to be misleading, inaccurate, or inconsistent with CARU's Self-Regulatory Guidelines for Children's Advertising, CARU seeks change through the voluntary cooperation of advertisers. CARU has also been at the forefront of children's issues in the interactive world. Its guidelines also contain a section that highlights issues, including children's privacy, that are unique to the Internet and online sites directed at children age twelve and under.

APPENDIX A: RESOURCE ORGANIZATIONS

Center for Media and Public Affairs (CMPA)
2100 L St. NW, Suite 300
Washington, DC 20037
Phone: (202) 223-2942
Fax: (202) 872-4014
Web site: www.cmpa.com
E-mail: cmpamm@aol.com

Founded in 1985, CMPA is a nonprofit, nonpartisan research and educational organization that conducts scientific studies of the news and entertainment media. The CMPA is one of the few groups to study the important role the media plays in communicating information about health risks and scientific issues. The CMPA has emerged as a unique institution that bridges the gap between academic research and the broader domains of media and public policy. Founded by Drs. Robert and Linda Lichter, the CMPA has become an acknowledged source of expertise in media analysis.

Center for Media Education (CME)
2120 L Street NW, Suite 200
Washington, DC 20037
Phone: (202) 331-7833
Fax: (202) 331-7841

Web site: www.cme.org
E-mail: cme@cme.org

A national nonprofit organization dedicated to creating a quality electronic media culture for children and youth, their families, and the community. The CME's research focuses on the potential—and the peril—for children and youth of the rapidly evolving digital media age. Examining the issues and framing the discussion surrounding this emerging new media culture to move responsibly into the digital future is the CME's major thrust.

Center for Media Literacy (CML)
4727 Wilshire Blvd., Suite 403
Los Angeles, CA 90010
Phone: (800) 226-9494 / (323) 931-4177
Fax: (323) 931-4474
Web site: www.medialit.org
E-mail: cml@medialit.org.

A nonprofit membership organization established in 1989, the center is dedicated to a new vision of literacy for the twenty-first century: the ability to communicate competently in all media forms, print and electronic, as well as to access, understand, analyze, and evaluate the powerful images, words, and sounds that make up our contemporary mass media culture.

Character Education Partnership (CEP)
1600 K Street NW, Suite 501
Washington, DC 20006
Phone: (800) 988-8081 (202) 296-7743
Fax: (202) 296-7779
Web site: www.character.org

CEP is a nonpartisan coalition of organizations and individuals dedicated to developing moral character and civic virtue in our nation's youth as one means of creating a more compassionate and responsible society. CEP also understands that the problems affecting youth reflect the broader social problems of our country as a whole and that it is the responsibility of all adults to model good character and help strengthen civic and moral foundations.

Children Now
1212 Broadway, 5th Floor
Oakland, CA 94612
Phone: (510) 763-2444
Fax: (510) 763-1974
Web site: www.childrennow.org
E-mail: children@childrennow.org

Children Now's Children and the Media Program works to improve the quality of news and entertainment both for children and about children's issues, paying particular attention to media images of race, class, and gender. Strategies include media industry outreach, independent research, and public policy development.

The Christophers
12 East 48th Street
New York, NY 10017
Phone: (212) 759-4050
Fax: (212) 838-5073
Web site: www.christophers.org
E-mail: mail@christophers.org

A nonprofit organization founded in 1945, the Christophers promotes a message to people of all faiths and of no particular faith to encourage individuals to recognize their abilities and use them to raise the standards in all phases of human endeavor. Their motto, "It's better to light one candle, than to curse the darkness." They depend on the initiative of individuals. There are no chapters, meetings, or dues.

The Dove Foundation
4521 Broadmoor SE
Grand Rapids, MI 49512
Phone: (800) 968-8437 / (616) 541-5000

APPENDIX A: RESOURCE ORGANIZATIONS

Fax: (616) 541-5006
Web site: www.dove.org
E-mail: movies@dove.org

A nonprofit organization established to encourage and promote the creation, production, and distribution of wholesome family entertainment. The foundation, free from commercial pressures, awards a blue and white Dove Seal to any movie or video that is rated "family-friendly" by its film review board. The Dove Seal is essentially a seal of approval for family entertainment. The Dove Foundation is working with the entertainment industry to help them identify and serve people who are eager to watch high-quality, wholesome movies. The Dove Seal makes it easy for customers to identify titles that are safe for family viewing.

Federal Communication Commission (FCC)
Enforcement Bureau
Investigations and Hearings Division
445 12th Street SW
Washington, DC 20554
Phone: (202) 418-1420 / (888) 225-5322
TTY/TDD: (888) 835-5322
Web site: www.fcc.gov
E-mail: fccinfo@fcc.gov

The commission documents complaints of indecent or obscene broadcasting it receives from the public. It does not independently monitor broadcasts. Complaints should be directed to the address above and include a tape or transcript of the program or significant excerpts, the date and time of the broadcast, and the call sign of the station involved. (Note: All information provided becomes part of the commission's records and can not be returned.)

The Henry J. Kaiser Family Foundation
2400 Sand Hill Road
Menlo Park, CA 94025
Phone: (800) 656-4533 / (650) 854-9400
Fax: (650) 854-4800
Web site: www.kff.org

This foundation engages in independent national healthcare philanthropy and is not associated with Kaiser Permanente or Kaiser Industries. In February 1999 the foundation published a study titled *Sex on TV: Content and Context* on the entertainment media and public health, which was conducted to examine the impact of entertainment media in society, and to work with entertainment industry leaders to help them convey important health messages to the public.

APPENDIX A: RESOURCE ORGANIZATIONS

Mediascope
12711 Ventura Blvd., Suite 440
Studio City, CA 91604
Phone: (818) 508-2080
Fax: (818) 508-2088
Web site: www.mediascope.org
E-mail: facts@mediascope.org

Founded in 1992, Mediascope is a national, non-profit research and policy organization working to encourage responsible portrayals in film, television, the Internet, video games, music, and advertising. Mediascope provides tools and information to assist the creative community to be more socially responsible without relinquishing creative freedoms. For example, the organization initiated some of the first studies on media ratings and their influence on children's media selections, and administered a major contextual content analysis of violence in television and film, which resulted in broadcast and cable leaders agreeing to rate television programs. Mediascope's resources and services are used by screenwriters, producers and media executives; journalists and critics; and researchers, educators, government officials, advocacy groups, parents, and students.

Morality in Media (MIM)
475 Riverside Drive, Suite 239
New York, NY 10115
Phone: (212) 870-3222
Fax: (212) 870-2765
Web site: www.moralityinmedia.org
E-mail: mim@moralityinmedia.org

This national interfaith organization was established in 1962 to combat obscenity and to uphold decency standards in the media. MIM maintains the National Obscenity Law Center, a clearinghouse of legal materials on obscenity law.

National Association for the Education of Young Children (NAEYC)
1509 16th Street NW
Washington, DC 20036-1426
Phone: (800) 424-2460/ 202-232-8777
Fax: (202) 328-1846
Web site: www.naeyc.org
E-mail: naeyc@naeyc.org

Founded in 1926, The NAEYC is the nation's largest and most influential organization of early childhood educators and others dedicated to improving the quality of programs for children from birth through third grade. The NAEYC approaches its seventy-fifth anniversary with over 100,000 members and a national network of nearly 450 local, state, and regional affiliates. The NAEYC has issued a position statement on the effects of media violence in children's lives (available at their Web site), which includes recommendations for parents, teachers, broadcasters and policy makers.

National Coalition on TV Violence (NCTV)
5132 Newport Avenue
Bethesda, MD 20816
Phone: (301) 986-0362
Web site: www.nctvv.org
E-mail: kmrco@mediaone.net

The NCTV and the Teachers for Resisting Unhealthy Children's Entertainment (TRUCE) offers parents and teachers useful information to help reduce the problems created for our children and for society in general due to violence in the media. The NCTVC helps children, parents, and teachers develop community-wide efforts to deal with media violence as a serious public health issue.

National Institute on Media and the Family
606 24th Avenue South, Suite 606
Minneapolis, MN 55454
Phone: (888) 672-KIDS / (612) 672-5437
Fax: (612) 672-4113
Web site: www.mediafamily.org
E-mail: information@mediafamily.org

The institute, founded by David Walsh, Ph.D., is a national resource for teachers, parents, community leaders, and other caring adults who are interested in the influence of electronic media on early childhood education, child development, academic performance, culture, and the spread of violence. The institute offers a number of unique resources including: movie, television, and video game content ratings; media awareness programs; and helpful hints for parents and families to evaluate their media use.

National Parent Teachers Association (PTA)
Headquarters
330 N. Wabash Avenue, Suite 2100
Chicago, IL 60611
Phone: (800) 307-4782
Fax: (312) 670-6783
Web site: www.pta.org
E-mail: info@pta.org

APPENDIX A: RESOURCE ORGANIZATIONS

Washington, DC, Office
1090 Vermont Ave. NW, Suite 1200
Washington, DC 20005-4905
Phone: (202) 289-6790
Fax: (202) 289-6791

The National PTA is the oldest and largest volunteer association in the United States working exclusively on behalf of children and youth. It has been promoting the education, health, and safety of children and families for more than a century. The mission of the National PTA is to support and speak on behalf of children and youth in the schools, in the community, and before governmental bodies and other organizations that make decisions affecting children; to assist parents in developing the skills they need to raise and protect their children; and to encourage parent and public involvement in the public schools of this nation.

Parents Television Council (PTC)
600 Wilshire Blvd., Suite 700
Los Angeles, CA 90071

Phone:	(213) 629-9255
Fax:	(213) 629-9254
Web site:	www.parentstv.org
E-mail:	editor@parentstv.org

VULGARIANS AT THE GATE

The PTC was established in 1995 as a nonpartisan, nonprofit group offering private–sector solutions to restore television to its roots as an independent and socially responsible entertainment medium. The mission of the PTC is to bring America's demand for positive, family-oriented television programming to the entertainment industry. The PTC yearly produces a variety of studies and analyses on the content of prime-time network TV. The organization publishes a monthly newsletter, as well as its own "Family Guide to Prime-Time Television."

APPENDIX B
MEDIA CONTACTS

ABC Entertainment
Mr. Stuart Bloomberg, Co-Chair
Mr. Lloyd Braun, Co-Chair
500 S. Buena Vista Street
Burbank, CA 91521
Phone: (818) 460-7477
Web site: www.abc.com
Email: netaudr@abc.com

Alliance of Motion Picture & Television Producers
   (AMPTP)
Mr. Nick Counter, President
15503 Ventura Blvd.
Encino, CA 91436
Phone: (818) 995-3600
Web site: www.amptp.org

CBS Television
Mr. Leslie Moonves, President & CEO
7800 Beverly Blvd.
Los Angeles, CA 90036
Phone: (323) 575-2345
Web site: www.cbs.com
E-mail: audsvcs@cbs.com

Comedy Central
Mr. Larry Divney, President & CEO
1775 Broadway
New York, NY 10019
Phone: (212) 767-8600
Web site: www.comedycentral.com

E! Entertainment Television
Ms. Mindy Herman, President
5750 Wilshire Blvd.
Los Angeles, CA 90036
Phone: (323) 954-2400
Web site: www.eonline.com

APPENDIX B: MEDIA CONTACTS

Entertainment Software Rating Board
Mr. Arthur Pober, President
845 Third Avenue
New York, NY 10022
Phone: (212) 759-0700
Web site: www.esrb.org

Fox Broadcasting Co.
Ms. Gail Berman, President
10201 W. Pico Blvd.
Los Angeles, CA 90035
Phone: (310) 369-1000
Web site: www.foxinc.com
E-mail: askfox@foxinc.com

Home Box Office (HBO)
Mr. Jeff Bewkes, Chairman & CEO
1100 Avenue of the Americas
New York, NY 10036-6737
Phone: (212) 512-1000

Mr. Chris Albrecht, President,
    HBO Original Programming
2049 Century Park East, Suite 4100
Los Angeles, CA 90067
Phone: (310) 201-9200
Web site: www.hbo.com

Infinity Broadcasting
Mr. Mel Karmazin, President & CEO
40 West 57th Street, 14th Floor
New York, NY 10019
Phone: (212) 314-9200
Web site: www.infinityradio.com

Interactive Digital Software Association
Mr. Douglas Lowenstein, President
1211 Connecticut Ave. NW #600
Washington, DC 20036
Phone: (202) 223-2400
Web site: www.idsa.com

Motion Picture Association of America (MPAA)
Mr. Jack Valenti, President & CEO
15503 Ventura Blvd.
Encino, CA 91436
Phone: (818) 995-6600
Web site: www.mpaa.org

MTV Networks
Mr. Tom Freston, Chair
1515 Broadway
New York, NY 10036
Phone: (212) 258-6000
Web site: www.mtv.com

NBC Entertainment
Mr. Jeff Zucker, President
3000 West Alameda Avenue
Burbank, CA 91523
Phone: (818) 840-4444
Web site: www.nbc.com

National Association of Broadcasters (NAB)
Mr. Edward Fritts, President & CEO
1771 N St. NW
Washington, DC 20036
Phone: (202) 429-5300
Web site: www.nab.org

National Association of Recording Merchandisers
Ms. Pam Horowitz, President
9 Eves Drive, Suite 120
Marlton, NJ 08053
Phone: (856) 596-2221
Web site: www.narm.com

National Association of Theatre Owners
Mr. John Fithian, President
4605 Lankershim Blvd., Suite 340
N. Hollywood, CA 91602
Phone: (818) 506-1778
Web site: www.hollywood.com/nato

National Cable Television Association (NCTA)
Mr. Robert Sachs, President & CEO
1724 Massachusetts Avenue, NW
Washington, DC 20036
Phone: (202) 775-3669
Web site: www.ncta.com

Odyssey Network
Ms. Margaret Loesch, President & CEO
12700 Ventura Blvd., Suite 200
Studio City, CA 91604
Phone: (818) 755-2400

Paxson Television Network (Pax TV)
Mr. Jeff Sagansky, President
601 Clearwater Park Rd.
West Palm Beach, FL 33401-6233
Phone: (561) 659-4122
Web site: www.paxtv.com

Recording Industry Association of America (RIAA)
Ms. Hilary B. Rosen, President & CEO
1330 Connecticut Avenue NW, Suite 300
Washington, DC 20036
Phone: (202) 775-0101
Fax: (202) 775-7253 fax
Web site: www.riaa.com

APPENDIX B: MEDIA CONTACTS

Showtime Networks Inc.
Mr. Matthew C. Blank, Chairman & CEO
1633 Broadway
New York, NY 10019
Phone: (212) 708-1600

Mr. Jerry Offsay, President
10880 Wilshire Blvd.
Suites 1500 & 1600
Los Angeles, CA 90024
Phone: (310) 234-5200
Web site: www.showtimeonline.com

United Paramount Network (UPN)
Mr. Dean Valentine, President & CEO
11800 Wilshire Blvd.
Los Angeles, CA 90025
Phone: (310) 575-7000
Web site: www.upn.com

USA Networks
Mr. Barry Diller, Chairman & CEO
1230 Avenue of the Americas
New York, NY 10020
Phone: (212) 413-5000

8800 W. Sunset Blvd., 4th Floor
West Hollywood, CA 90069
Phone: (310) 360-2300
Web site: www.usanetworks.com

Viacom
Mr. Sumner Redstone, Chairman & CEO
Mr. Mel Karmazin, President & COO
1515 Broadway
New York, NY 10036-5794
Phone: (212) 258-6000
Web site: www.viacom.com

Video Software Dealers Association (VSDA)
Mr. Crossan Anderson, President & CEO
16530 Ventura Blvd., Suite 400
Encino, CA 91436-4551
Phone: (800) 955-8732
Web site: www.vsda.org
E-mail: vsdaoffice@vsda.org

Warner Bros. Network
Mr. Jamie Kellner, CEO
4000 Warner Blvd., Building 34R
Burbank, CA 91522
Phone: (818) 977-5000
Web site: www.thewb.com
E-mail: faces@thewb.com

RECOMMENDED READING

Facts About Media Violence. American Medical Association, 1996.

"Television Code of the National Association of Broadcasters," 1st Edition, 1952; 22nd Edition, 1981. Encyclopedia Britannica Online: www.eb.com.

Whatever Happened to Childhood? The Problem of Teen Pregnancy in the United States. National Campaign to Prevent Teen Pregnancy, May 1997.

The National Televison Violence Study. Universities of: California, Santa Barbara; Wisconsin, Madison; North Carolina, Chapel Hill; Texas, Austin. Mediascope, 1996.

Allen, Steve, *Dumbth: The Lost Art of Thinking.* Prometheus Books, 1998.

Baird, Robert M., William E. Loges, and Stuart E. Rosenbaum, eds. *The Media & Morality.* Prometheus Books, 1999.

Baker, William F. and George Dessart. *Down The Tube: An*

Inside Account of the Failure of American Television. Basic Books, 1997.

Beckwith, Francis J. and Michael E. Bauman, eds. *Are You Politically Correct? Debating America's Cultural Standards.* Prometheus Books, 1992.

Berry, G. and C. Mitchell-Kernan, eds. *Television and the Socialization of the Minority Child.* Academic Press, 1982.

Berry, Gordon L., and Joy Keiko Asamen. *Children & Television: Images in a Changing Sociocultural World.* Newbury Park, California: Sage, 1993.

Bianculli, David. *Teleliteracy: Taking Television Seriously.* Touchstone, 1994.

Brown, Les. *Television: The Bu$iness Behind the Box.* Harcourt Brace Jovanovich, 1977.

Cantor, Joanne. *Mommy, I'm Scared: How TV and Movies Frighten Children and What We Can Do to Protect Them.* Harcourt Brace, 1998.

Carlsson, C., and C. Von Felitzen, eds. *Children and Media Violence: Yearbook from the UNESCO International Clearinghouse on Children and Violence on the Screen.* Nordicom: Goteborg University, 1998.

Cowan, Geoffrey. *See No Evil: The Backstage Battle Over Sex and Violence in Television.* Simon and Schuster, 1978.

Dyson, Michael Eric. *Reflecting Black: African-American Cultural Criticism.* University of Minnesota Press, 1993.

Federman, Joel. *Media Ratings: Design, Use and Consequences.* Mediascope, 1996.

RECOMMENDED READING

Federman, Joel. *Television Violence Study, vol.3.* University of California, 1998.

Gelernter, David *Drawing Life: Surviving the Unabomber* Free Press, 1997.

Greenfield, Patricia Marks and Jerone Bruner, Michael Cole and Barbara Lloyd, eds. *Mind and Media: The Effects of Television, Video Games, and Computers.* Harvard University Press, 1984

Grossman, Lt. Col. Dave and Gloria DeGaetano. *Stop Teaching Our Kids To Kill: A Call To Action Against TV, Movie & Video Game Violence.* Crown Publishers, 1999.

Heaton, Jeanne Albronda and Nona Leigh Wilson. *Tuning In Trouble: Talk TV's Destructive Impact on Mental Health.* Jossey-Bass Publishers, 1995.

Hewlett, Sylvia Ann and Cornel West. *The War Against Parents: What We Can Do For America's Beleaguered Moms and Dads.* Houghton Mifflin Company, 1998.

Josephson, Wendy. *Television Violence: A Review of the Effects on Children of Different Ages.* Ottawa: National Clearinghouse on Family Violence,1995.

Kent, Nicolas. *Naked Hollywood: Money and Power in the Movies Today.* St. Martin's Press, 1991.

Levine, Madeline. *Viewing Violence: How Media Violence Affects Your Child's and Adolescent's Development.* Doubleday, 1996.

Medved, Michael. *Hollywood vs. America: Popular Culture and the War on Traditional Values.* HarperCollins Publishers, 1992

Minow, Newton. *How Vast the Wasteland Now?* Gannett Foundation Media Center, 1991.

Newton, Michael. *Killer Kids.* Loompanics Unlimited, 2000.

Prothrow-Stith, Deborah. *Deadly Consequences.* New York: HarperCollins, 1991.

Roe, Yale. *The Television Dilemma: Search for a Solution.* Hasting House, Publishers, 1962.

Stein, Ben. *The View From Sunset Boulevard: America as Brought to You by the People Who Make Televison.* Basic Books, Inc., Publishers, 1978.

Steyn, Mark. *Broadway Babies Say Goodnight: Musicals Then & Now.* Routledge, 1999.

Tinker, Grant and Bud Rukeyser. *Tinker In Television: From General Sarnoff To General Electric.* Simon & Schuster, 1994.

Valenti, F. Miguel. *More Than A Movie: Ethics In Entertainment.* Westview Press, 2000.

Walsh, David. *Selling Out America's Children: How America Puts Profits Before Values-and What Parents Can Do.* Minneapolis: Fairview Press, 1994.

INDEX

ABC, 47, 48, 85, 96, 98, 152, 399

Action, 115, 117

advertising industry, 141, 232

Advocate, The, 191

Alcoholics Anonymous, 149

Allen, Fred, 75

Allen, John, 75

All in the Family, 63

All My Sons, 300–302

All Things Considered, 345

Alliance of Motion Picture & Television Producers, 399

Ally McBeal, 340

American Academy of Pediatrics, 294, 383

American College of Forensic Psychiatry, 294

American Medical Association, 384

American Psychiatric Association (APA), 291, 385

American Psychological Association (APA), 385–86

America Online, 190

America's Most Wanted, 66

Annenberg Public Policy Center, 119, 171

Anti-Defamation League, 193

assassinations, 70–71

audience. *See* market

Auletta, Ken, 111–12, 355

Austin Powers: The Spy Who Shagged Me, 116

authority, 340–42

awards. *See* Emmys; Oscars; Tonys

Banks, Sandy, 92

Banned in America: The World's Sexiest Commercials, 88

Basic Instinct, 164, 196

Batman Returns, 214

behavior

  deviant, 187

  standards of, 50, 69, 103, 136, 140, 146–49, 267, 333, 342, 354, 374

Bendall, Jennifer, 160

Bennett, William, 260–61, 270

Benny Hill Show, 41

Better Business Bureau, 386

Beverly Hills Courier, 300

Beverly Hills 90210, 46

Body of Evidence, 195, 196

books, influence on children, 139–42

boycotts, 368

Bozell, L. Brent, 114–17

Brady Bunch, The, 86

Bray, Stephen, 189–90

Broadway Babies, Say Goodnight, 244

Brownback, Sam, 159–60

Brown, Helen Gurley, 132

Brown, Les, 75

Bruce, Lenny, 222

Buzz, 130

Byrd, James, Jr., 90

cable television networks, 84, 151–52

Caesar, Sid, 45, 52

Canadian Broadcast Standards Council, 231

Carter, Bill, 166

Carter, Jack, 45

Casino, 360

CBS Viacom, 47, 53, 55, 75, 76, 84, 85, 106, 152, 223, 231–32, 233, 312, 315, 348, 400

censorship, 21–22, 38–39, 118, 122, 140, 303–22, 335, 346–50, 358, 359

Center for Media and Popular Culture, 28

Center for Media and Public Affairs, 387

Center for Media Education, 387–88

Center for Media Literacy, 388

Center to Prevent Handgun Violence, 345

Character Education Partnership, 389

Charlie Brown Christmas, A, 76

Charlie's Bar, 54–55

Cheers, 63

Chicago Sun Times, 165

children, 102–106, 107, 149, 180, 216, 217, 229, 249–50, 261–63, 295, 307, 309–11, 318–19, 330, 335, 336, 346, 357, 372, 375–76. *See also*

role models
media influences on, 72, 139–42, 166–73, 277–78, 283, 290
State of Children's Programming Television Report (1998), 171
violent, 288–89, 294, 350–55
Children Now, 389–90
Christophers, the, 390
civilization, fragility of, 133–37
Clay, Andrew Dice, 39, 44, 181
CNN, 52
code of conduct, media, 20–21, 38, 118, 125. *See also* Canadian Broadcast Standards Council; Hays Office Code; Voluntary Movie Rating System
Cohen, Alexander, 95
comedy. *See* humor
Comedy Central, 400
Conan O'Brien Show, 264–66
conscience, 135–36
Cooper, Abraham, 192
corporate responsibility, 132
Cosmopolitan, 132
crime, 67, 103–104, 142–44

Daily Variety, 86, 95–96, 106, 164, 234, 242, 337, 373, 378
David Letterman Show (March 31, 1994), 198–212, 312
DeGaetano, Gloria, 292–93
delinquency, juvenile, 350–55
democracy, 103, 169, 320, 326
Dennis, Reginald, 274
Detroit Free Press, 191
Detroit News, 195
Diagnosis Murder, 379
Disney corporation, 129
Dove Foundation, 355–58, 390–91
D'Rasmo, Stacey, 46
Drawing Life (Gelerntner), 143–44
Dumbth (Allen), 67

E! Entertainment Television, 400
Eminem, 253–57, 270
Emmy magazine, 62, 150
Emmys, 95, 96, 349
entertainment industry, 19, 22, 73, 118, 128, 160–62, 163, 182, 277–78
Entertainment Software Rating Board, 401
Entertainment Weekly, 116, 190
environmental degradation, 81
Eszterhas, Joe, 164

family, 19, 22, 37, 71–72, 132, 240, 337, 338–40, 366
Federal Communication Com-

mission (FCC), 118, 172, 234, 235, 241, 242, 295, 381, 391–92
Federal Trade Commission (FTC), 160, 311, 314, 372–76
First Amendment, 125, 126, 127, 183, 297, 298, 308, 319, 334, 336
Fox network, 57–58 , 63, 64, 85, 88, 96, 114, 115, 117, 236, 340, 401
Frasier, 64
freedom of speech. *See* First Amendment
free enterprise system, 30, 81
Friars Club, 44–45

Gandhi, Mohandas (Mahatma), 135
Gelerntner, David, 143
Godfrey, Arthur, 347
Goldberg, Whoopi, 96
Gore, Al, 163
Graham, Jefferson, 240
Greeniaus, H. John
  letter to (May 23, 1995), 155–57
  letter to (July 20, 1995), 158–59
Grossman, David, 292–95
gun control, 290, 345

Hall, Arsenio, 236
Hardisty, Jean, 78
Hays Office Code, 121–24
HBO, 45, 48, 50, 51, 401
Henigan, Dennis, 345
Henry J. Kaiser Family Foundation, 392
Herzog, Doug, 115–16
Hettrick, Scott, 330–32
Hewlett, Sylvia Ann, 71
Hollywood Reporter, 102, 196, 230, 238, 330, 334, 377–78
Holocaust, 168–69
Holston, Noel, 226
Humanitas Prize, 365–66
humor, 37, 43

Ice-T, 264–66, 275
I Love Lucy, 43
Infinity Broadcasting, 402
Interactive Digital Software Association, 402

Jerry Springer Show. See Springer, Jerry
justice. *See* social justice
Just Shoot Me, 93, 94

Kansas State Board of Education, 306–307
Karmazin, Mel, 234
  letter to (May 16, 2000), 238–39

Kempley, Rita, 124
Killer Kids (Newton), 289
King, Larry, 52
Koscielak, Ruth, 340

language
  politically correct, 312
  vulgar, 41, 51, 154, 173–76,
    183, 214, 222, 251–53,
    255–57, 312, 331, 337, 359,
    378–79, 380, 382
Leo, John, 168
Lethal Weapon, 298–99
Lieberman, Joe, 163–64
Link, William, 295–99
Littleton, Colo., 18
Lofton, John, 191
Los Angeles Daily News, 377
Los Angeles Times, 42, 62, 63, 92,
    163, 223, 234, 235, 263,
    271, 275, 293, 329, 373, 377
    (September 17, 1990), 35–39
Luce, Clare Booth, 186

Mad About You, 64
Mademoiselle magazine, 197, 198
Madonna, 180–213, 214, 215,
    257, 312, 334, 335
Mad TV, 236
*Man Who Turned Back the Clock,
  The* (Allen), 65
market, 31, 42, 166, 173, 181,
    184, 299, 372–76
Married . . . with Children, 35, 58,
    63, 64
Mask, The, 358
Matoian, John, 58, 59, 66
  letter to (October 2, 1995),
    60–65
McCaffrey, Barry, 161
McCain, John, 310
Media Access Project, 232
Media Advisors International,
    150
Mediascope, 393
Meeting of Minds, 186
Meet the Press, 293
Melrose Place, 46
Mifflin, Lawrie, 166
Miller, Henry, 184
Minneapolis Star Tribune, 226
Minnow, Newton, 381
Misery Loves Company, 56
Mobilizing Resentment (Hardisty),
    78
Moonves, Leslie, 106, 233–34
Morality in Media, 394
moral standards. *See* behavior,
    standards of; codes of con-
    duct, media; pornography;
    sin; societal collapse
moral values, strengthening,
    362–65, 371
Moritz, Neal, 87

Morton, Gary, 43

Morton, Robert, 212

Motion Picture Association of America (MPAA), 122, 163, 373–74, 402

motion picture industry, 121, 161–62, 167, 283, 290, 292, 356

MTV, 108, 191–92, 402

Murdoch, Rupert, 57, 66
letter to (October 2, 1995), 57–60

Museum of Television and Radio, 233

music
jazz, 246–47
popular, 119, 129, 243–76
rap, 243–68
violence and, 268–76

Nabisco Foods, 155–57

National Association for the Education of Young Children, 394–95

National Association of Broadcasters, 19, 403

National Association of Recording Merchandisers, 403

National Association of Television Program Executives, 240

National Association of Theatre Owners, 403

National Cable Television Association, 404

National Coalition on TV Violence, 395

National Endowment for the Arts, 38

National Geographic, 75, 76

National Institute on Media and the Family, 396

National Parent Teachers Association, 396–97

National Public Radio, 345

National Review, 341

NBC, 47, 65, 85, 93, 118, 152, 240, 339, 403

New Orleans Times Picayune, 192

Newsweek, 49, 190, 240, 244, 275, 303, 329

Newton, Michael, 289

New Yorker, The, 111, 355

New York Post, 116, 234

New York Times, 44, 46, 166

New York Undercover, 66

NYPD Blue, 48

O'Donnell, Rosie, 95, 197

Odyssey Network, 404

Omaha World-Herald, 112

Oscars, 94, 96

parent-guidance rating system, 119

parenting, 19

Parents Music Resource Center, 119

Parents Television Council (PTC), 110–14, 371, 397–98

Parker, Sarah Jessica, 46, 49

Pax TV Network, 337, 404

PBS, 152

People magazine, 195

Peoria, Ill., 101–102

Philadelphia Enquirer, 49

picketing, 368

Planned Parenthood, 83, 315

polls, 18, 40, 83, 104, 244, 288, 290

pornography, 91, 141, 249, 263, 307, 310, 311, 319

poverty, 68

Prince, 214, 215

prisons, 68

profit motive, 29, 30, 34, 41, 56, 68, 78, 80, 84, 86, 133, 184, 237, 261, 274, 299, 325–26, 335, 356, 357, 372

public service announcements, 162

racism, 137

radio, influence on children, 139–42

ratings, 36, 68, 74, 76, 106, 234, 240, 242, 348–49, 361, 380

Reagan, Ronald, 242

Rechtshaffen, Michael, 377

Recording Industry Association of America (RIAA), 119, 160, 404

Redstone, Sumner, 84, 85

religions, 137, 145, 281–82, 342, 344, 363, 369

Richmond, Ray, 86–87

Rogers, Will, 188

role models, 50–51, 180, 186, 216–17, 263

Russell, Bertrand, 342–44

Sahl, Mort, 42

Saint Laurent, Yves, 189

Satcher, David, 293

Saturday Night Live, 39, 93, 236

schools, 19

Schwartzman, Andrew, 232

Seinfeld, 64

self-policing, 118

sex acts

in films and television, 85, 141, 144–45, 162, 167, 214, 215, 277, 356, 359, 380

in popular music, 244

Sex and the City, 45, 47, 48–50, 51

sexual harassment, 153–54, 313

Shakur, Tupac, 253–55

Shasta McNasty, 86–87

Sheldon, Sidney, 304

Showtime Networks, Inc., 405

Sikes, Gini, 46

Simon, Robert, 168–69

Simon Wiesenthal Center, 192

Simpsons, The, 332

sin, 107–10

Singer, Jerome, 290

slavery, 136, 279, 344

social action, 366–76

social justice, 70, 134, 136, 279, 344

social policy, 32

social problems, 77. *See also* crime; delinquency

social progress, 134

social responsibility, 31, 129–64, 261, 289–92, 325

social unrest, 350–55

societal collapse, 65, 67–68, 73, 77, 107, 109, 168, 196, 243–76, 248–49, 285–88, 332, 354, 376

Sommers, Christina Hoff, 169–70

Sopranos, The, 48

Source, The, magazine, 274

South Park, 108, 115, 116, 152, 329–30, 332

Spade, David, 93

Special Committee on American Culture, 159–60

sponsors. *See* advertising industry

Sports Illustrated, 141–42

Springer, Jerry, 170, 239–42

Spy, 130

standards of behavior. *See* behavior, standards of; codes of conduct, media

Star, Darren, 46, 47, 49

Stern, Howard, 55, 116–17, 150, 154, 170, 220–39, 334, 347

Stevenson, Adlai, 165

Steyn, Mark, 244

Stop Teaching Our Kids to Kill (Grossman and DeGaetano), 292–93

Storyteller, The, 296–98

Strauss, Bob, 377

Talk of the Nation, 345

Tauzin, Billy, 102

Taylor, William W., letter to, 150

Teachout, Terry, 143

television industry, 33, 161, 328, 381

influence on children, 28, 139–42, 172, 283, 290–92

standards for, 130–31

Television: The Business Behind the Box (Brown), 75

terrorism, 137

There's Something About Mary, 116

Thomas, Kevin, 377

Thompson, Jack, 335

Time magazine, 189, 212, 271, 329

letter to Board of Directors (1992), 213–17

Tinker, Grant, 240

Toastmasters, 39

tobacco, 120, 127, 277

Tom Green Show, 152

Tonight show, 236, 347

Tonys, 95

Tracht, Doug, 89

Travelena, Fred, 360

Tucker, C. Delores, 260–61, 263, 270

TV Guide, 87, 88, 115, 117, 223, 238

2 Live Crew, 251–52, 257–58

Unabomber, 142–44

UPN television network, 86, 405

US, 46

USA Networks, 405

USA Today, 85, 221, 240, 315

U.S. News & World Report, 168

Valdes-Rodriguez, Alisa, 271–76

Valenti, Jack, 138, 163, 164, 371, 373–74

values, shared, 22

Van Dyke, Dick, 379–80

Vanity Fair, 189

Viacom, 406

Video Software Dealers Association, 406

violence in entertainment, 19, 21, 29, 141, 173, 214, 244, 259, 261, 277–302, 356, 379, 382

music and, 268–76

Voluntary Movie Rating System, 123

W magazine, 212

Wall Street Journal, 332

War Against Parents, The (Hewlett and West), 71–72, 336

Warner Brothers, 406

motion pictures, 358

records, 193

Washington Post, 124, 329

Weaver, Pat, 65

West, Cornel, 71

Whipped, 377–78

White House Office of National Drug Control Policy, 161

Will, George, 165

Winslow Boy, The, 378–79

Wired magazine, 310

X-Files, 66

Youngman, Henny, 44